A BLOODY BUSINESS

A BLOODY BUSINESS

America's War Zone Contractors and the Occupation of Iraq

Colonel Gerald Schumacher
United States Army Special Forces (ret.)

ZENITH PRESS

First published in 2006 by Zenith Press, an imprint of MBI
Publishing Company, Galtier Plaza, Suite 200, 380 Jackson Street,
St. Paul, MN 55101-3885 USA

Zenith Press titles are also available at discounts in bulk quantity
for industrial or sales-promotional use. For details write to Special
Sales Manager at MBI Publishing Company, Galtier Plaza,
Suite 200, 380 Jackson Street, St. Paul, MN 55101-3885 USA.

ISBN-13: 978-0-7603-2355-7
ISBN-10: 0-7603- 2355-0

Printed in the United States of America

To the memory of Wolf Weiss, the Consummate Warrior,
and to all the men and women who do not wear a uniform yet
go into harm's way to serve our country.

Table of Contents

One would think that civilians who have taken jobs to work in Iraq would be anxious and open to discussing their experiences. They are anxious but most are not open. Although many want to express themselves, the media has not been kind to these men and women or the firms they work for. They are warned by their employers to stay far away from the press, and they are often restricted by their contracts. Many are afraid of losing their jobs if they tell their story without their employer's approval. A number of contracting firms refused to cooperate in the making of this book without screening the stories, which was out of the question. The filter of "official" involvement would have compromised the stories. These are not official accounts; they are reality.

Two companies stepped up to the plate without imposing any restrictions or conditions and without any threats or guidance to restrict their employees' voices: MPRI and Crescent Security. They did not ask for editorial review nor did they stage any dog-and-pony shows. They were accommodating, candid, and honest. Their employees were permitted to speak freely. I sincerely appreciate their help and respect the risks they took. Thank you Rick Kiernan, director of media relations for MPRI. Rick paved the way for this book by opening MPRI's doors and coordinating my trip to facilities in Kuwait and Iraq, which then led to subsequent contacts in those countries.

A big thanks to Larry Word, the retired army colonel who runs Team Viper at MPRI's training base along the Kuwait-Iraq border. After spending several days with his team, and without any advance notice, I interrupted a formal meeting and informed Larry that I was headed north into Iraq with another contracting firm. I recall him looking at me with great concern. Then he looked around the room and said, "Gentlemen, I think this is a good time for a break." He turned to one of his men and ordered, "Get this man some gear for his trip." Next thing I knew I was being loaded up with body armor, helmets, and other equipment that would help keep me alive. This was one of those moments in which an American just does something for you because you are a fellow American.

I owe a special debt of gratitude to Renee Taylor, the wife of a KBR contract truck driver. Renee spent countless hours researching information, getting me in touch with other drivers, and reviewing stories for accuracy. Her limitless and energetic support of her husband, Mark, truckers in Iraq, and their families is a tribute to her selfless character. Thank you, Renee. Thank you very much.

Many thanks to Mrs. Sheila Powell, whose husband, Steve, was a diesel mechanic in Iraq. Throughout the course of writing this book, Sheila sent me articles, stories, contacts, and information about contractors and their experiences. Her undying love, respect, and support of Steve was reflected in everything she did. He's a lucky man.

To Franco Pecco, the owner of Crescent Security, and his director of security, Scott Schneider, I extend my heartfelt appreciation. Not only did Franco and Scott let me bunk with them and allow their people to talk with me freely, Scott took me along, riding shotgun on the roads in Iraq. Scott went through great lengths to make sure that I saw whatever I wanted to see and that I lived to write about it. They never rested until we were safely back inside the wire at some military base or crossed the border into Kuwait. They are a tireless and professional crew, and I would not hesitate to trust my life to them. Thank you.

Two very important people who warrant special recognition are Jake Guevarra and Charles Rudolph, U.S. security contractors in Iraq. Thank you for all your help in putting together the details of your moments of terror and exhilaration. Your honest and humble insights show the truly human nature of facing inner demons and struggling with the prospect of impending death. Your contributions to this book were enormous.

I offer my appreciation to Ken McDonald, Mark Taylor, and Jeff Dye, Iron Pony Express truck drivers who contributed much to this book. For the townspeople of Paris, Illinois, who turned their little community upside down to welcome home their "kids," you represent the finest traditions of the American people. And to the families from Paris, Illinois, whose sons and daughters paid the ultimate sacrifice, the United States is forever indebted to you.

Prior to leaving for Iraq, Roy Hamilton opened his home and marksmanship facilities to me in Pyramid Lake, Nevada. Roy was kind enough to provide loads of ammo and an assortment of weapons to practice with. As it turned out, this stop en route to the Middle East proved to be far more valuable than I would have predicted. I really appreciate the opportunity to have the rust shaken out of my spokes.

Thanks much to Hans Halberstadt, the author of numerous military special operations books, who got me started in this whole business of writing. Time and again, Hans was there as a considerate friend through countless episodes when I pestered him about this endeavor. Thanks to Ben Parsons, my friend and business associate, who I force to read everything I write and always accommodates me with a smile and a pointed, educated review. My acknowledgments to Steve Gansen, my editor, who took such a deep personal interest in making this book come together. Steve, you contributed much, and I sincerely appreciate all your effort and concern.

I'd like to proffer a deep and very personal thanks to my mother, Grace Hendrickson, who, many years ago, nudged me into creating and editing my eighth-grade newspaper, *The Magpie*, at Saint Margaret's School in Chicago. Your intellectual acumen and your voracious appetite for literary works have been an inspiration and source of strength throughout my life. Thank you to my wife, Deb, my son Kevin, our friend Tosca, and my daughters Tamara and Ashley, who read or listened to the many drafts and lent your opinions, as different as they may be. I appreciate the fact that you never cut me any slack. You are truly an acid test, and I wouldn't trade a one of you.

Many Americans believe that war should be the exclusive purview of soldiers. This thinking ignores the realities of insurgent warfare, the requirements of nation building, the complexities of battlefield technologies, and the willingness of volunteers to join a downsized military in the absence of a national draft. Some people might be surprised to know just how many civilian contractors are out there working in the shadows, performing high-risk jobs in training, equipping, and developing foreign troops, and who are influencing battle plans in dozens of countries throughout the world.

Since the first Gulf war in 1991, the proportion of private forces to military personnel has more than quadrupled, and today the number of private contractors employed by the Pentagon is more than seven hundred thousand by some estimates. The soldier of fortune has taken on an entirely new dimension in the modern war zone. When the political environment is not conducive to the deployment of U.S. forces, our government hires civilians to execute its foreign policy. This makes them more than a surrogate army in indirect support of U.S. combat operations; they are a virtual surrogate government.

Historically they have been called *mercenaries*, an unsavory term in today's war zone contracting community, and mostly inaccurate. However, mercenaries do still exist, conducting morally and legally questionable combat operations, assassinations, and personnel recovery outside the scope of U.S. military authority and unaccountable to the U.S. government.

Few, if any, Department of Defense contractors would be party to mercenary operations (or admit to it if they were).

In the purest sense, the term *mercenary* applies to those who are employed to kill others for money. But with a few notable exceptions, not many modern contractors fit this Wild West "hired-gun" stereotype. The complexity of the myriad job requirements on the modern battlefield dictates the direct involvement of tens of thousands of highly skilled civilians. Today they are sought from nearly every occupation imaginable. But any historical discussion of war zone contracting must begin with its mercenary origins. Mercenaries have been employed by tribes, communities, and governments around the world since the beginning of humankind as a quick and dirty way to build an army. The Carthaginians, for example, employed a foreign force of chiefly Libyan mercenaries against a Roman army of landowning patriots during the Punic Wars. The concept really came into vogue during the Italian Renaissance in the fifteenth and sixteenth centuries. Encouraged by money, a significant number of men emerged who had no qualms about fighting for the highest bidder.

The popularity of mercenaries decreased as nation-states promoted the idea of patriotic duty. Developing nations fostered the romantic notion that fighting for one's country was an honorable thing to do, and that foreigners with no attachment to the soil or history of a land for which they were fighting could not be depended on for their loyalty. Mercenaries fell into disfavor, but for many of the same practical reasons they are still in use today, and have never disappeared.

Many of today's private contractors, like the mercenaries of old, are driven by money into war zone employment.

A BLOODY BUSINESS

Contracting to accomplish vital missions and jobs in war-torn countries is big business. Jobs once restricted to the Defense and State Departments are now replicated by civilian agencies contracting their services to the U.S. government. In many cases, their services offer critical skills that could not be readily procured from within our military and government personnel pool. In other cases, their services provide the United States with the ability to publicly distance itself from an otherwise unsupportable commitment of U.S. forces.

While the economics cannot be discounted, most contractors will insist that patriotism also ranks high on their list of motivations. That today's nation-states are any less motivated by economics than individual contractors is hard to dispute. Simply put, it is cheaper to pay big money for temporary help than it is to maintain a large standing military. Another factor influencing the use of civilian contractors is the growth of non-nation-states, insurgencies, and terrorism. Religious, cultural, tribal, and ethnic combatants—and especially terrorists without national affiliations—are confronting conventional armies with unconventional tactics. For them, it is less about winning than it is a waiting game, a test of wills to see who can hold out the longest. In addition to creating general mayhem and disorder through kidnappings, beheadings, car bombs, gun battles, and assassinations, these unconventional forces make maximum use of technology, including computers, the Internet, encryption equipment, and the media, both to terrorize civilians and to recruit more jihadists to their cause.

Private contractors have skill sets uniquely suited to provide military support services in an unconventional environment, skills you won't find at the local army firing range. They are able to provide a wide range of basic and sophisticated services that support both U.S. military and political objectives.

Construction contractors provide infrastructure services like basic subsistence, housing, utilities, and industrial rehabilitation. *Trucking contractors* keep supplies moving to the soldiers and the construction sites. *Training contractors* provide small-unit combat training, law enforcement training, and battle-staff training for mid-level military officers. *Technical assistance contractors* keep communications networks, radar sites, tanks, and aircraft functioning. *Security contractors* provide the first level of safety to all the rest of the contractors. And, of course, there is that unsavory kind of contractor, that rare object of much controversy and fascination that we discussed earlier—the *mercenary*.

Private military contractors (PMCs), such as Military Professional Resources, Inc. (MPRI), Science Applications International Corporation (SAIC), and Blackwater USA, annually book millions of dollars in government contracts and would not be inclined to accept any assignments that were in contravention to U.S. foreign policy. Such rogue behavior could jeopardize their future contracts. If they are involved, it's a sure bet that our government is directly or indirectly supporting their activity. That is not to say that we would always know that they were involved. These are highly professional organizations.

Contractors are fast, reliable, skilled, efficient, and largely anonymous. It is no stretch to call contractors the United States' "shadow army." They come from every branch of the military, government, business, industry, and academia. The contracting workforce is comprised of ex-military, former law enforcement officers, dog handlers, electricians, and drilling rig and pipeline specialists. There are truck drivers, cooks, clerks, technicians, trainers, media professionals, engineers, architects, surgeons, former general officers, and think-tank academics. Although their employment is temporary, given the United States' inclination to influence world events, it is unlikely that there will be any shortage of employment opportunities in the foreseeable future.

In the early 1990s, when Croatia fought to maintain its independence from the Serbs, their outlook for success was bleak. In battle after battle, they were soundly defeated. For a variety of reasons, the United States was reluctant to openly support Croatia.

Following a period of withdrawal and reorganization, the Croatian army launched a highly skilled and successful battle campaign that resulted in ejecting the Serbian aggressors from that country. How did Croatia go from a country on the verge of losing its independence to one with a force capable of defeating the Serbian military machine? War zone contractors, working at tactical and strategic levels, brought in the expertise to plan and train with the Croats and had a positive impact on the outcome. Afterward, there were no parades, no victory celebrations, no medals, no media attention, only the successful conclusion of another war. A few contractors returned to normal jobs, while others moved on to Bosnia, where more conflict meant more demand for their specialized expertise.

Some contracting firms have been censured recently for their employees' alleged gun-slinging behavior. In June 2005, nineteen private contractors from Zapata Engineering operating in Iraq were arrested by U.S. Marines and accused of having fired automatic weapons indiscriminately, consequently endangering coalition forces and innocent civilians. Although the allegation was never substantiated, the story took on a life of its own in the press. Most security firms are careful to thoroughly screen and establish clear guidelines on the conduct of their personnel. Future contracts depend in large measure on professionally and quietly accomplishing their mission.

Contracting firms are as versatile and different from one another as the men and women they hire. Some contracting firms provide logistical expertise, others, such as Blackwater USA, have a reputation for furnishing personal security guards, and some, like SAIC, focus on port security. One firm, MPRI, employs more than twelve thousand professionals with skills ranging from humanitarian assistance to law enforcement, democracy transition services, military training, technical support, and force development planning.

In the United States, the Posse Comitatus (Latin for "power of the country") Act, where able-bodied individuals can be called upon to assist law enforcement, places restrictions on the application of active-duty military units in civil-police law enforcement activities. Contractors, who are not so restricted, are seizing the employment opportunity and filling the voids in homeland security. They are able to execute reconnaissance and intelligence collection operations that would normally be tied up in bureaucratic red tape between competing law enforcement agencies. They are available for "advisory" and training assistance contracts with any given agency in the United States or other countries. They have also been employed in U.S. responses to natural disasters and are helping to resolve issues related to illegal immigration.

Historically, U.S. Army Special Forces have provided training to the Colombian military. Now with U.S. forces stretched too thin by other conflicts, hundreds of contractors are involved in counter-drug training and operations in Colombia. They are training national police forces, military units, and paramilitary operatives. The contractors are, for the most part, former Green Berets, Navy Seals, retired intelligence agency personnel, and police officers. Some are pilots and others are handlers for tracking dogs. They are fulfilling vital objectives of U.S. foreign policy. Their activities are closely monitored for compliance with U.S. and international standards. Although they are directed to avoid direct combat, it is impossible for them to maintain a noncombatant posture if their personal safety is threatened. Sometimes firing in self defense is a necessary evil of the job.

From unobtrusive U.S. locations, with signage intended to mislead an unwary public and stave off curiosity seekers, government contractors execute aerial reconnaissance and defoliating missions into places such as Colombia, Bolivia, Peru, and the Andes. They are actively engaged in dangerous counter-drug operations. Some political activists and media personalities have alleged that these contractors are conducting counterinsurgency operations. When pilots, crew chiefs, or maintenance personnel are never heard from again, the famously less-than-candid contracting firms don't exactly hand deliver telegrams to the victims' relatives. Individual contractors understand the dangers and have no expectations for flags to fly at half mast for the ultimate sacrifice.

Uncle Sam is by no means the only employer of war zone contractors. Contracting agencies offer services to companies and allied governments around the world that require their expertise in executive protection, hostage rescue, language translation, strategic defense planning, airborne security operations, building oil pipelines, securing Africa's diamond mines, and, in the case of Sierra Leone, the ousting of a renegade government from power.

In 1998 in Sierra Leone, the elected government had been overthrown by a handful of merciless senior military officers. They began brutally executing all opposition forces. Public executions of elected officials and former government employees were conducted on a daily basis. The United States could not muster the public support required to assist, so the United Nations was asked to intervene. The United Nations made a feeble attempt to punish the renegades by imposing a trade embargo. When that didn't work, a country with interests in the region hired a contracting agency. In this rare instance of contractors initiating direct combat actions, the rebel officers were quickly eliminated, and remnants of Sierra Leone's elected government reassumed power.

This episode left little doubt that wholesale slaughter cannot be prevented with trade sanctions and embargoes alone. Absent an effective force, the United Nations is often rendered impotent without outside help. But nations are loathe to publicly support the use of contractors in helping resolve international problems. Still, UN Secretary General Kofi Annan reportedly admitted that the contractors in Sierra Leone saved lives, and if they had been allowed to do the job sooner, a hundred thousand people might still be alive. In yet a later humanitarian disaster, London's *Financial Times* reported in November of 2003 that Annan was considering the use of private contractors to address the slaughter taking place in the Democratic Republic of the Congo (DRC). There was no support anywhere within the

United Nations. "The world may not be ready to privatize peace," Annan concluded.

The United Nations has been reluctant to employ private contractors to resolve international security issues. Such considerations have frequently been labeled as immoral. However, their reluctance begs the question: Is it moral to do nothing? The morality of employing private contractors, or the lack thereof, is succinctly summed up in an article by David Shearer, in which he states, "There is a serious question here: if a private force, operating with international authority and within international law, can protect civilians, how moral is it to deny people protection just because states can't or won't find the forces to do it? Or put another way, is the means of response more important than the end for which it is used particularly where a failure to respond results in the death and abuse of civilians?"

In spite of these objections, government contracting agencies are thriving. The Defense Logistic Agency is attempting to privatize most of its $1.6 billion network of warehouses and distribution facilities. The government has reported that nine hundred thousand government employees are doing work that could be performed by private firms. Private military contractors are working with at least forty-two countries, and that number is growing by the month. Future growth projections are exponential. Revenues from the global international security market are expected to rise from $55.6 billion in 1990 to $202 billion in 2010, according to private industry projections. The *Pittsburgh Post-Gazette* (February 2000) reported that private security companies with publicly traded stocks grew at twice the rate of the Dow Jones Industrial Average in the 1990s. Governments and businesses that employ their services get the short-term benefit of their expertise without the long-term investment in recruiting, hiring, training, employing, and insuring the lives of these personnel, who are the combat equivalent of account temps.

When the work is there, they do it. When it's not, they return to a less profitable—if less life-threatening—existence. It is hard to imagine a job with the risk of being beheaded, like the unfortunate Turkish truck-driver contractor, or the contractors in Fallujah who were burned and hanged naked from a bridge. In another incident, thirty contractors were wounded in a targeted car-bomb attack. More than three hundred American contractors have been killed in Iraq alone. We haven't heard much about most of them. Most war zone contractors know they have a thankless job; they ask for little sympathy, and receive even less. Their deaths are looked upon by most of the world as a natural consequence of the job. It's all blood money, anyway, so why should it come easy? They know the risks they face, and if they touch a hot stove, they should expect to get burned.

But one question hardly ever seems to get asked—where would we be without them?

This book will introduce you to a number of contractors in Kuwait, Jordan, and Iraq for whom, you will find, it is rarely about money. We will explore the legal, moral, ethical, and practical questions they face every day. To mention a few:

What is the legal status of a contractor in a war zone? How much flexibility do they have to operate in a war zone? Can contractors be restricted or prohibited from going certain places within a hostile country?

Contractors in high-risk areas have gotten into the target countries but found themselves without weapons, without properly shielded vehicles, without body armor, and most importantly, without access to intelligence information. How well do soldiers and contractors interact and communicate? Who do contractors call when they get into trouble? How do contractors get information on the current friendly and enemy situation, such as if the U.S. Army is planning an attack in the area, or if an aerial reconnaissance drone has detected an improvised road mine planted during the night on the route they will be traveling?

Does being privy to too much information make a contractor a security risk? If a contractor is taken prisoner by enemy forces, does he have an obligation to resist interrogation? Is he protected under the Geneva Convention?

Soldiers can receive a court-martial for failure to respond to orders—is there a similar disciplinary action for contractors? For instance, if a technician contractor is working on ground-surveillance radar equipment in support of an army unit, and that unit comes under attack, must the contractor respond to directives from military personnel?

Are all contractors allowed to carry weapons? When should a contractor take offensive action against a person who appears to be the enemy? What happens to a personal security contractor who mistakenly shoots innocent civilians? Who adjudicates the incident?

Perhaps most importantly, to whose authority do the various categories of war zone contractors answer? It is worth noting that the U.S. Constitution prohibits military authority over civilians except when war has been declared, but as you will read, contractors have pragmatic reasons for not rocking the military's boat.

What happens when the contractor and the military get their signals crossed? Consider this scenario: You are a contractor. Remember that you are in the war zone to help a local government, military, or law enforcement agency. You cannot assume they will let you do your job without occasional interference, intentional or otherwise. That may not seem like a problem until you get in a situation where their actions place your own life in serious danger. A group of armed security contractors are traveling in a Toyota SUV. It's nighttime. All of them are dressed in civilian clothing. They stumble onto a military checkpoint or, worse yet, a military operation. An aircraft circling overhead observes them through the onboard thermal imaging system. A thermal device is not capable of distinguishing national or ethnic identity. The contractors are merely human figures emitting a heat signature with weapons in hand. The aircraft reports to the ground troops that they have identified a vehicle with armed, nonuniformed personnel. Can you fault the U.S. Army for firing a Javelin missile at such a threatening target?

In spite of the high risks involved, the line of U.S. and foreign applicants willing to become war zone contractors gets longer every day. According to a statistic reported by the PBS series "Frontline," there are well over one hundred thousand civilian contractors working in Iraq. A recruiter for Kellogg, Brown & Root, a major war zone construction company, reported having more than sixteen thousand applicants in a month to fill two thousand job openings in Iraq. Even after a thorough orientation, including exposure to images of blown-up contractors' living quarters, personal war stories, and the fact that construction sites are attacked on the average of two dozen a week, only one in five applicants withdraws.

No question, the military is losing many of its most highly skilled personnel to contracting firms, but the great majority of contractors are not direct transfers from the military. In fact, many have never served in the military, but they believe in the cause or they need to fill some void in their life. For many, it's a chance to fulfill a patriotic sense of duty they missed by not joining the service when they were military age. Perhaps many men and women feel the need in their lifetime to have done something for their country, something above average, something beyond the norm. Maybe it's just for the adventure. While the risk to life and limb is essentially the same, it probably doesn't hurt that the pay is much better than in the military, and contract work comes without any long-term obligation.

As you read this book, you will meet men and women who are not much different than your next-door neighbor. You'll travel with them through a typical day in the war zone. You'll be with them in their best and their worst times, sharing moments of grief and joy. You'll discover their varied reasons for being in Iraq, their fears, their mistakes. Sometimes they'll gloat in celebration over a successful mission; sometimes they'll hang their heads in failure, sometimes they'll question whether victory was worth the price.

This is no whitewash, no glorification. These are not perfect people, but they are real. I've tried to convey their reality as objectively as possible. Perhaps we can all benefit from an open-eyed assessment, discard our preconceived notions, and take a fresh look at these civilians willingly engaged in a truly bloody business.

Chapter 1

The Growth of War Zone Contractors

When the U.S. government experiences battlefield deficiencies, it proposes institutional, organizational, and training changes that take years to implement. But the U.S. public seems to want quicker, easier solutions than the military can deliver. The political pressure to keep wars short is intense, and capitalist business practices tend to emphasize efficiency—in other words, quick and easy solutions. Perhaps, then, the merger of war and business would inevitably lead to the employment of more and more war zone contractors.

Capitalists are one step ahead of our government's request for assistance. Unlike government institutions, a business has an obligation to make profits for its shareholders and investors. In the constant pressure to act in the best financial interest of the firm, they must fulfill contractual obligations efficiently or go out of business.

The U.S. government has proven to be less than agile in adapting to wars that don't go its way. In Vietnam, we were surprised by the resiliency of the enemy, the lack of support for a corrupt South Vietnamese government, the level of empathy for the North Vietnamese leader Ho Chi Minh, and our failure to understand the needs of the people. This shortsightedness generated opportunities for contractors to fix the problems our government had not anticipated. As the war progressed, we hired more and more contractors for infrastructure construction, political development, agricultural enhancements, education, intelligence collection, and combat-support activities. When the United States was a day late and more than a few dollars short, contractors picked up the slack.

In Iraq, the United States was once again caught off guard by the scope and dimension of the counterinsurgency battle and the requirements of that dirty word the administration doesn't like to use—*nation-building*. Assumptions about the availability of oil revenues, active support of the Iraqi people, and the limitations of outside groups to influence events were entirely incorrect.

For some reason, pundits and politicians in Washington seemed surprised by the lack of active post-war support. Much of this lack of support can be attributed to the U.S. abandonment of an Iraqi uprising a few years earlier, adding to an already blemished track record from Vietnam, Lebanon, and Somalia. Once again, civilian contractors were required to fill a void in government planning. It is often stated that the U.S. government is always prepared to fight the last war. In fact, our preparedness is worse than that. We are not prepared to fight even the last war. The U.S. government is prepared to fight only a World War II–style conflict. With the exception of our combat action on behalf of the tiny island of Grenada in the fall of 1983, it's a stretch to call any conflict since the end of World War II a victory for U.S. forces.

Even the first Gulf conflict, where we soundly defeated Saddam Hussein on the battlefield, the United States did not win the war; we won only a series of battles. Iraqi soldiers may have left Kuwait, but Iraq and Saddam continued to be a threat to world peace. To keep them out of Kuwait and under some semblance of control, we had to conduct combat air patrols up to and through the next set of battles: the second Gulf war. The number of years it will take the U.S. government to adjust to its own deficiencies is anyone's guess.

In the meantime, war zones continue to present opportunities for enterprising businesses. The resurgence of contractors is both a reflection of the changing nature of war and the inability of nations to adjust. While the magnitude of contractor employment is on the rise, the history of contractors is legendary. Following the death of Alexander the Great, the Greeks employed mercenaries to advance Hellenistic civilization. In 755, the Chinese T'ang Dynasty was nearly overthrown by mercenaries from Indian pastoral tribes. England used Flemish mercenaries for several decades in the twelfth century. In the sixteenth century, the Pope employed the Swiss Cantons, now called the Swiss Guards, who made available more than fifteen thousand of the finest warriors of their time. So good were they in battle that the Pope titled them, "The Defenders of the Church of Freedom."

In the American Revolutionary War, a group headed by none other than Benjamin Franklin, Thomas Jefferson, and Benjamin Harrison hired mercenaries to conduct intelligence operations overseas. The British hired more than thirty thousand mercenaries, many of them Germans, to fight against the colonists. In a twist of history, many German mercenaries switched sides and ultimately fought against the British. During the United States' two great wars, the use of mercenaries declined, but in the early

1960s African nations incapable of defending themselves reinvigorated mercenary employment. At the same time, private contractors in Vietnam, such as Air America, were experiencing rapid growth.

Air America has roots in an organization formed in pre–World War II days. When Japan invaded China, a group of freelance pilots, called the American Volunteer Group, flew missions against the Japanese. Later this group, renamed the Civil Air Transport, supported Chiang Kai-Shek's nationalists in combat against Mao Zedong's communists. Air America and its cousins by various names (Air Asia, Southern Air Transport, Civil Air Transport, etc.) flew operations in support of the French at the conclusive battle of Dien Bien Phu. All were U.S.-sponsored contractors assisting in the implementation of U.S. foreign policy, doing what contractors do: executing missions where U.S. military presence is not politically supportable.

During Vietnam, Presidents Johnson and Nixon repeatedly affirmed that there were no U.S. troops in Laos or Cambodia. However, neither of them are known to have denied that there were Air America contractors in Laos or Cambodia. The truth was that Air America helicopters and DC-3s were flying missions daily throughout those two countries. Air America was so commonplace in Vietnam, Laos, and Cambodia that one could identify their silver aircraft coming and going at nearly every airfield in the region. Only the most naïve visitors to Vietnam actually thought that Air America was a noncombatant civilian air transport company. Air America crews were running search-and-rescue missions to recover secret operatives and teams behind enemy lines. They were dropping food and ammunition to paid tribal mercenaries. And they were dying on a daily basis.

During the first Gulf conflict, one in fifty personnel "in country" were American contractors. Many of them were involved in technical support and reconstruction of Kuwait. In the second Gulf conflict, that number rose to one in fifteen. Granted, part of that growth is due to the scope of nation-building activities launched after the end of major hostilities, as they were called. Nevertheless, the number of contractors in the second Gulf conflict is double that of the first conflict, with less than half the number of U.S. forces involved. In addition to the numbers of contractors, of particular note, are the dangers in unprecedented proportions that all contractors now face. Unlike Kuwait, which provided a secure environment for construction contractors, there are no safe environments in Iraq.

Countries with abundant natural resources and poorly trained, ill-equipped, and untrustworthy armies hire agencies such as Executive Outcomes to protect their wealth, or in some cases, to recover it. In exchange, security firms get a cut of the action. This resembles the classic mercenary profile, which has come into greater prominence in the last thirty years, especially in Africa. Africa's contractors, some of whom are U.S. citizens, fit the stereotype of taking any side that will pay them well. Many of these contractors are former members of the South African army's Buffalo Battalion, a notorious group with an unsavory reputation for perpetuating apartheid. Executive Outcomes insists that it performs work for only legitimate governments, but there are a fair number of skeptics to this claim.

The increased power of contracting firms in Africa and expansion into other businesses has been the subject of much controversy in the United Nations and elsewhere. Contractors have been accused of competing not just for contracts, but for vital interests protected by other firms in the less visible war behind the war. They are alleged to be wielding their influence and power to colonize nations. Some of these contracting agencies have even launched public relations campaigns to clean up their image.

To stem the flood of mercenary activity in Africa, several nations have passed laws prohibiting their citizenry from involvement in military actions outside their borders. In Zimbabwe, more than sixty mercenaries were imprisoned for a plot to overthrow the government of Equatorial Guinea. Conversely, the requirements and opportunities in Africa for mercenaries continue to grow. Some are even being retained to shoot wildlife poachers. In spite of efforts to curtail contractor activity in Africa, the law of supply and demand will continue to drive a robust contracting business for many years to come.

By contrast, contractors conducting business on behalf of the U.S. government would like nothing more than to avoid the hit-man designation. That is not to say that the United States does not have a few mercenary-type contractors, nor is it beyond consideration that a foreign government might request mercenary services from a U.S. firm. This type of activity operates beneath the radar of public scrutiny, with good reason. If caught, they can kiss the possibility of future contracts—and their business—good-bye.

That said, some U.S. firms have a Teflon-like ability to conduct direct combat operations without leaving a telltale signature. Contractors' slipperiness keeps them in business. For instance, the contracting agency involved in planning and executing Croatia's successful campaign against the Serbs in the

1990s publicly denies any direct combat involvement to this day. Their explanation—training assistance—is hard to refute without any evidence. But the fact that some of these training exercises with Croatian forces turned into hostile encounters with the enemy hardly seems coincidental.

Construction and infrastructure contractors are the most diverse and come from every conceivable trade, skill, profession, avocation, and career. They are clerks, cooks, truck drivers, carpenters, bridge builders, engineers, machinists, communications specialists, computer technicians, utility installers, and oil drillers. For reasons known only to them, they are willing to risk life and limb in a war zone. They develop companionships similar to those typically found only in combat military units. Contractors share experiences on the Web, in chat rooms, and around their often abysmal living conditions. Even after returning home, they keep in touch with one another and on occasion host contractor reunions.

Military hardware has become exceedingly high tech. Units are equipped with computers, lasers, biological sniffers, mass spectrometers, robots, night-vision systems, people sensors, satellite radios, video recording equipment, and ground and aerial surveillance radar. Helicopters use advanced microchips and firing systems. High-tech gear is placed in the hands of the military years before the Department of Defense can develop the training programs to provide the required maintenance experts. Contractors are hired in droves to keep these critical battlefield devices operating. They live and work with the military units they support. There is constant pressure to reduce turnaround time on broken equipment. Increasingly, they are brought farther forward on the battlefield. The idea is to fix and repair as close to the user as possible. Increasingly, they are placed in harm's way.

Civilian logistics, infrastructure, trucking, and technical contractors are caught in the conundrum of modern war. They are prohibited from carrying weapons. When the rules were made, war zones and the geographical employment of these contractors was perceived to be something different from the realities of counterinsurgency conflict now taking place in countries like Iraq. The law was meant to prevent contractors from losing legal protections afforded noncombatants and to reduce the chances that civilian contractors will shoot the wrong people. These prohibitions do not sufficiently resolve the environmental realities these men and women face. Today's enemies do not respect a civilian's noncombatant status. The enemy shoots civilian contractors as casually as they shoot soldiers.

When the military is unable to provide civilian truck convoys with even a token armed escort, as is often the case, the convoys must employ private security companies to protect their personnel, supplies, and vehicles. But with convoys frequently stretching long distances over winding roads, one or more segments might face enemy fire with escorts unaware or unable to respond.

The number and complexity of logistics and construction operations in Iraq stretches the army too thin to adequately provide daily protection to these activities, so utility and construction firms are forced to employ private security contractors. The war zone proliferates with civilians protecting civilians. These contractors quickly become streetwise to nuances of war, developing a keen sense of danger and planning for all contingencies.

The thought of having to shoot one's way out of an impending ambush leaves many contractors on edge. Employees want to get home to their families, and it gets expensive for companies to replace the ones that get hurt. Fueled by survival instinct and simple economics to use the very best weaponry, protection, and employees, firms turn to ex-military and law enforcement personnel to give them the upper hand.

Former special forces, Navy Seals, Marine Force Recon, Air Force pararescue, and law enforcement personnel are flooded with opportunities to join the war zone contracting industry. Many become trainers, personal-security agents, and asset-protection guards. Security and training contractors often seek and receive permission to carry weapons. If they are not authorized to carry a personal firearm, they get around this limitation by theoretically having to conduct firearms training, twenty-four hours a day. They have been attacked while training police or military units or protecting their assignment. Under these conditions, they are authorized to use lethal force to subdue their attackers. And they do.

Although they are not official combatants and are not subject to the same law of war/armed conflict and rules of engagement as military personnel, they are restricted on the type of firearms they are authorized to carry. Theoretically, they will use weapons only in a self-defense mode. Other than the military and police-unit trainers, some contractors are not allowed to carry fully automatic weapons and some are restricted to handguns. These restrictions seem to change daily. This is yet another example of the U.S. government's failure to adapt to new exigencies. On the other hand, weapons manufacturers are not so slow at the draw. They are one step ahead of government and have recently been offering personal sidearms that tread a fine line regarding these limitations yet provide the user with a higher level of accurate, lethal firepower.

John Karuza, a military training contractor, tells a story of weapons being acquired in an unconventional way. Karuza spent a year training Iraqi soldiers, who bonded with him as their teacher—a kind of bond Iraqis are known for, one that crosses cultural, ethnic, national, and religious borders.

While training the Iraqis, Karuza had not been authorized to carry a personal sidearm. By the time of his subsequent return to Iraq, the soldiers he and his fellow contractors had trained were in leadership positions. They confronted the U.S. military, demanding that their friend Karuza and his fellow contractors be properly armed. Their demands were nonnegotiable. The confrontation concluded with the U.S. Army coughing up about a hundred weapons.

The United States continually struggles to keep control in the war zone. But the government's muddled bureaucracy is slow to recognize new developments and adapt accordingly. Politicians seem surprised by the organization, structure, and dynamics, or lack thereof, in the twenty-first-century war zone. The battlefield spirals out of control with insurgents armed to the teeth who mix with the Iraqi populace, with no telling friend from foe. Faced with the constant threat of being killed or captured, contractors have no illusions about a cavalry coming over the hill to rescue them. Self-sufficient and street-smart, many contractors, including truck drivers, technicians, and construction workers, have resorted to buying unauthorized weapons on the black market. It's every man and woman for themselves.

It doesn't do much good to fix training problems at the front lines, while leaving a country's leadership unchanged. In Vietnam, we saw example after example of corrupt or incompetent mid- to senior-level leaders. In that country, much of the military and political leadership was not fit to lead or employ the civilians and soldiers in their charge. There was a breakdown of confidence at every level, with the South Vietnamese army's morale in the toilet. The rural people were indifferent or opposed to the elected provincial and national leaders. To witness the void between Vietnam's leadership and the people, one only had to wander into a thatched hut in some rural village or hamlet. In accordance with the law, each hut was adorned with framed photographs of their president. A common image showed him in a suit and tie standing next to a Lincoln Continental. Little wonder that peasants and farmers related more to Ho Chi Minh than the government we were there to support.

The U.S. State Department and the Department of Defense have done little training of advisors for local and regional officials and senior-level military officers of developing nations in the time since Vietnam. They have deemphasized counterinsurgency training and focused more on conventional combat tactics. Many post-Vietnam special forces units were deactivated, and funding for these types of units was severely curtailed. The basic premise of military thinking was that nation-building was not part of the U.S. military's charter. Recently, the army has taken steps to expand the reserve component of civil affairs. But civil affairs soldiers remain limited in what they can do to help local civil, military, and law enforcement authorities in third world nations, and they know next to nothing about rebuilding decapitated militaries.

With the shortage of advisors, trainers, and strategic planners for these countries, it seems that the U.S. government has left these difficult tasks up to contract agencies. Firms like MPRI and SAIC have answered the call. Accordingly, the entrepreneurial vision of these companies has brought them a wealth of business in reconstruction and force development.

The president and founder of MPRI is former U.S. Army Chief of Staff General Carl Vuono. His right-hand man is retired General Ron Griffith, who, among his many distinguished assignments, was the army's vice chief of staff and commander of the 1st Armored Division during the first Gulf conflict. They are surrounded on a daily basis by a support staff of high-level government employees and accomplished civilian and military professionals, many with offices in the State Department, Department of Justice, and the Department of Defense. It is fair to call them part of the Beltway establishment.

MPRI projected a need and delivered the expertise to train and advise both senior civilian and military leaders in several conflicts. They assist and review military, political, tactical, and strategic objectives. MPRI is under contract to advise leaders in dozens of countries. Former U.S. colonels and generals teach principles of military decision making and leadership; provide feedback from their field-level operators, both civil and military; and act as a conduit for communication between leadership levels for their counterparts.

Organizing elections, developing governmental agencies, managing economic growth, developing new trade relationships, and creating impartial judicial processes are complex, sensitive, and often alien endeavors to war-torn countries. When elected officials and candidates for office in Afghanistan and

Iraq sought help in effectively communicating their messages to the people, U.S. advertising agencies came out of the woodwork, providing expertise and marketing savvy in a neutral—and sometimes clandestine—manner.

In January 2005, the Iraqi people were presented with a series of slick television ads that promoted unity among Iraq's three major parties. One video clip portrayed Shiites, Sunnis, and Kurds engaged in an angry exchange. Children from the three groups rush forward to hug one another. The adults in the video clip look on with embarrassment over their own prejudicial behavior. The ad ends with the message: "Divided, we won't conquer." No firm has stepped forward to take credit for the paid advertisements, and the stations themselves remain mum on the subject, but the skills behind them had all the hallmarks of a Madison Avenue ad agency.

U.S. law enforcement personnel, including senior officials such as former New York City Police Commissioner Bernard Kerik, continually contract their services to various foreign countries. These services include providing security for U.S. enterprises and developing the host country's police force. Sometimes they work directly for a U.S. government agency, other times as an employee of a government contracting firm.

Sometimes it isn't clear exactly who they are working for, a disquieting and not-so-infrequent experience in the extremely tight-lipped world of war zone contracting. Contractors are often hired for jobs that they assume represent U.S. interests, but being that the hiring party might be three or four rungs removed from the original contracting agency, they could be at cross-purposes to the United States and not even realize it. Dozens of firms in Iraq have been said to represent themselves as being associated with "the Agency"—the CIA. In fact, they are really with one of a number of other government agencies (OGAs) or sub-subcontractors, many levels removed from the original contracting firm or OGA. Unlike the CIA, the activities of numerous OGAs and subcontractors in the war zone are unaccounted for in Pentagon records.

The United Nations has proven to be slow and inefficient when it comes to planning free elections in newly democratic countries. When such bodies fail, contracting firms, including nonprofit organizations, frequently step in to fill the vacuum. They help plan elections, identify polling stations, design ballots, distribute election materials, and provide observers to monitor the voting process. One such nonprofit, the International Foundation for Election Systems (IFES), has rendered election assistance in more than 120 countries. Profit or nonprofit, it doesn't make much difference to the individual paid contractor.

War zone contractors are like baseball free agents—the best ones go to the highest bidder. In this environment, salaries and benefits packages have skyrocketed.

The demand for contractors is so high that it has spawned recruiting activity known as "contract jumping." Companies that lose employees this way lambaste it as corporate theft, but those that benefit call it fair competition. Firms that hire contractors on the cheap, they say, get what they deserve. In-country recruiters have been known to solicit employees from other companies right in the middle of the war zone. In one such scenario, a recruiter from ABC firm drives onto a base and approaches a contractor from XYZ company. The recruiter informs the contractor that if he gets into the car with him, he'll guarantee a 50 percent increase in his compensation package.

Sometimes they negotiate up to twice the salary, with a signing bonus to boot. It's no wonder contractors have a hard time saying no. While many firms consider this blatant thievery, they would have a hard time proving it in court. The offending companies are too clever about getting around the legal and ethical restrictions.

In business terms, the demand for contractors exceeds the supply. The result has been a deterioration of hiring standards and a flood of relatively unskilled and inexperienced contractors on the battlefield. We'll explore the consequences of this in a later chapter.

Chapter 2

Five Criticisms of Private Military Contracting

As the numbers of private military contractors (PMCs) has grown, they have been subject to more and more criticism. The public image of contractors might be near the bottom of any opinion poll, right there with lawyers and politicians.

While the critics are most vocal about the corporate entities themselves, the individual employees have also faced their share of criticism. Detractors apply the term *mercenary* in its most derogatory sense—money-grubbing opportunists who kill for money.

The criticisms might be divided into five general categories: *greed, cronyism, disproportionate role* in the mission, lack of *self-restraint* on the battlefield, and lack of *accountability*. Let's address them one by one.

Greed

Without a doubt, corporations and individuals are motivated by money to get into the war zone contracting business. But there is another aspect of human nature at play; people tend to gravitate toward what they do best. This is true of individuals, and it is true of corporations. One corporate example is Halliburton, which, along with its subsidiary Kellogg, Brown & Root (KBR), has been operating in the Middle East for decades.

As for individuals, there are plenty of military veterans who will jump at the money and bring a lot of skills to the table. The military's up-or-out promotion system for officers forces people into retirement at relatively young ages. It's common for a soldier to retire between the ages of thirty-seven and forty-seven. Employment opportunities are not abundant for them, so it's no surprise that they gravitate toward contracting for the Department of Defense. It's the area they know best.

Some talking heads have declared that the best military men and women are being lured out of the service for high-paying contractor jobs. Many highly skilled career soldiers feel insulted to have their loyalty questioned in such a way. There is little or no evidence to support this contention. The benefits of resigning a military career to pursue a contracting opportunity aren't as great as many people think. After years of specialized training, to jump ship, thus foregoing retirement pay and benefits for what is certain to be a short-lived financial opportunity, can be a very shortsighted decision. Contracting income is tied too closely to uncontrollable and unpredictable national and international developments. The most skilled soldiers are who they are and get to where they are because they are educated, analytical people.

That said, the U.S. Army has a well-documented history of throwing out great soldiers as soon as conflicts wind down. For example, following the Vietnam conflict, thousands of highly skilled helicopter pilots and special forces officers were forcibly discharged from the army. The peacetime military no longer required their services. It is reasonable to assume that the same thing will happen after the Iraq conflict. Those commissioned officers who joined the service to fly helicopters are pretty much out of a flying job once they attain the rank of captain. If they still want to fly in combat-type operations, their only choice is to sign on with a security contractor like Blackwater USA. When a soldier leaves the service now and goes to work for a contracting firm, he or she may be just a year or so ahead of the axe. For the most part, it's the U.S. military's fault for losing highly qualified people, not the compensation offers of contracting firms. Even our best-trained soldiers have little or no job security. It's foolhardy to believe otherwise.

Furthermore, all branches of the military send people to school with highly specific prerequisites that the service member will have x amount of time remaining on his or her enlistment following completion of the training. This ensures that U.S. armed forces get an adequate return on their investment. The military has the option of increasing the time requirements remaining after schooling is complete, or improving the pay and working conditions for highly skilled personnel.

Perhaps it isn't a bad thing that the Department of Defense is faced with some healthy competition. The U.S. Air Force, in particular, has had a tough time through the years retaining pilots who might be lured out of the service for much higher paying jobs flying commercial airliners. The DoD has addressed this problem, at least in part, by developing compensation and benefits packages, including fair pay, retirement, and a bonus system that recognizes the extraordinary demands of military service on the individual service members and their families. A more recent development is the DoD's effort to improve retention of special forces personnel along these same lines.

Salaries for contractors and especially security contractors are often exaggerated in the press. Like the stories about fourteen-hundred-dollar coffeemakers and three-thousand-dollar toilet seats, accounts of individuals making a thousand dollars a day are taken to represent the entire profession. While true in extremely rare cases, these stories don't accurately represent the usual compensation, nor do they take expenditures or costly sacrifices into account. Most U.S. citizens working in a war zone are skilled at their jobs and are making between $50,000 and $120,000 a year. Similar jobs in the United States would pay about 20 to 30 percent less. The few contractors who make more are typically in very dangerous assignments, such as the Blackwater USA contractors who provided security for Paul Bremer, the top U.S. man in Iraq at the time.

Most contractors say they would have gone to the war zone for half of their salary. Common motivating characteristics among these men and women is their desire for adventure, a sense of patriotism, and work flexibility not found in military service. They look for professionalism in their contracting firm of choice—the kind that keeps a person alive—with compensation a secondary factor at best. For most rational people, money alone could never be worth the risk that war zone contractors face on a daily basis.

Critics are quick to point out huge contracts and accuse contracting firms of bilking the U.S. government. If those critics were to ride shotgun in a KBR truck from Kuwait to Mosul for just one day, they might change their minds. Iraq is a scary place, and it tests one's values and deeply held convictions. When faced with the reality of what's going on, money alone is meager compensation. People who go there for the money often return home within a week after arrival. That's their prerogative. If it weren't for strict military discipline, many soldiers would be headed home right there with them, patriotism or sense of duty be damned.

KBR operates under cost-plus contracts. According to the General Accounting Office (GAO), they receive their actual costs plus 1 to 3 percent profit above and beyond their expenses. The awards are down from the 1 to 9 percent formerly awarded during the 1990s. This is in line with most defense contracts and is not extraordinary by any industry standards, even if they achieve their maximum profit potential.

Granted, that still amounts to a lot of money given that contracts for Halliburton and its subsidiary, KBR, are running into the billions of dollars, but it certainly does not fit the business model of most U.S. enterprises. Especially when taken into the context of the job KBR is performing, the profits are marginal. According to Alfred Neffgin, a KBR CEO, during his congressional testimony in July 2004, his employees, equipment, and construction sites in Iraq were enduring forty to eighty enemy attacks per week. Since then, insurgent attacks have consistently increased and those numbers have gone up substantially.

Some security companies bill $1,500 to $2,000 per day, per contractor. These billing charges are unrelated to the individual contractor's compensation. After factoring in extraordinary expenses—overhead such as the cost of health and life insurance, everyday transportation in and out of the war zone, lodging, and specialized equipment—the profits don't look so profitable. And it's nearly impossible to gauge the long-term health of private military contractors, given the volatility of the international political situation. Only a handful of PMCs survive in this volatile business environment.

And if not for ready, willing, and able civilian contractors, who else would do it? Critics often fail to calculate the true cost of maintaining a large enough military force capable of responding to the full spectrum of potential conflicts. By some estimates, a soldier earning $35,000 to $40,000 a year actually costs the government about $25,000 a month. Contracting secures badly needed talent without the long-term economic or political costs.

Those individual contractors who do survive and grow accustomed to the missions seem to have trouble leaving. When they do leave the war zone, they often return home and find themselves walking in circles. Nothing seems to make them happy or content. They've lived on the edge too long and now find it hard to cope with regular life. It sounds strange, but many head back to the war zone not for the money, but for the experience of closeness with fellow human beings, that special camaraderie that comes from facing danger together on a daily basis.

The real difference between soldiers and contractors is that contractors have more experience. Some would argue that the civilian contractor should not only get paid for it, he should get paid well. As with any profession, experience is a highly valued commodity. Whether the contractor is a long-haul trucker or a former drill sergeant, he's been doing his job for years. He is damn good at it. He has developed a lot of skills. And most importantly, he isn't any less a patriotic citizen than those in uniform.

Cronyism

Kellogg, Brown & Root's geographical dispersion, core pool of skilled personnel, and equipment designed for the Iraq war zone are virtually unmatched. Their subcontractors know the drill, and they understand the nuances of working with U.S. military units. The learning curve for a new low-bid contractor is painful at best and can cost lives at worst. KBR has a reputation for getting the job done. For whatever reasons, KBR received so many initial contracts, one can find little fault in their ability to meet government requirements in a professional and expeditious manner. The U.S. military is reticent to send an unseasoned unit into the war zone, and it follows that we would not want to send in unseasoned contractors.

Major Thomas Palermo knows something about the real cost of trying to run a war in a competitive bidding scenario. He commands NAVISTAR, a dusty convoy staging base on the Kuwait-Iraq border. "When I first came to the Middle East I was not a KBR fan," Palermo admits. "But now that we have been forced to award building and trucking contracts to other low bidders, I have truly come to appreciate what KBR brings to the table. Most of the new firms are just clueless as to how to get the job done. They bluffed their way into a contract as a 'qualified' bidder and now we are paying the price. At least you felt with KBR that they were just an extension of your military unit. They know what to do and don't gripe at every turn. They are truly a 'can-do' operation."

KBR began as Brown and Root, founded in Texas in 1919 by siblings George R. Brown and Herman Brown and their brother-in-law, Dan Root. Its first job was supervising the building of naval warships. KBR's start-up scenario is similar to that of its younger contracting peers: a couple of retired generals founded the company, then got their foot in the door with the help of the active-duty generals who were their understudies in years past.

Many believe this is a classic old-boy network, and thus should be subject to a fairness evaluation process; if the fair-haired stepchild gets the war zone contract, it should be disallowed. All things being equal, yes; however, all things are not equal, particularly when it's about life and death. Objectivity is not the highest priority in a war zone strewn with roadside bombs and the threat of beheadings. When it comes to training coalition forces or protecting the interim Iraqi president, one questions whether the trust that comes from only personal, first-hand knowledge of a contractor's experience should be outweighed by another contractor's low bid.

The growth of modern contracting is a relatively new phenomenon—easy to criticize, but hard for policy makers to wrap their arms around. They have yet to digest all the implications and seem light years away from any real solution to the issue of fairness in hiring contractors. Perhaps there needs to be some elaborate proving ground that will demonstrate and test the abilities of trainers and armed war-zone contractors. Meanwhile, the cronyism charges will continue as the old-boy network thrives, some would argue, by life-or-death necessity.

Disproportionate Role

In March 2004, four Blackwater USA contractors ran out of luck on a mission into Fallujah. Crowds ambushed and killed a team of former Navy Seals and U.S. Army Rangers, suspending two of their lifeless bodies from a bridge, leaving the other two dead, burned, and dismembered at the scene of the ambush.

Blackwater asserted that the four men were security contractors, providing protection for a food truck on its way to a U.S. military base, and reports of their being mercenaries on a mission to snatch insurgents were false. Much of the world refused to make the distinction. Security contractor is just another name for paid mercenary, and the general feeling outside the United States is that they got what they deserved.

Overwhelmingly, the majority of security contractor missions in Iraq consists of convoy protection, personal bodyguards, and critical-site protection. For them, the label *mercenary* is misleading and unwarranted. Every day in Iraq, dozens of security contractor firms are engaged in protecting mail, food, supplies, and fuel shipments throughout the country. The use of civilians to accomplish these tasks frees soldiers to do what they are there to do—fight enemy insurgents.

In the last sixty years, civilians working in a war zone generally fit one of two categories. Either they were defense contractors like Halliburton, employing personnel to rebuild a war-ravaged country's infrastructure, or they were mercenaries. Although the public doesn't seem to hold either in great favor, at least the lines between the two were very distinct, until now. New developments blur those distinctions: the military is overtaxed and war-zone contractors are in far greater danger than ever before. They are forced to provide their own security, and they often take up arms themselves or hire people to provide protection. Additionally, there are myriad jobs that never existed in previous wars, and everyone working in Iraq or Afghanistan requires personal security.

During the first Gulf conflict, Red Adair Company and others entered Kuwait and Iraq to put out the hundreds of oil rig fires. Back then, most of the public was supportive, if not always approving. That military units alone could not accomplish the job without the help of contractors seemed obvious. Much like the immediate aftermath of 9/11, firefighters in the Gulf had the status of true heroes.

This was only the beginning, and the business of contracting was about to explode.

While the military focused on combat preparedness for the diverse nature of future conflicts, it fell behind in the demand for the countless peripheral services that would be required in the evolving war zone. Protecting military convoys is one thing, but providing daily protection for thousands of civilian trucks pouring supplies into rebuilding a country is quite another. Even if the DoD had predicted personnel needs with 100 percent accuracy, it would still have had to outsource the countless support jobs, from providing security for local, national, and international political representatives to driving a steady stream of trucks and moving supplies under constant enemy fire. With the public's unwillingness to support a national draft, the military will increasingly look to the private sector for the foreseeable future.

Thousands of individual contractors come from countries other than the United States. Military contracts frequently result in the hiring of third world nationals as truck drivers. This is a source of great anxiety to U.S. military forces assigned to provide security to these convoys of what are known pejoratively as "Haji drivers," for they are completely unpredictable, particularly in an ambush situation. There could be any combination of a dozen or so languages flying around all at once. The language barrier makes the resulting chaos all the more impossible to control, so U.S. gun-truck escorts are thrilled when they see U.S. drivers at the helm.

Training military personnel to survive and win at war is a huge endeavor, and must be constantly improved and updated as the nature of war evolves. Military training commands are operating at maximum capacity. U.S. Army Reserve and National Guard training units have been spread especially thin. Therefore, our government continues to outsource military and nonmilitary training to the private sector. In so doing, it makes sense to give special consideration to former military people who understand the growing complexity of the war zone.

Training another country's entire army is complicated to say the least, especially when that foreign army will be going straight into combat. Civilians with previous military training experience are desperately needed to fill the void. Some will be used to train foreign soldiers and others will be used to conduct specialized training for coalition force units.

Building an entire national police force largely from scratch in a country that has known only a ruthless dictatorship for decades is no easy task. Moreover, it has never been part of the U.S. military's mission until now. Instilling a strong rule of law into the new Iraqi police force (the kind dedicated to the principle of innocent until proven guilty, and one in which even the most hardened criminals have rights) will require years of training and monitoring. Not to mention that fire departments, hospitals, schools, elections, and political and judicial processes require civilian contractors willing to risk their lives in the interests of U.S. foreign policy.

The U.S. armed forces were not designed for the kind of conflicts and security issues that the United States now faces.

We can only hope that U.S. defense strategists are planning a redesign of the military force structure. The required changes will take years to implement. In the interim, civilian contractors are more than a stopgap solution and will become only more essential as our enemies present us with new threats.

Self-restraint

Security contractors have been frequently cited for shooting first and asking questions later. In one incident, a private military contractor was escorting a convoy through a U.S. Army checkpoint by helicopter. The contractor allegedly teargassed the soldiers managing the checkpoint to accelerate movement. There is no question that some civilian security firms have gotten out of hand at times. The lack of self-restraint has the potential to jeopardize U.S. objectives. And things may get worse before they get better, as new security firms pop up faster than quality-control programs can be implemented.

War zones are chaotic environments. Accurate, factual stories are hard to come by. Even the participants themselves rarely give the same accounting of events. Allegations about undisciplined military operations materialize on a daily basis. Many have a kernel or more of truth, but others are the by-products of fertile imaginations. The same can be said for allegations of misconduct on the part of civilian contractors.

The Internet is full of stories of resentment and discrimination on the part of military personnel against high-paid civilian contractors in the war zone. In some cases, military units have treated contractors poorly and with disdain. Documented cases of mistreatment of civilian contractors by soldiers or marines have emerged, but they are rare in the scheme of things.

In those few isolated cases, the mistreated contractors are often themselves former soldiers or marines. It is highly improbable that these veterans would flagrantly disregard or jeopardize the lives of military personnel. But young soldiers and marines who feel underpaid and underappreciated have a hard time suppressing their jealousy toward contractors, veterans and otherwise. They view them all as civilians with guns, living in hotels, and driving SUVs, while they, by contrast, are forced to rough it. These young servicemen and women do not always fully accept or understand the critical roles that experienced contractors fill on the battlefield.

In the rush to meet battlefield requirements, some contracting firms, whether inadvertently or by necessity, find themselves working in isolation from military units. It's no wonder that both groups feel alienated from one another. On the other hand, relationships between contractors and military units tend to flourish when there is better communication, education, and closer working relationships. In such cases, the friendship, respect, and support for one another can be remarkable. They demonstrate all the characteristics of a team. Throughout Iraq, civilian security contractors and military personnel share information about the enemy on the roads ahead. Military homecomings, like the one held in Paris, Illinois, in June 2005, often include both civilian contractors and their counterpart soldiers.

To deter undisciplined incidents and assist the military development of standards for contractors, reputable firms have worked hard at self-regulation. A group of contractors now subscribes to the code of conduct established by the International Peace Operations Association (IPOA). This code requires that private military contractors and their employees conduct themselves in accordance with key international and human-rights laws governing conduct while involved in peace or stability operations. It also requires complete openness with the International Red Cross. The document holds PMCs accountable in conflict and post-conflict environments, and the signatories are required to fully cooperate with all investigations conducted by relevant authorities. While the consequence of failure to follow the code is merely dismissal from the organization, it is, nevertheless, a positive step in the right direction. Membership is, at a minimum, a criterion the U.S. government might apply in the selection of PMCs.

The flip side of this problem is that the rules of engagement are designed around the application of conventional military units on the battlefield. In Iraq, these rules are established by the Coalition Forces Land Component Command (CFLCC) and do not seem to have considered that every civilian contractor is a potential enemy target. Although security contractors are becoming better armed and equipped every day, few of them possess the weapons and combat support of units normally associated with military operations. This lack of needed equipment makes them more vulnerable to an effective attack than their counterparts in uniform.

PMCs may or may not have Kevlar helmets, individual body armor, bulletproof glass, armored cars, medical evacuation helicopters, attack aircraft circling overhead, trained medics, and a quick reaction force that can bail them out of trouble. If a security contractor thinks he may be fired upon with small-arms fire, there can be no delay in his reaction time. Riding in standard SUVs or trucks without armored plating, contractors are very exposed. And they know it! They compensate by asserting a level of aggressiveness that they hope will ward off would-be attackers. The challenge is to keep their aggression within the bounds of the rules of engagement. This is a fine line to walk.

One might rationally argue that the equipment issue is their problem, and so it is. To outfit a PMC like an army unit is going to cost a lot of money, and that translates into bigger and bigger contracts and all the attendant issues. We return to the problem of low bidders entering the conflict unprepared to do the job. You get what you pay for. In fact, more and more third world countries are jumping into security contracting. They drive roads guarding convoys with equipment that suggests that they surely believe their employees are highly expendable. The problem is that not only do the foreign contractors get killed but every person in the convoy is in grave danger when ostensibly protected by such poorly trained and poorly prepared security companies. Another illustrative example was the sight of a personal bodyguard contractor walking around with his client in the insurgent-infested city of Fallujah, with nothing more than a .38-caliber revolver in his pocket—no body armor, no extra ammunition, no radio, no backup. One would have thought he was guarding an ice cream stand at Disneyland.

Critics of armed civilians on the battlefield also point out that carrying weapons voids any protections afforded noncombatants by the Geneva Convention. As a theoretical matter, they are correct, and many countries are in various stages of proposing new guidelines concerning protection and conduct of civilian contractors. However, as a practical matter, the United States is fighting enemies that have no respect whatsoever for the protections of the Geneva Convention. Any number of *unarmed* civilians have been tortured and executed by insurgents in Iraq. As a protection for U.S. civilians working in the war zone, the shield of the Geneva Convention is useless.

In spite of the fact that terrorists disregard every moral convention of war and international law, some would suggest that we follow them to the letter. As to the portion of the Geneva Accords regarding being armed, no sane person travels through Iraq without a weapon or an abundance of security guards. This does not translate into combatants looking to do battle with the enemy. Carrying a weapon or being surrounded by people who do, does not make a journalist, a mail carrier, a trucker, or a personal bodyguard, fair game to be executed if captured.

Accountability

After counting U.S. forces, civilian contractors represent the next largest contributor of personnel to coalition forces in Iraq. The expanded use of contractors on the battlefield has moral, ethical, political, and economic implications. To many, it's all negative and spells disaster in the making. They perceive the expansion of war-zone contractors as the abdication of military power from the state to the private sector. As PMCs get better and better organized and equipped, who will control them in the international market? Who is going to disarm them and when? Are they legitimate businesses performing vital services to many countries? Their employee makeup is becoming multicultural. Where are their loyalties? Does their loyalty rest with whoever is their client, be it a nation, religion, tribe, or ethnic group?

Clearly, the potential for PMCs to ignore national interest and pursue business interest is very real. It's almost unfortunate that war-zone contractors are so good at what they do. This burgeoning business enterprise has provided military expertise that allows governments and private parties to launch military operations without the full support of their population. Because contract operations do not get the visibility that military operations do, the true cost, in terms of lives and impact on U.S. foreign policy, is disguised. As a concerned public, we need to be far more aware and informed about where, when, and how the United States employs these firms.

PMCs offer a big advantage in terms of efficiency. They can tailor personnel resources for nearly any given job, almost on the spur of the moment. They can bring skill sets and institutional knowledge to numerous foreign policy challenges. If the loyalties, conduct, ethics, and armament of PMCs can be controlled, their use is a very practical solution to many military and humanitarian contingencies.

As to the future application of PMCs, consider an argument advanced by David Gwydion, a U.S. historian at a London University: "Muslims in North Sudan are butchering non-Muslims in the South and West. In the aftermath of the Iraq debacle, we cannot expect that any western state will intervene militarily to put an end to this particular chapter of human misery. Nor can we count on any non-military multilateralism to be of much help. Sanctions anyone? Soft power?" He continues: "Why don't liberal humanitarian interventionists simply club together, raise the cash, and send a bunch of PMCs over to Darfur to protect women and children from the Janjaweed currently butchering them? . . . [F]uture PMCs will probably be our only option for projecting power abroad for humanitarian purposes."

Most PMCs are not mercenaries. They are a new breed of military trainers, technicians, advisors, drivers, consultants, medical, and security personnel. The negative connotations of the past must be abandoned and replaced with a more intellectual analysis of the best methods to control and utilize this resource. The only alternative would be to double the size of the military, and that is neither desirable nor necessary. We need to adjust to, and get comfortable with, the expansion of private military contractors, which will continue to thrive as an extension of the U.S. Department of Defense and a major player in modern warfare.

Chapter 3

Becoming a Contractor

"Take a close look at these images," the contracting firm recruiter directs his group of job applicants. He flips through a series of slides depicting gunshot wounds, dead bodies, and blown-up buildings. "These little prefab buildings will be your new home. Of course, we've repaired the buildings since these pictures were taken, but you never know when they'll be attacked again." The recruiter flips the slides to an image of the burning hulk of a tractor trailer. "Here is one of our trucks that was hit just last week. The driver lost a limb and his eyesight, but he'll live." Perhaps it's a macho thing, but aside from the occasional grimace and one individual's sprint to the bathroom, most applicants showed little indication of being deterred by the barrage of grisly images flashing before their eyes.

This kind of screening is standard for most reputable contracting firms. It costs a lot less to weed out people before they deploy than it does to bring them back home later. Nearly all defense contracting firms have an orientation and training program to prepare their new hires prior to leaving the States. Inevitably, nearly all the orientations begin with visual projections of the true face of war. Experienced contractors who have recently served in the war zone tell it like it is to the new recruits. In the earlier days of the war, firms were somewhat timid about exposing job applicants to the horrors of combat.

Today, for the most part, it's a no-holds-barred presentation. Also surprising, only about 20 percent back out.

Frequently Asked Questions

Prospective war-zone contractors often ask the same questions: How do I get hired? How long is the term of a contract? What are training and preparation like? Will I be covered by life insurance? Who takes care of me if I am injured or wounded? Will I receive long-term medical care for a serious injury? What if I can't work? Can I carry a gun? If yes, can I bring one with me? How do contractors get weapons? How long is a typical contract? What if I need to break my contract? How frequently can I leave the country for a visit with my family? Do I have to pay my own travel costs if I go home for a family visit? Can my PMC cancel my contract without notice? Will I have a computer and Internet access? Will I have a phone? Are my telephone calls paid for? Where do I eat? Where do I sleep? What clothing should I bring? Will I be given body armor and a helmet? What happens if I die?

Some of these questions can be answered definitively, but most of them have no standard answer. I hope the reader will accept a few generalizations and examples of how some major contracting firms have addressed these questions and how they have attempted to resolve these problems.

Unfortunately, very few of these issues are covered by any laws or regulations. Benefits packages and the cost to an individual contractor will vary from company to company. Applicants for contractor jobs should, at a minimum, know the range of possibilities and common practices.

Getting the Job

The best way to land a war-zone contracting job is to network, to "know a guy who knows a guy." Contractors who have served in a war zone are eminently qualified to determine the type of person who will function and survive in a war zone. Often they can read the *right* personality in a heartbeat. The volume of people pestering for endorsements for each opening can inundate the well-connected individual. It is not uncommon for casual contacts to ask veteran contractors for personal endorsements, pleading "Hey man, get me a job over there." Rather than tell most of them the hard truth—that they don't have the right stuff—many vets keep their war-zone experience a closely guarded secret.

Most contractor veterans won't refer riffraff to the war zone. They know what kind of team effort surviving requires and they feel an obligation to those who are over there. For these reasons, recruiters are very responsive to applicants who come along with a personal referral, either verbal or written, attached to the inquiry. Inexperienced applicants should not pressure a veteran for a referral. If he or she does refer you, consider yourself one of the very fortunate.

In the back of this book is a listing of security contracting firms. All of them have websites, most of which have a recruiter contact link. If you have a relevant background, summarize your experience and attach a résumé or complete the online application form—mail it at the same time for extra insurance. A week or so later, follow up with a phone call. Leave a message that refers to your having sent an application by e-mail and/or regular mail. This gives the recruiter an opportunity to find it before he or she returns your call. If you just call and you're lucky enough to get a live human being on the phone, at least have a summary of your experience in front of you during the conversation. Expect that you will be asked to mail or fax that summary to the recruiter.

Compensation and Length of Contract

Compensation is the most challenging topic to draw any generalizations about. Not only is it different for each contracting firm, but as personnel resources become harder to acquire, companies are changing their pay rates to attract qualified candidates. Many war-zone compensation packages have some version of three major components: a base salary, an area bonus (called a work area differential), and hazard pay. The work area differential pay takes into account the hardships associated with living in a particular foreign country, and the hazard pay can best be defined as the additional money you get for being shot at!

The area differential and hazard pay are a percentage calculated on your base pay. Base pay is usually somewhere between $2,000 and $6,000 a month, with both area and hazard pay being 25 percent each. For hospitalized, missing, or captured contractors, their pay will normally continue at whatever their average pay had been in the preceding months while they were on contract. As you might have guessed, in addition to base pay, both area and hazard pay will continue during medical recovery, captivity, or detention.

In addition to the three types of compensation previously discussed, some contracting firms offer what is called a foreign service bonus. This is generally a percentage of *base* pay only and may be paid monthly, quarterly, or annually, depending on the specific contract. At least one major contractor computes this bonus as 5 percent of base and pays it on a monthly basis.

Most contracts are written for twelve-month periods and can be terminated at any time by either party. However, if you terminate early, your ride home may be charged to your final paycheck.

Medical and Life Insurance

All U.S. contractors and subcontractors working in a war zone are required to cover their employees with a form of workers compensation insurance known as the Defense Base Act (DBA) insurance. U.S. firms are required to show proof that they have acquired this insurance before they can be awarded a contract. DBA covers medical treatment and lost wages as a result of injuries incurred on the job. The cost of DBA is risk proportionate to the location and job being performed. As you can imagine, security contractors in Iraq are at the high end of the cost spectrum.

Many war zone contractors receive extended insurance under the War Hazards Compensation Act (WHCA). If a contractor is injured, killed, or captured as result of war-related risk, WHCA reimburses the insurance carrier for claims made by the contractor or his family. The claims do not have to be job related. Just the fact that the contractor was on contract in a declared or undeclared conflict is sufficient. An organization called the Employees Compensation Fund is responsible for war-hazard compensation. The fund, like so many other aspects of the war in the Middle East, could not have anticipated the volume of claims emerging from the Iraq conflict. This is a federally funded program that receives about $2 billion a year. How Congress will address the issue of dwindling resources remains to be seen.

Expect to pay around $200 to $300 a month for medical and life insurance premiums. That'll buy you a million dollar health insurance policy with about a maximum of $2,000 out-of-pocket expenses. The attached life insurance will probably contain a $25,000 or $50,000 death benefit. In country, U.S. military bases have medical facilities that will take care of you for routine medical problems such as colds, flu, insect bites, sprained ankles, dysentery, infections, broken bones, shrapnel, and minor gunshot wounds. Yes, many shrapnel and gunshot wounds are minor problems in this environment. The workload managed by military medics and doctors is overwhelming. In the last couple of years, they have treated more than fifteen thousand military and civilian combat injuries and tens of thousands of routine ailments. They don't appreciate whiners, so be prepared to suck it up, and don't take up their time unless you absolutely have to.

If your wounds or injuries are serious, you will be evacuated by military aircraft to a more advanced echelon of care at a military hospital, such as the one at Ramstein Air Base in Germany. At some point, you may be sent back to the States. Often, you are simply patched up and sent back to finish your contract. Many wounded contractors do a lot of soul searching during their recovery and are not anxious to jump back on a plane to the war zone. Still others can't wait to get back; this is a common phenomenon among many combat veterans. If your injuries require a return to the United States, your care will be transferred to a civilian facility, and your health insurance coverage will begin picking up the tab.

Disability claims are not easily approved, and many civilian contractors have found themselves mired in years of complicated litigation attempting to secure war-related disability payments. Especially when it comes to mental problems such as post-traumatic stress disorder (PTSD), contractors will find the burden of proof to be very difficult.

If you should die while in the war zone, the military will place a toe tag on you identifying your contracting firm (e.g., KBR, Blackwater, Vinnell, DynCorp, etc.). It is your contracting firm's responsibility, not the military's, to arrange to have your remains properly identified and shipped back to your family. Major contracting firms have personnel whose sole job is to help the family with final pay, insurance, and burial arrangements. Some do this better than others. The level of service will vary significantly from firm to firm.

Unfortunately, there are no military honor guards for most contractors. There are no medals for heroism. There are no bugles sounding "Taps." Rarely do contractors' deaths get any attention in the press beyond the obituary column. It is a sad fact that these men and women are largely unrecognized for their contributions. Families struck with grief over their father or husband's death, and unprepared for the cold reality of public opinion surrounding contractors, will experience tremendous pain. These issues need to be discussed with and understood by your family before you sign on for the dangerous work of becoming a war zone contractor.

Orientation and Training

When you arrive at the contracting firm's headquarters, you will be staying at a nearby hotel. You might walk or be bused to the training facility each morning. Travel, lodging, and meals are covered by the contracting firm. Training is accomplished in groups. Your group members will be more experienced in some subjects than others. A few may have already been to Iraq with another contracting firm. Like most groups, at least one or two people will be storytellers. Their stories will make for interesting evenings, but be careful to not place too much stock in their fables.

Your orientation and training will consist of many components. Each orientation and training segment will vary in length from a few hours to several days. They typically consist of an introduction to the war zone, physical examinations, passports, administrative issues, insurance and banking paperwork, area and cultural awareness, military defensive response training, characteristics of working with the military, security issues, prohibitions, and restrictions.

Before you depart from home, you will get a recommended list of what to bring and what not to bring. You need to leave your camouflage hunting gear at home. You cannot wear anything that might resemble a military uniform. Dressing anything like a soldier will void your Geneva Convention protections and will be cause for termination of your contract. As an exception to this policy, many MPRI contractors do wear desert camouflage uniforms when they are on their training installation in Kuwait or Iraq, but when they leave the base, they are required to change into civilian clothing.

Expect an entire day of getting poked and prodded. Contractor physical examinations are pretty thorough and include a chest x-ray, pulmonary function test, EKG, a blood test, drug screen, vaccinations, vision, and hearing tests. If you test positive for drugs, and quite a few applicants do, there is no more discussion. You will be on the next flight home. You will not have a second chance to come back.

If your prospective job is part of a State Department contract, you will have to complete a ton of paperwork and qualify for a minimum of a "secret" security clearance. Bring your birth certificate and/or other proof of citizenship. Be prepared to furnish dates and locations of every address you have ever lived at, every school you have attended, and every country you have ever visited. You should also have with you the names and addresses of relatives, neighbors, and friends. You will need all of this information to complete the required forms. All U.S. contractors are issued a special contractor identification card. State Department security contractors will be also be issued diplomatic passports.

Cultural-awareness training will lay the foundation for how you conduct yourself when mixing with the local population in the Middle East. This is about how not to be an "ugly American." For example, do not take pictures of local nationals without their permission. Many Arabs consider the act to be evil. Do not point your finger at anyone. Pointing a finger is considered a threat. Do not put your feet up on furniture. The bottoms of your feet are considered the dirtiest part of your body and are insulting to others. Do not touch or pet a dog. According to Muslim law, dogs are filthy animals. The left hand is traditionally part of the toilet routine, and is considered unclean. If you hand something to an Arab with your left hand, you are insulting him.

On day two or three, you will receive a security briefing. Here you will be exposed to the many ways in which the release of seemingly harmless information can in fact place military operations and people's lives in great danger. You will also develop an awareness of chance meetings with a person who could be a spy trying to acquire information on you, your team, your operations, or your base. You will be instructed on how to recognize and handle suspicious individuals. Never attempt to determine for yourself how much you should or shouldn't say. As a general rule, don't tell anybody you don't know about anything!

One security firm applicant had this to say about his first week of orientation and training, "Our group was training to be part of the Diplomatic Security Services (DSS). That is, we would be assigned to protect high-level government officials. We initially started with over thirty operators from various military and law enforcement tactical backgrounds. Our experience ranges from military special operations, counterintelligence, and SWAT. Over the past few days, we've lost almost a third of our class. Most of the washouts were due to psychological or background deficiencies. This course wasn't designed to have a high attrition rate. It was designed to have the best qualified candidate for the job. During the training and orientation, we learned that the terrorists have placed a fifty-thousand-dollar reward for capturing a security contractor. Their intent is to have a televised beheading. I don't foresee that happening to me ... at least not being taken alive."

Inevitably, contractor applicants raise the question concerning how many civilian contractors have been killed or wounded. The old axiom "statistics don't lie, but people do" often applies. Many contracting firms are reticent to talk about specific numbers. Also, you may want an answer that encompasses all the company's casualties, not just U.S. casualties. Remember, these firms hire a lot of foreigners to do the same work they are hiring you to do. Watch carefully how the questions are asked and how they are answered. Few companies are very candid.

Day by day, the seriousness of this new job venture sinks into the applicants. Job applicants become aware of the frequency and severity of contractor casualties. More and more, each of them questions the strength of his or her convictions and motives. Every day, there are fewer applicants present for training. There are few, if any, macho attitudes here. Only a fool is macho. Quitting is a deeply personal decision. Rarely is it discussed at the evening meals. No one is proud to quit, but no quitter is scorned. No one knows for certain who made the best decision.

Depending on your job, your military defensive response training segment will vary in length and composition. Nearly all contractors will receive military-oriented protective posture (MOPP) training. This training prepares a contractor to be able to operate under conditions of a nuclear, biological, or chemical (NBC) threat environment. In the case of NBC, nuclear refers to any release of radioactive material on the battlefield, such as a radioactive dirty bomb. Applicants are taught about the type of chemical and biological agents that could be used and how to put on, wear, eat, drink, eliminate body fluids, and continue to function wearing a protective mask and suit.

Security contractors will be exposed to considerably more training on small arms, convoy-escort procedures, executive protection, communications, close-quarters combat (CQC), and close-quarters marksmanship (CQM). Most trucking contractors will receive the balance of their military defensive response training when they arrive in Kuwait on their way to Iraq. The drivers will go through the defensive driving course. This is a rather benign name for what amounts to how-to-survive-an-ambush training. It consists of subjects such as tactical distances, convoy speeds, night driving, communicating, and driving with a shooter riding shotgun. Some of this training may seem simple enough, but try to imagine what it's like to be driving at night with explosions on your right and left, hot brass from the shooter's automatic rifle bouncing all over the cab and down the back of your neck with enemy bullets and rocket-propelled grenades breezing past your windshield.

Living Conditions

Very few contractors live in splendor. For most, the conditions are harsh, bordering on brutal by U.S. living standards. Often your bed is a metal cot in a dusty steel building or tent. If you are a truck driver or your job takes you to multiple locations in the country, expect that sleeping accommodations will be on a catch-as-catch-can basis. What you get and who you share space with will change from night to night. Even contractors who routinely bunk out in the same location every day sometimes find themselves sleeping in strange places. It's not uncommon that a contractor working outside the wire won't be able to get back to his or her home base at the day's end. If insurgent activity has developed on the road network between you and your home base, you are going to be headed in a different direction for the night.

Sand fleas will be biting at your legs all night, the drinking water will be almost hot enough to burn your mouth, showers will have long lines, and privacy will be a foreign concept (so will convenience, as you stumble out to the port-a-let in the middle of the night). Breathing is a luxury, as your sinuses will be constantly clogged with sand, and you'll wake up in the morning feeling like you've been inhaling coal dust all night long. It's one thing to endure these conditions for a week or two, it's entirely another to live with it for six months to a year. Those contractors who live in hotels or homes in the local communities are at much greater risk of being killed or captured. It's a tradeoff; take your choice. There are no free passes in a war zone.

A contractor in Iraq talks about the water, "Running water— our running water at home always works! In Baghdad it's a crapshoot. Along with that the water flow fluctuates. Some days it works and other days you're SOL. I have no idea where our water source comes from, and I don't want to know. The water is nonpotable and visually unappealing. One look at the public lakes tells you where the water comes from. In small amounts, it looks clear, but in larger amounts it looks like brewed tea. If you drink it, be prepared to be the pilot of a toilet seat for a few days." U.S.-produced bottled water is abundant; plan on sticking with that.

As for traffic laws in Iraq—simply put, there aren't any, at least none that are enforced. For the most part, there aren't any traffic lights, stop signs, or speed limits. Everyone does their own thing. Cars will cross over the median strip and, in what seems like a game of chicken, will head directly at you. Donkey carts full of propane gas travel interspersed among the vehicles on the road. People and bicycles clog the roads. Sometimes you'll even encounter a Volkswagen racing alongside you in *reverse*!

Food

Most civilian contractors in Iraq will eat at military dining facilities called DFACs. They used to be called mess halls, but someone decided that DFAC sounded more appetizing. It's common practice in the military that when something doesn't work right, they simply change the name—and presto!—the problem disappears. However, in the case of DFACs in Iraq, the food is great!

Ironically, the dining facilities are managed by contractors too, very often KBR. In fact, KBR serves more than 450,000 meals daily to coalition force personnel. U.S. servicemen and women, contractors, Iraqi employees, Iraqi soldiers, and Iraqi police often eat side by side in huge dining facilities with every imaginable cuisine from hamburgers and hot dogs to roast beef, spaghetti, cold sandwiches, and a dozen choices for dessert and liquid refreshments. Everything, that is, except alcohol. Alcohol is strictly forbidden in the Middle East. The food is more digestible if you avoid thinking about the Iraqi soldier who wore a bomb vest into the dining facility and killed twenty-six people during a noon meal.

Not all dining facilities are managed by U.S. food contractors. Some, like several of those at hotels inside the international zone are serviced by contracting companies from any number of other countries. If your home-base dining facility happens, for example, to be run by an East Indian company, you will find a disproportionate number of meals that smell like curry. Sure, they will attempt to Americanize the way they prepare meals, but other than the occasional hot dogs, don't expect a major departure from their inclination for native cooking.

If your job in Iraq requires travel outside the wire, expect that you'll be taking along meals ready to eat (MRE). If you are lucky and schmooze the DFAC manager, you might get some cold sandwiches to toss into your cooler. It really doesn't matter a whole lot because when you are dining outside the wire in sweltering temperatures and watching for insurgents, nothing tastes very good.

R&R

Expect about ten days of rest and recuperation (R&R) about three times a year. This too, will vary based on the company you are with. Most contracting firms will offer a fixed dollar amount to cover the cost of a plane ticket to your R&R destination. This may or may not be sufficient to get all the way back to the United States. Regardless of how much they contribute for air fare, travel time often eats up a lot of the vacation time. In addition, contractors will frequently take advantage of the opportunity to visit another country. Many prefer to meet their spouse and spend their vacation in Europe or at a Middle East resort. If you do go home on R&R and decide not to go back to the war, and some do, your plane fare will be deducted from your final pay.

Carrying Weapons in a War Zone

Most civilians applying for war zone contractor positions think they can carry a firearm. They are wrong. Only special categories of contractors can carry a weapon. Their company must be approved to carry weapons by both the Iraqi Ministry of Internal Affairs and the Coalition Forces Land Component Command. Approvals are normally reserved for security contractors and executive protection services. With the possible exception of a few high-level officials, you cannot take your personal firearm into Iraq. Nor can you possess a firearm while in country. The caveat on the latter restriction: it is not strictly enforced, but it could be.

If you choose to carry a firearm in violation of the restrictions, you could lose your job, be subject to legal recourse, and be promptly removed from the country. Unauthorized use of a weapon might also void your insurance. Of course, this isn't much of a consideration when a group of insurgents opens fire on you. No one has ever heard of a contractor, when under intense enemy fire say, "Sorry I can't shoot back because my life insurance could get cancelled." In some countries you could be imprisoned by the local authorities for carrying an unauthorized firearm. In Iraq, U.S. military commanders have the authority to disarm and arrest you. And they have in fact arrested civilian contractors in some isolated cases.

Companies or individuals wanting to take weapons into a foreign country are required to obtain a license from the U.S. State Department. The licensing process is cumbersome and can often take many months to gain approval. The limitations and updating requirements are a bureaucratic nightmare that is not flexible enough to accommodate the fast pace of changing requirements in Iraq. Consequently, many security contractors have simply opted for a commonly used shortcut. They purchase weapons on the black market in the host country.

In Iraq, pistols, assault rifles, and machine guns are readily available from the corner store. For less than a hundred dollars, you can pick up a Russian-made AK-47 assault rifle and for not much more you can buy a full-fledged machine gun. Even non-security contractors, who are officially prohibited from carrying weapons, frequently pick up a personal sidearm in the thriving arms business of Iraq's black market. When the contractors leave Iraq, they usually sell their weapons to newly arrived contractors or simply sell their weapons back to the local vendor.

State Department contractors are exempt from many of the restrictions and prohibitions on carrying weapons. In fact, Blackwater and DynCorp contractors working for the U.S. Department of State are armed to the teeth. A DynCorp contractor describes his armament: "Our equipment is state of the art and each operator is issued roughly ten thousand dollars' worth of gear. Our vehicles are also 'up to spec.' We have modern, luxury-type SUVs with bulletproof glass and armored panels. Our humvees are all 'up-armored' and outfitted with the latest radio gear. In the 'Special Ops' world we would be called 'Gucci' or pretty. I guess we are.

"Each operator has equipment that is designed and worn for his own operational needs and capabilities. We wear what works. None of us wear stuff that would be considered 'Hollywood'; no Rambo knives, peace and love pins, or stuff like that. We select our equipment based on three criteria: it must be reliable, durable, and operator friendly. So we do end up with a lot of 'Gucci' stuff that might be called faddish back home, but that's not the reason the stuff was selected. I guess, if the truth be known, when you put all that equipment on, the testosterone just ekes through your pores."

Here is a typical list of equipment worn or carried by State Department contractors:
- Level III close-quarters battle (CQB) ballistic helmet with infrared capabilities
- Level IV multiple-hit body armor
- HSG Wasatch special forces modular chest rig
- Colt government M4 rifle with aimpoint red dot reticle
- 14 thirty-round M4 ammo magazines (420 rounds)

- Glock 19, 9mm pistol with three high-capacity mags loaded with Hydra-Shock ammo
- 1 U.S. high-concentrate smoke grenade
- 2 U.S. M67 fragmentation grenades (25-meter kill radius)
- Encrytped squad radio
- Cell phone

Family Support and Communication

For many would-be contractors, the biggest challenge they face is family support. During the training and orientation, reality of the endeavor also begins to sink into the contractor's family. Second thoughts creep into the minds of the family left behind, be it wives, husbands, girlfriends, or children. While job applicants struggle through orientation with their own fears and doubts, they are often confronted with phone calls from home that resurface questions about their imminent departure. Wives will often experience negative comments about their husbands' venture from friends and neighbors. Feelings of isolation and abandonment begin to overwhelm some families.

Contracting firms do not normally get into issues of wills or power of attorney documents. Families are often reticent to discuss funeral preferences. Pretending that the worst won't happen isn't the answer. The avoidance of these unpleasant discussions will place an inordinate burden on family members if fate deals a bad card. These are important tasks that should be taken care of before a job applicant departs for orientation. Also, facing these possibilities beforehand will help develop a sense of seriousness that can be a catalyst for surfacing objections sooner rather than later.

Very few contractors will have their own personal Internet connections. Contracting firms often provide employees access to their corporate computers to send e-mails to family and friends. Of course, there's always a waiting line. To complicate matters, the contractor has to be very cautious of what he or she says on the Internet or phone. Internet and phone communications are monitored by Department of Defense intelligence units. Contractors can be in serious trouble if they reveal information on the Web or phone that is considered classified. A simple and seemingly innocent remark like, "We'll be picking up supplies in Jordan tomorrow," would be a clear violation of secrecy regulations.

Many contractors have satellite or cell phones issued by their employer. Often these companies will permit outgoing international phone calls to be made on their equipment, and the calls are routed through their home base—such as KBR in Houston. Cell phones are a primary means of communicating within the country, and consequently, many contractors run around Iraq with two mobile phones, one cell and one satellite. If the contracting firm doesn't provide you with a phone, there are several inexpensive ways to get a satellite or cell phone from a local supplier.

It isn't a good idea for families to call contractors operating in the war zone. Unless there's a family emergency, the individual contractor is in a much better position to determine when he or she is in a secure area and can safely place a call to the States. Also many military convoy escort units operate jamming equipment that is designed to screw up your phone conversation. The reason for jamming cell phone frequencies is because the enemy frequently uses cell phones to detonate explosive devices.

Soldiers get some modicum of support from Americans. Contractors get next to none. Quite the opposite, civilian contractors are frequently denigrated for their decision to work in a hostile country. It is critical that contractors know that at least their family is behind them and can handle the day-to-day challenges during their absence. Finding contractor family-support groups on the Internet can be a great help and a source of comfort during a spouse's absence.

If a contractor's family is incapable of genuine support and dealing with issues at home without burdening her spouse, she will be placing the person she loves in great danger. A contractor in Iraq cannot allow himself or herself to be distracted with worries and concerns about domestic problems while at the same time remaining focused on staying alive in the war zone. Staying safe in a combat environment requires incredible focus and attention that will sap the energy out of the most prepared human being. Don't add to the problem.

Chapter 4

A Drive through the War Zone

It's hot in Iraq. Not hot like Arizona. Not hot like Death Valley. Furnace Creek, California, is a poor cousin to the scorching heat of Iraq. Your eye-socket fluid dries up. Your lips crack and parch. Your mouth feels like you've been eating cotton. Sand blows across the roads and piles up on everything. Many times the sky is filled with blowing sand and forms a brown haze that obliterates the sun. On windy, cloudless days, the sun looks more like the moon in a daylight sky, a faint orb.

The air chokes newcomers' lungs. Desert temperatures routinely exceed 130 degrees Fahrenheit. You drink water by the gallon, 130-degree water. It evaporates off your body as fast as you pour it down. Except for the drenching wetness beneath your thirty-pound flak vest, your sweat evaporates instantly. When you remove the vest, you are almost embarrassed by the soaking wet dishrag that your shirt has become. Not to worry; you will be dry in minutes.

Want to know what it's like in Iraq? Fill your oven with sand, put a fan inside, turn on the heat full blast, and stick your head in. Every breath is superheated, sand-filled air. You can't imagine how anyone survives this hellish climate.

The debilitating effects of the climate shock army units arriving from the States. When they departed their home base, they were full of vim and vigor and ready to bring death to the insurgents. Everyone thinks they know what to expect. They believe they are prepared. They quickly learn that it can't be imagined. It can't be trained for. It can only be experienced. One army unit, freshly arrived in Kuwait, had more than fourteen heat casualties on their first day, before crossing from Kuwait into Iraq, the infamous Berm (a 1,690-mile-long system of defensive walls around which is the biggest concentration of land mines in the western Sahara). Besides "crossing the Berm," this border crossing is also called "going through the gate."

Regardless of what it's called, everyone who crosses the Berm feels a chill go through them. They know that at any moment they may be under fire. They may see a brilliant flash of light in a split second as an IED detonates on a vehicle in their convoy—maybe their vehicle. The .50-caliber machine gunner standing up in the humvee knows that he risks being sliced into two pieces if he is standing up and fails to see explosives on the road ahead. Gunners now hunker down behind a steel turret until enemy contact is made. There are no safe havens in Iraq. Only a fool assumes some area of the country to be safe. Every day such assumptions are proven false.

In Iraq, there are seventy to eighty insurgent attacks a day. On any given day, you may hear about three or four of them in the news. Most of these incidents don't make the mainstream press. Most media people are bedded down at hotels in Baghdad. If they learn of an insurgent attack at the local marketplace, they rush down, with plenty of security vehicles to file their on-the-spot report. They are not privy to the information on the dozens of attacks elsewhere in Iraq. The coalition forces are not inclined to tell them what they don't know. Even if they were informed, few would venture the high-risk trip to the scene.

About a mile into Iraq, you come into the town of Safwan. Life is cheap here. It's not just that insurgents lurk in the shadows; it's also the bandits who will kill for almost anything of value. It's a lawless region: insurgents, bandits and thieves (known locally as "Ali Babas" after the eponymous hero of "Ali Baba and the Forty Thieves"), and kids. The kids ride their bikes next to your vehicle trying to cut a deal for anything you may want. This town took a physical beating during both Gulf conflicts and not much has changed since. As you journey north, encountering danger is not only possible, it is probable. You had better be mentally prepared for every imaginable ruse, and some that are not imaginable. You are in Iraq. This is a war zone.

Herds of camel and sheep wander the desolate countryside. Bedouins tend to their herds without notice of the passing convoys of trucks carrying supplies to sustain the war and rebuild the country. Beetles plant their eggs in camel dung and roll them into a protective fold, not dissimilar to a taco. Baby camel spiders, which are known to grow to more than a foot in diameter charge at you, stop, and suddenly retreat as if they sized you up and determined that you are not an appropriate meal. Lizards, called dubs, scurry around the desert chasing God knows what. They are quick, but they have enough energy for only a forty-yard dash. Keep them from retreating to their hole and they will quickly exhaust themselves. After their forty-yard dash, you can then walk up to them, pick 'em up, and dine on their chicken-flavored tails.

In southern Iraq, the only water you see is the shimmering turquoise water of the aqueduct that, periodically, can be seen alongside the road. You might muse over the thought that it is a wonder the water hasn't totally evaporated in the incredible heat. Everywhere is sand and limestone gravel. Remnants of war are ubiquitous: a burned-out Iraqi tank here, a blown-up building there, hundreds of rusting war vehicles clumped together. These are graveyards of sorts. Thousands of Iraqi soldiers died in them during the first and second Gulf conflicts. Iraq is littered with grim reminders of war.

People are living in the skeletons of one-story buildings and some have just pitched a tent, seemingly in the middle of nowhere. Nearly all have a satellite dish. A van will be pulled over to the side of the road, and you will see five or six women, dressed in their black garb, kneeling on a rug in the sand. Often they have stopped for prayer. Sometimes they are eating, a roadside picnic of sorts. Remember, it's 130 degrees.

As you approach small towns, children appear everywhere along the road. They wave and extend their hands, looking for whatever tokens you might toss them. When you throw them a water bottle or candy bar, they will quickly put it with the rest of their stash in a hole, or behind a mound of earth, and run back to the road to continue begging. Sometimes, when you don't give them anything, you can watch in your sideview mirror as they extend their middle finger at you. If you stop in a town, even what appears to be a deserted town, a child or two will approach you immediately begging for a handout. You'd better have a case of handouts because within seconds there will be dozens of children appearing out of thin air.

In the small towns and the cities, you occasionally spot a couple of military vehicles stopped with children gathered around the soldiers who are passing out candy or bottled water or MREs. Soldiers can't seem to resist kids. All kids, but especially

81

children in a war zone, seem to tug at the heartstrings. Some soldiers have lost their lives while performing these humanitarian gestures. It's unlikely, though, that they will ever stop treating children with kindness, regardless of the threat.

You come upon the remnants of a burning fuel tanker, obviously from an earlier convoy. It was hit by an IED. You slow down and pass cautiously. There are no security forces in the area. The truck is engulfed in a ball of flame. As you cruise by and feel the searing heat, you notice a dozen Ali Babas working feverishly. They are stealing everything and anything of value on the truck. Several are removing the tires before they melt. Two or three are waiting in line, draining the fuel into five-gallon cans. A couple of others are scouring the cab. You notice the windshield and side windows are riddled with holes, broken glass everywhere. Someone was hurt here. You guess that he probably died. This is not your problem. You continue your journey.

The six-lane highway you are traveling is separated by a large sandy median. Cars and trucks, for any number of reasons, routinely cut across the median strip and drive straight at the oncoming traffic. At times, even entire convoys cut across the median and drive in the oncoming traffic lanes. They may have good reason. They may have learned of some danger ahead on their side of the highway. Every twenty or thirty miles you encounter highway checkpoints with Iraqi police (IP), Iraqi National Guard (ING), U.S. military, or some combination of these. Often the checkpoints are set up in the shade of a highway overpass.

Frequently, just past the checkpoints, will be a collection of five or ten 10-by-10-foot "Haji shops" (or, in more politically correct terms, shops run by local merchants). They are separated from each other by about twenty yards. Vehicles passing through the checkpoints will pull over and shop with the vendors for food, drinks, or other sundry items. It is a cause for some alarm when a checkpoint is hastily established and has no Haji shops nearby. Insurgents and bandits will sometimes kill the police and dress in their uniforms or simply just put on uniforms and set up a checkpoint.

Haji shops exploit the opportunities created by the traffic flow near checkpoints. If one or two shops are set up alone near an overpass where there is no checkpoint, it is yet another cause for alarm. Isolated Haji shops at the edge of the road have, on occasion, been found to contain rocket-propelled grenades (RPGs) that are linked to a trip wire running under the overpass. The trip wire is rigged to fire several RPGs simultaneously. If you don't detect the trap, you will surely be blown apart. You quickly become suspicious of everything.

Convoys of trucks are rolling down this highway constantly. Many have twenty or thirty trucks. A few have been known to run more than a hundred vehicles. Some are purely military vehicles with army escorts, and others are civilian trucks with army or private security contractor escorts. Smart convoy drivers will keep their vehicles spaced 75 to 100 meters apart. They know that when an attack occurs, this separation will reduce the possibility of losing two trucks from a single explosion. Convoys try to roll at a high rate of speed. Insurgents will have a harder time hitting them if they are moving fast.

The convoy security teams (military or civilian) often wave at one another when passing in opposite directions. Everyone is scanning the surrounding area with automatic rifles and machine guns poised to fire.

Far out in the desert you make out the faint image of a tractor trailer billowing up dust as it moves away from the main highway. You deduce that bandits culled out the vehicle from another convoy, shot the driver, and stole the truck. No one is in pursuit. There is a good chance that the driver directly behind the stolen truck was helpless to tell anyone that a truck was being taken. His convoy just rolled on. He rolled on. Even if his security elements saw the theft, there is not much they can do. They certainly can't abandon forty trucks and go chasing across the desert after the thieves. Shit happens in Iraq.

In southern Iraq, the military escorts may be U.S., British, Australian, Japanese, Italian, or Iraqi. As you go farther north, the military units are almost exclusively U.S. or Iraqi. Private contractors, like Blackwater, Hart, TDL, Triple Canopy, Crescent, and dozens of others, run the whole country without regard to geography. These firms are a highly flexible resource providing expedient solutions to everchanging war zone requirements.

As you proceed farther north, you begin to encounter more nonlethal threats, such as children or adults throwing rocks. This might seem benign, but given your level of tension, a rock smashing against your vehicle can be quite unnerving. The vegetation picks up here, and the temperature drops a few degrees. At first, even a few scattered trees and bushes are a welcome site, but then you realize that the brush and trees afford the insurgents more hiding places. Your ability to see a head bob over a berm or out of ditch is diminished. You'd rather have the bland desert back. Better to be bored with the scenery, but alive.

While driving the roads, your entire body is on full-scale alert. You watch for broken-down vehicles on the side of the road. They may be filled with explosives. The trouble is that there are hundreds of broken-down vehicles on the highways. You watch for vehicles with tinted windows full of young men. Insurgents frequently travel in such groups and often execute a drive-by shooting of your vehicle. You look for trucks and cars that sag too much in the rear end; they may be loaded with explosives. You watch for vehicles that won't leave the center lane of the road, they may be straddling the center lane because they suspect or know a bomb is just ahead. Iraqi citizens know to stay in the right or left lane. The center lane is primarily for use by convoys.

A garbage bag alongside the road, a piece of Styrofoam, a dirt mound, a patch of new pavement, a pothole, a clump of tires, or a pile of brush may all be disguises for roadside bombs. Explosives, aimed at the ground, have been found in the crook of a tree branch. Dog carcasses have been packed with explosives and propped up to appear to be alive. They are placed along the shoulder of a road and detonated with a remote triggering device.

At times even donkeys are wandering the area packed with explosives. The donkeys nibble on the vegetation in the ditches alongside the highway. When a target vehicle rolls by, the donkey, the truck, and the personnel inside blow up together. Afterward, it's a challenge to distinguish whose parts belong to whom. The military even has a name for these devices: donkey-borne improvised explosive devices (DBIEDs). The ruses are endless.

Insurgents routinely plant explosives on the backside of guardrails. The guardrail on the outside corner at the bend of a highway exit ramp has often been selected as a location to plant bombs. Trucks have blown up coming off the ramp, and as other trucks pass on the inside corner, they too have been blown up by a second set of hidden explosives. Bait devices appearing to be explosives are sometimes planted on the highway. A convoy will slow, stop, or change lanes to avoid the bait and will either run into the actual explosives or come under attack from hidden insurgents. At times the insurgents open fire from both sides of the road.

If a vehicle mixes into the middle of your convoy and doesn't make a dash to get ahead or fall behind, you have a high potential of a developing insurgent attack. If a pickup truck approaches at high speed from a perpendicular desert road, you need to brace yourself. The Iraqi people are well informed about how to, and when not to, approach a convoy. They are supposed to stay at least 100 meters away from convoys. Many don't. The rules of engagement permit the military and security contractors to open fire when a vehicle has been warned to stay back but continues to close in on them. It is a testimony to self-restraint on the part of both military units and U.S. civilian security contractors that more innocent people have not lost their lives for foolishly ignoring these rules.

The sight of human bodies lying on the road near a blown-up vehicle can have a disarming effect. You have to fight your natural tendency to rush forward to help in whatever manner might be possible. It is not uncommon that the bodies have been planted there by insurgents and subsequently booby-trapped. It defies human inclinations that you must first recon the area to make certain an insurgent isn't lurking nearby with an explosive detonator in hand. Even when approaching seemingly lifeless bodies, care must be taken. This could be a suicide bomber wearing a military uniform with an explosive vest under his shirt. Finally, when moving bodies, you have to be alert for grenades, ready to explode, that may have been planted among them. Nothing is sacred in this war—nothing.

Whether you live or die in Iraq is often about personal friendships and not so much about whose side you represent. Iraq is full of people from different religious, ethnic, and tribal origins. Simply being on the same side of the war is insignificant to many Iraqis. They strongly resent anything that smells of U.S. arrogance. If you're smart, you'll go out of your way to befriend everyone you can along your route. You will pass this way again and again, and this won't be the last you see of these people. There's a good chance the day will come that your effort at being a "friend" may well save your life.

The Haji shop vendor, the border guards, the police, the Iraqi soldiers, the shepherds, and the kids are all important to your success. Periodically, along this route, stop and talk with them. You need to get to know them. They may not be inclined to help Americans, but they will often help a friend. Friendship in Muslim countries is a powerful cultural phenomenon that, on a comparative scale, is not found in Western society. A token gesture, a smile, a wave, a pause to ask them about their day promotes invaluable relationships. Your Iraqi friends will tell you things about the enemy and help you through complicated negotiations that would otherwise be a nightmare.

In the Middle East, most Arabs believe and practice an ancient tribal code of honor known as *dakhil*. That means: if you seek the help of another and he commits to protecting you, regardless of your transgressions, under the traditions of dakhil, your protector must, even at risk to his own life, provide you security. He cannot allow any harm to befall you. You need only ask for dakhil. If you have been extended protection under dakhil and are betrayed, the betrayer will be forever disgraced by his family and his tribe.

In the cities, look to see if people are congregating on one side of the street and not the other. They know what you don't. If you are in a traffic circle, and the vehicle in front of you stops for no apparent reason, all your senses go on edge. One of your greatest fears is getting stuck in a traffic jam. A stopped vehicle is a target. Hundreds of insurgents drive the roads looking for "targets of opportunity." This is especially true of stopped vehicles with Americans in them. Perhaps the insurgents believe that their heavenly rewards will be greater if they terminate the life of Americans. It doesn't take long to become exhausted from the intensity of the situation and the adrenaline drain. You cannot allow yourself to become complacent. Complacency is a death knell. There are no naps on this road trip.

At night you will see fires burning throughout the desert. Some are burn-offs from oil wells. Others are the result of oil pipeline attacks, and some are the remnants of blown-up vehicles that may be a dozen or so miles ahead of you. Some fires are from tires placed on the road to soften the highway for a later emplacement of an IED. The insurgents are busy throughout the night. At times they will bury as many as twenty-seven explosive devices in a row. The coalition forces are busy too. The war never sleeps.

A mile or two ahead you see a burst of light followed by a dull thump sound. You see a few streaks of light crisscrossing the horizon. You know the flash and thump was either an artillery, mortar, or possibly an IED. You know the streaks of light are bullet tracers. Someone is shooting at someone. Your fear factor skyrockets. You begin to slow down. This is not good. Slowing down exposes your vehicle to well-aimed enemy fire. You speed up. Stopping is not an option. You reason that stopping at night on an Iraqi highway is more dangerous than driving into the potential maelstrom ahead. Your eyes are as big as saucers as you peer into the black desert landscape and scan the fireworks on the horizon. It's an eerie feeling to know that a few miles ahead, someone may be dying and others are engaged in fighting for their life, and you are headed in their direction.

Ahead you see orange-and-green sticks being waved in circles. As you get closer, you realize this is a checkpoint, and the Iraqi police are waving chemical lights in their hands. At least you hope these are Iraqi police. You slow down and talk with the police. They give you a heads up on the enemy activity ahead and ask if you can spare a few extra chemlights. You give them a dozen from your stash and a few bottles of cold water. They smile. They thank you. They wave you on through the check-point. For them, this is as routine as some cop in the States advising you of ice on the bridges ahead. Everything is relative. And after all, this *is* a war zone.

A couple miles farther, you see a cluster of military humvees along the road. In the darkness you make out the silhouettes of some Bradley fighting vehicles in the desert. Overhead you hear the *whop-whop-whop* sound of helicopters, circling in the night sky. They may be gunships, but at least one may be a medical evacuation chopper. Several soldiers standing on the road wave you through and motion for you to proceed slowly.

About a hundred yards off to your right flank, a .50-caliber machine gun lets off a burst of fire at some distant target. The unintelligible sound of radios crackling can be heard everywhere. You see a group of personnel carrying a stretcher bolting through the darkness. You have no idea what just happened. You only know it involved good guys and bad guys. If this were a highway in New Jersey, you'd be a gawker. Not here! You have only one thought: *I want to get through this area.* You clear the area and put the pedal to the metal.

It's about midnight now and you are entering Baghdad. Curfew began at 9 p.m. and the streets are deserted. Every now and then you see the figure of a person dart through the shadows. You suspect they are insurgents. You watch the overpasses more carefully than ever. The streets are void of the thousands of people, kids, cars, and bicycles that clog the roadways during the day. You pass ornate palaces and mosques and wonder who's inside. You wonder who's watching you. You wonder if some street ahead will be blocked by insurgents.

Some buildings are decimated shells and others look like they were built last week. The city is a contrast of poverty and wealth, destruction and construction. Military combat vehicles scurry about the deserted streets as if they were late for an appointment. Every one of them takes notice of you. Some point their weapons in your direction. At times you fear they are going to open fire. You are stopped frequently. You don't dare move without their direction. Nerves are on edge and fingers are on triggers.

North of Baghdad you enter the city of Baqubah. A local power plant was blown up yesterday and there are no streetlights. Without power, the homes are pitch black. This elevates your fear level again. You ponder that perhaps the blackout was just phase one of an enemy plan. You start wondering whether or not you are driving into hell's kitchen. For a short time, you decide to turn off your headlights. Tense and exhausted you drive as quietly as possible through the town. You feel like you're creeping through a pit of sleeping snakes hoping not to wake any of them. Finally, you arrive at Camp Anaconda, a large military base just south of Tikrit. Just the sight of it causes you to take a deep breath. Until this moment, you hadn't realized how tired you were. Now you can hardly wait for a simple pleasure like a cot to sleep on.

As you approach the main gate, the guards go into full-scale alert. A half-dozen automatic rifles and machine guns are ready to fire on you. You move very slowly through the zigzag maze that is the entry check point (ECP). You listen for, and follow, every direction from the soldiers at the gate. Finally, you open your vehicle glove compartment and center console, then slowly step out of the vehicle leaving all doors open and your hands visible. The guards approach cautiously. They check identification and inspect your vehicle with mirrors and dogs. When you are cleared to proceed, you feel as if the guards are looking at you like you are some poor crazy fool. And maybe you are.

The expression on the faces of the gate guards suggests that they are asking, "Who in their right mind would be driving through Iraq in the middle of the night?" By now, you're probably asking yourself the same question. You'll catch six hours of sleep, and at "0 Dark Thirty" in the morning you'll be headed south for Kuwait or maybe the Jordanian border. It'll be just another day driving through the war zone. Perhaps you'll stop for the night at Cedar II (Tallil Air Base) just north of Basra. There you can grab a meal and another couple hours of rest. As one MPRI contractor put it, "Driving the roads through Iraq is like placing your life in a crapshoot. You just never know which day your luck will run out." As you close your eyes, you think to yourself, *Well, at least Cedar II has a great mess hall.*

Chapter 5

Trucking Contractors

I. An Overview

Participants in war have been historically defined in one of two ways: those who are assigned to direct combat units and those who are in logistics support roles. In past conflicts, support roles were considered to be relatively safe. In Iraq, this distinction has disappeared. Support soldiers and the civilians who work with them are frequently under attack. In fact, they are often the primary targets of insurgent battle plans. There are thousands of incidents where support units have been attacked. However, in this war, those who operate outside the wire, versus those who largely remain inside the wire, define the real differences. Truck drivers operate outside the wire every day in Iraq.

There is a certain glamour attached to the big-rig driver in the United States. As the rebel hero of 1970s' music and movies, he has become part of the country's popular folklore, and at the same time, a target for controversy. In many ways, truckers are modern U.S. cowboys; they herd their trucks from town to town, drop one load and pick up another, then hit the trail for some distant city. They leave their wives and families behind and criss-cross the open roads for weeks at a stretch. They wrangle with each other, but when an interloper butts in, they unite as if they never had a quarrel among themselves. By and large, they are red, white, and blue U.S. patriots. And this is the real reason many of them have gone to Iraq.

Most of these drivers make no more money than they would in the same job back home. Granted, they work a lot more overtime in Iraq, and consequently accumulate quite a bit of money, and they have some tax benefits. But as one driver put it, "If I had worked these hours back in the States, I would have made close to the same paycheck and I wouldn't have been shot at nearly every day." He's not complaining; he's just stating the facts.

What would be called trucking terminals in the United States are called staging bases in Kuwait and Iraq. The sheer number of trucks and the volume of cargo that is being moved into and through Iraq on a daily basis would defy the imagination of most people. Convoy after convoy rolls out of Kuwaiti ports every hour. They stage at a military base on the Iraq-Kuwait border called NAVISTAR. Every day, ten, twenty, or thirty convoys, each with dozens, sometime hundreds, of trucks wait to roll north into Iraq. The coalition forces would starve without this vital cargo. The reconstruction of Iraq would screech to a halt. Soldiers wouldn't get mail. Repaired vehicle and aircraft engines would rust. Desperately needed ammunition wouldn't make it to U.S. fighting forces. In short, without these truckers, the war would be lost in a week.

Officially, U.S. truck drivers are prohibited from carrying personal firearms. That is the "official" line. As to whether or not U.S. trucking contractors are armed, don't creep up on one in the middle of the night to find out. The soldiers who escort them often have a version of the "don't ask, don't tell" philosophy. And when the shit hits the fan, every shooter on your side is your new best friend.

For whatever reasons these individuals choose to place themselves in harm's way, they will be quick to tell you that their reasons for staying in Iraq were all about the team. Combat has a way of bonding people that exceeds by light years any other lifetime experience. The job quickly becomes all about those who risk their lives with you. The team becomes family—more than family. The ideologies of governments clearly take second place to their deep-rooted sense of obligation and commitment to one another.

*　　*　　*

Mark Taylor (a.k.a. Ugly Puppy), Ken McDonald, and Glenn Collins share the same occupation, driving big rigs in and out of military bases, day-in and day-out, in the Iraqi war zone. Besides their skill at handling big rigs, they shared a common reason for entering the fray. Each of them being successful in their own right before 9/11, it wasn't money that compelled them, but the need to do something for their country.

Once in Iraq, they were assigned to transport U.S. mail over Iraq's treacherous back roads, streets, and highways. In the ultimate dedication to the post office motto, "Neither snow, nor rain, nor heat, nor gloom of night [nor flying bullets, nor roadside bombs, nor enemy ambush] would stay these couriers from the swift completion of their appointed rounds." They vowed to never allow two things to happen: first, they would never leave one of their own behind on the battlefield, and second, they would never let a soldier's personal mail fall into enemy hands.

Mark Taylor and his wife, Renee, owned a thriving trucking operation. Home base was Warren, Arkansas. Mark is in his early forties, six feet tall, and reasonably fit at about 230 pounds. He has short black hair, is unassuming and low-key with a soft-spoken southern drawl. He is introspective, well read, and articulate. As an independent long-haul owner-operator, Mark frequently writes articles on trucking issues for *Landline*, a trucking industry magazine for members of the Owner Operator Independent Drivers Association (OOIDA). Since becoming a trucker in the mid-1980s, he has been active in working through print, radio, Internet, and television media to improve the public image of truck drivers. His own small company consisted of five tractors and five trailers. His wife, partner, and best friend, Renee, is an activist, founder, and leader in several U.S. contractor family support groups. She is a feisty, outspoken, uninhibited hundred-pound ball of fire.

When 9/11 occurred, Mark and his wife were on the open road in Utah driving across the country on a routine freight haul. They listened on the radio to the reports of a plane striking one of the World Trade Center towers. Mark lumbered his rig off the highway and turned on his satellite TV to see the breaking news. They were just in time to watch the second plane strike the other tower of the World Trade Center. A week later, Mark tried to join the army. They wouldn't accept him. At thirty-eight, he was too old.

Ken McDonald was hauling sensitive government cargo when the United States was rudely awakened by the al-Qaeda attacks. Ken is a rugged outdoor-looking guy in his early thirties, suntanned, muscular, with a medium build, medium height, short blond hair, and a mustache. He has a gregarious life-of-the-party personality. When he walks into a room, everyone knows he's there and everyone is glad to see him. He's a risk taker, but no fool. He thrives on bailing people out of trouble, a trait that he subsequently put to good use over and over again in Iraq.

Roadside sign, Baghdad, Iraq (Camp Victory)

↑ Abu Hyder's guard is taken prisoner and interrogated by the team during their raid to uncover where hijacked trucks and drivers are being held.

↓ Some people in the Middle East haven't forgotten. This sign is along a major highway in Kuwait just south of the Iraqi border.

↑ Mark Taylor (Ugly Puppy) at the JMMT, Baghdad International Airport. In the background are new up-armored Mercedes trucks that have just arrived for the Iron Pony.

↓ Iraqi machine gunners who vie for the rear gunner position mount and load their Russian PKM machine guns onto the back of Chevy Avalanches.

↑ Ken McDonald and Jodi Rund hug each other during the party at Malfunction Junction. Jodi, a U.S. Army soldier, manned a .50-caliber machine gun on one of the 1544th's gun trucks.

↓ Ben Strickland takes a moment out from driving his KBR big-rig to try his skill at camel driving.

↑ Greg Garsjo (Montana), a twenty-six-year retired army vet, now delivers mail to soldiers in Iraq.

↓ The Iron Pony Express. Left to right: Greg Garsjo, Ben Strickland, Kendall Hardwick, Abraham Lee, Charles Wilcox, Jeff Dye, Herbert Walton, Phil McCall, Mark Taylor, Mike Humphrey. (Photo by Arthur "Gunny" Alessandro)

↑ Kevin and Randy (driving) at NAVISTAR, along the Kuwait-Iraq border, just finishing up a three-day mission in Iraq.

↓ Left to right: Ben Strickland, Jeff Dye, Greg Garsjo.

Major Thomas Palermo, known as the "Mayor of NAVISTAR," commands this sprawling convoy staging area along the Kuwaiti-Iraqi border.

In front of one of Saddam's blown-up palaces in Baghdad: Mark Taylor, Sergeant Joshua Cox, and Specialist Michael Jordan on the top rail.

↑ Soldiers from the 1544th stand in formation at a welcome home awards ceremony in Paris, Illinois.

↓ Mark Taylor hugs a soldier who ran the roads with him in Iraq.

In front of the National Guard Armory
building in Paris, Illinois. Throughout Paris
are memorials to the local young men and
women who didn't come home.

Jeff Dye stands next to the cab of his truck
after one of the many IED attacks on the road
to Balad (Camp Anaconda).

↑ MPRI's training is serious business. Here soldiers react to a simulated firefight and casualty care.

↓ A young soldier takes cover behind the wheel of a giant heavy-equipment transport during MPRI's training at Camp Yankee just a few klicks south of the Iraqi border.

Paul Collins, MPRI, conducts a training
review with soldiers from the Wisconsin
National Guard.

↑ Curtis Acton and Larry Word meet with army training coordinators to discuss the rotation of coalition force units through Camp Yankee.

↓ Bill Bratten, an MPRI trainer, monitors the radios at Team Viper's operations center.

Tariq, a Pakistani gate guard and translator,
with the author at the entrance to MPRI's
Camp Yankee about ten miles south of the
Iraqi-Kuwaiti border.

← Larry Word, MPRI's program director at Camp Yankee, reviews the projected training plans for coalition force units deploying through Kuwait to Iraq.

→ Soldiers scramble to the helicopter landing zone during a mock medevac training exercise at MPRI's Camp Yankee.

Soldiers killed in action from the 1544th Army Transportation Unit—
Specialist Jeremy Ridlen, Sergeant Jessica Cawvey, Sergeant Ivory
Phillips, Sergeant Shawna Morrison, and Specialist Charles Lamb—are
memorialized in the high school gymnasium in Paris, Illinois.

Ken's career as a trucker encompassed a lot of high-security work. At times he hauled radioactive waste, but when 9/11 occurred he had been trucking cash around the country for the U.S. Treasury Department. This type of sensitive work was clearly not in the low-wage-earner bracket.

His job took on new significance following the series of 9/11 attacks. The Treasury Department wanted sufficient cash available across the country for banks that may have a run on withdrawals from panicked customers. Additionally, the fear that major Federal Reserve Banks might be the target of a terrorist attack motivated the government to disperse its cash throughout the country. The day after the attacks, Ken jam-packed his rig with pallets of hard currency at the New York Federal Reserve Bank. As he was driving through the Washington, D.C., area, he stopped his big rig near the devastated Pentagon. Acrid smoke still filled the air. His senses were struck by the unmistakable smell of burning flesh. As the odors permeated his soul, he realized he needed to be a bigger part of the solution.

Glenn Collins was a log hauler from Arizona. His father had served in Vietnam, and Glenn had felt a calling to serve his country. He had unsuccessfully attempted to join the army several times but had been rejected for physical reasons. Glenn is in his twenties and younger than either Mark or Ken. He is fair skinned, round faced, almost Swedish looking, usually quiet: a listener type. He is slow to trust people, but when he does, he has been known to burst out with feelings, emotions, and stories in a most sincere and unpretentious manner. His experiences in Iraq have left him emotionally scarred. He is coping the best he can, but fear of driving at night may be an albatross on his back for many years to come. Following 9/11 he stumbled across his opportunity to serve his country without having to wait for the army's blessing. One of Glenn's friends had driven trucks in Kuwait and Iraq. His buddy hooked him up with a KBR recruiter. He was packing the next day.

Word was spreading fast through the CB radios of the U.S. trucking industry: KBR desperately needed drivers. The truckers went through the initial screening process with KBR in Houston, followed by several weeks of area orientations, psychological evaluations, pay processing, and filling out forms. At about the same time, across the country in the small town of Paris, Illinois, an Army National Guard unit received their orders to deploy for Iraq. The 1544th Army Transportation Unit would be assigned security responsibility for trucking convoys. Before year's end, the drivers in Houston and the soldiers in Illinois would become family. This improbable combination of Americans would come to be known throughout Iraq as the Iron Pony Express.

II. The Mail Run

One by one, alarm clocks ring in the middle of the afternoon. It's 4 p.m. and another hot, dusty day in Iraq. The Iron Pony drivers stretch, yawn, moan, and peer out of their metallic boxes they call their hooches. Over time, each driver has developed his or her own special nickname. Some names they chose for themselves, and others, the group just gave them with or without their consent: Jeff Dye—"Diehard," Phil McCall—"Tumbleweed," Paul Reed—"Romeo," Scott Thomas—"Tex," Tony Moreno—"Ninja Turtle," Mark Taylor—"Ugly Puppy," Pete Satterstrom—"Bones," Tom Meade—"Too Tall," Elzie Norman—"Gunsmoke." These are the KBR drivers who make up the Iron Pony Express. They are a proud group and not a one would trade places with a trucker back in the States. They actually like what they do. They feel they are part of the solution and not part of the problem.

They begin getting their gear ready for another night's mail run. Each has his own personal ritual. Some, like Mark, go for a run, others jot out a note or two to their family. Still others wake up wondering if being in Iraq was just a bad dream. Eyes closed, lying on their crude cots, for just a moment, some envision themselves back home in the States. No, this isn't home, this is purgatory. Reality creeps into their brain cells as the waking drivers absorb where they are. This is no time for self-pity, and they just suck it up and get ready to do what has to be done.

It's time now. The bus is waiting. Drivers board a military bus and head over to the Joint Military Mail Terminal (JMMT), the convoy staging area at Baghdad International Airport (BIAP). For the next several hours, drivers hook up trailers, pull maintenance, and go through the pretrip checks of their Italian Iveco and German Mercedes trucks. Like pilots going through a preflight inspection, attention to detail is paramount. Woe to the driver who doesn't spot that coolant leak and breaks down in an insurgent-infested neighborhood.

Finally, Kevlar helmets and body armor are checked and placed in each cab. The drivers have a little extra time; some use the KBR computers to check e-mail, others catch up on a little reading, and other drivers write letters home.

It's about midnight now, and humvee gun trucks, under the command of Staff Sergeant Frey, from the 1544th Army Transportation Unit, begin to arrive in their desert-camouflaged vehicles. Sergeant Frey has brought along Captain Tackett. Tackett is the company commander, but on this night, technically, Tackett is a "strap hanger," meaning the officer is just along for the ride as an observer. Sergeant Frey is running the show. The soldiers have been doing their pre-mission checks.

Compared to the drivers, most of the soldiers are just kids. Fresh-scrubbed faces and broad smiles. Some are teenage girls barely out of high school. This is an Army National Guard unit. These are part-time soldiers in full-time combat. They come from the small corn-fed town of Paris, Illinois. Most of these young soldiers went to school together. Unlike active-duty military units that have a mix of soldiers from across the country, these kids have been neighbors and friends since they were born.

Mark Taylor looks at them and reflects to himself, "Yeah, they may be kids but they have 'been there and done that.' We have run these roads with them before, and they know how to get out of crap when it happens." No one in this mix of civilians and soldiers thinks of the other in any sort of demeaning manner. This group has an abundance of mutual respect. They are a team: middle-aged men and young soldiers. The team is going outside the wire again. No one knows what will happen. Maybe nothing, but *nothing* can never be assumed. To the contrary, they assume the enemy will attack. They are as ready as they can be.

The drivers gather around a few homemade picnic tables they have constructed from scrap wood. As they wait for the rest of the 1544th soldiers to arrive, a few personal jabs and light-hearted jokes are exchanged. This helps diffuse and disguise the tension and apprehension that each driver struggles with every evening. Tony Garcia, the KBR night foreman, speaks first. He reviews safety standards such as wearing seatbelts and using battle gear. He verifies that every driver had completed his pretrip checks and that all vehicles are fueled and ready to go. Tony confirms that every truck is loaded with emergency equipment, including a medical bag, a stretcher, a towbar, chains, a case of water, and a functioning Qualcomm unit. Qualcomm will allow headquarters to track, via satellite, the exact location of every truck on the road.

Tony steps back and the briefing takes on a more ominous tone. Like all convoys that mix soldiers and civilians, it has both a military and a civilian convoy commander who work side by side. Each will brief the entire group. Sergeant Frey begins, "Tonight we will be headed to Rasheed, Falcon, and the Green Zone. You will get the latest enemy situation report from Specialist Poss, after Mr. Reed and I complete this briefing. Friendly Situation: We have three gun trucks and seven tractor trailers rolling tonight. Our order of march is . . ." This is the sequence in which vehicles will be lined up. Frey continues, "We'll have one bobtail driven by Mark Taylor. He will be in the rear of the convoy. Friendly roving patrols can be expected in the vicinity of RP 3, 6, and 8. Our QRF (quick reaction force) is on standby at . . . and can be contacted on the emergency frequency.

"The weather is clear, no moon, and the temperature will be about 85 degrees. In the event of enemy contact, our TSOP [tactical standard operating procedure] is in effect. Our route tonight will take us north on . . . The primary radio frequency is . . . Alternate is . . . The medical evacuation frequency is . . . Emergency frequency is . . . Every vehicle should have a case of MREs, a MOPP suit, and all your 'battle rattle' [body armor, helmet, load-bearing equipment, etc.]. Ammunition is per SOP." Paul Reed steps up and begins KBR's total safety task instructions [TSTI] brief: "Drivers will maintain tactical night driving distance. Radio traffic for mission critical information only. Let's go back over the route checkpoints. . . . Everyone needs to watch the turnoff at RP 12. It's easy to miss, and we don't need half the convoy touring Baghdad at 2:30 in the morning. If you think a driver has missed an exit or made a wrong turn, don't wait to report it. Get on the horn immediately. No one gets lost out there tonight! Do not permit any vehicle to penetrate the convoy. If this happens, take evasive action immediately. At this time of night, we shouldn't be seeing any civilian vehicles on the road. If you do, report it. Do not allow any vehicle to accelerate up the ramp. If one tries, the gun trucks will take it out. Just be aware that there have been several ramp attacks by VBIEDs [vehicle-borne improvised explosive devices] this week. Drive around, not through, potholes. Avoid coming close to any debris and watch the overpasses carefully." He concludes with, "Look out for wires stretched across the road, and again, stay away from any and all debris!"

Specialist "Kitty" Poss, an intelligence specialist from the New York National Guard and assigned to the 56th Personnel Service Battalion steps up: "Howdy y'all. In the last twenty-four to thirty-six hours the following enemy activity has occurred in your area of operation. IED found at 22A, 25, and 26A, extreme risk. 'Handcuff' (QRF)16A, call 5957, inform Thunder battle space (air support call sign) is 16A–20A. Beware of Racks off overpasses. VBIED on Irish near CP 5. IEDs in potholes, IEDs connected to gators. Watch the overpasses." Kitty's briefing may seem Greek to most people, but to the soldiers and drivers, every word and number helps put together the complex puzzle of information on recent enemy activity.

Specialist Poss ends her briefing with tonight's flare codes. These are the color of flares shot into the air that reveal to friendly forces in the area what to expect ahead. Red might mean an engagement with enemy forces and green could mean all clear. They could also mean just the opposite. The codes are routinely changed so that if the enemy were to learn the codes, they could not use them to their advantage. Everyone takes mental notes and hopes that the flares tonight are good omens.

The briefing ends. The three briefers stand there for a moment. Sergeant Frey asks, "Does anyone have any questions?" Someone asks, "Where did you say the VBIED was and what kind of vehicle was it?" A few other questions bounce around. Each briefer answers those questions relevant to his or her area of responsibility. The group falls quiet. There are no more questions. Sergeant Frey asks, "Sergeant Wetherell, will you lead us in a prayer?" All heads bow. Wetherell, in a solemn voice, begins Psalm 91. He ends with, "God protect us and keep us safe." Mark thinks to himself, *I wonder if somewhere out there tonight is a group of insurgents asking Allah to help them kill Americans. I hope God's on our side.*

Final checks are under way. The convoy lines up. The humvee gun trucks slide in between the huge tractor trailers. Everyone puts on their body armor and tightens down the chin-straps on their helmets. The last couple cases of water are tossed into the waiting vehicles. Engines are running. Final radio checks are conducted. Tonight, Paul Reed, the KBR convoy commander, has designated all trucks begin their call sign with the word *Romeo*. The drivers begin their radio checks: "Romeo six, this is Romeo three, radio check, over." "Romeo three, got you five by" [loud and clear]. The soldiers are completing their radio checks too: "Gun one this is gun two, how do you copy?" "You're squealing gun two, turn down your power." Everyone finishes fine-tuning their radios.

Tony Garcia, his crew, Specialist Poss, and a handful of support soldiers who will be staying behind watch as the Iron Pony mounts up. It's their job to maintain the vigil and monitor the radios until Iron Pony is back safely inside the wire. Some smile and give a thumbs-up. Others shout out a few words of encouragement. A couple of drivers toss chemlights at the farewell party. Some others just nod as you hear over and over again, "Keep your head down." Someone else yells out, "Hey, Ugly Puppy, don't be stopping for any trinkets at the Haji shops." They exchange grins, each quietly wondering if they will see one another again.

There's not much talk now. Sergeant Frey barks out, in a commanding voice indicative of military verbal orders, "Lock and load." The order can be likened to an umpire at a baseball game shouting "Play ball." Only here the game has much higher stakes. Throughout the length of the convoy, the unmistakable metallic sound of bullets being jammed into M16 rifle chambers echoes through the night air. Gunners on the humvees ratchet back the charging handles on their .50-caliber machine guns and slam the bolts forward loading in the huge rounds. You can cut the tension in the air with a knife. This is a no-shit moment. It's 0115 hours and the first truck begins to roll out of the gate.

The "twelve volt" convoy creeps out of BIAP and into the dark, deserted Iraqi streets like a fox leaving its den on a night hunt, only the fox is the hunted. Mark describes the night: "I was the bobtail recovery vehicle toward the back of the convoy. As we left BIAP, all nonessential radio clutter stopped, all weapons were loaded and ready. Everyone was tense. We were headed to our first stop, Rasheed. We were checking off the rally points (RP) as we passed them. Around RP3 and RP4 we encountered some friendly patrols. Everything continued smoothly. We had now been on the road about forty-five minutes. We were nearing RP12, and exiting off of MSR [main supply route, or how the military refers to major highways] Irish on a cloverleaf and entering onto MSR Senator." MSR Irish is the highway between downtown Baghdad and the airport.

Mark continues: "Coming down off the ramp and onto the next highway, I spotted a deserted humvee off to the side of the road and what appeared to be an Iraqi local in a blue jumpsuit or coveralls. He was wearing an interceptor flak vest. I grab my radio and report the sighting to Sergeant Frey. Frey acknowledges with the comeback, "Good Copy," and not a second later an IED detonated in front of Phil McCall's rig.

Jeff Dye (Diehard), a six–foot-six-inch, 280-pound trucker from O'Fallon, Missouri, often called "Gentle Giant," also remembers the night well: "We were coming off a highway exit ramp. So far, this had been an uneventful mail run. Ugly Puppy called in that he spotted someone in body armor. A few seconds later, there was a thunderous explosion and a blinding flash. Pete's trailer in front of me was lifted and moved over a lane. Phil's truck in front of Pete's suddenly jolted to the left and headed for the median. In front of me and to the right, there were two more explosions in rapid succession. Shrapnel rained down on the front of my truck. I heard the pinging of metal and saw sparks flying off the protective window cage.

"Now, directly in front of me, Phil's truck blasted through the guardrail sideways, his left side tires four feet off the ground.

I knew he was going to flip over. I hit my brakes, anticipating I needed to stop and pull him from the wreckage. Suddenly, I couldn't see anyone or anything. We were in a complete whiteout of dust. I yelled into the radio, 'McCall is down!'

"My truck was still moving, and as I emerged from the dust bowl, to my shock, Phil was right side up and plowing down the highway on the opposite side of the road in the oncoming traffic lanes. Phil popped up on his radio correcting my statement, 'I'm not down but I am hit.' Mark, our bobtail, started calmly reassuring Phil that we were watching him and we weren't going to leave him. We stick by our motto, 'No one gets left behind.' "

Mark recalls: "The entire team responded just like we had trained to do. Phil relayed his status and that of his vehicle: 'Windshield is blown in, dash warning lights all coming on, I'm losing coolant, I'm hit in the shoulder but have no idea how badly and still moving.' The other drivers began their accountability reports. Everyone was still alive; everyone was together. Several trucks were damaged but could still roll. I stayed alongside Phil's crippled truck, and the rest of the convoy slowed down for us to catch up.

"We stopped briefly. Paul Reed, our KBR boss, took over driving Phil's truck. During the transfer of drivers, I inspected Phil's wounds. Thanks to his body armor, he did not appear to have a serious wound. Later, the medics would pluck out some shrapnel from his shoulder that he now uses as a key-chain decoration. We continued on. Paul eventually drove Phil's truck back over the median and the vehicle was placed in the front of the convoy. The explosions had knocked out the street lights, but evidently backup generators were now getting the lights back on and we headed toward Rasheed."

En route to Rasheed, Mark attempted to report events to the operations center and prepare them to receive the convoy. Despite continuous attempts to raise someone at KBR operations, all he could get on his cell phone was "Your call cannot be completed at this time." At Rasheed, Mark scrambled to transfer Phil's trailer to his own bobtail. The mail still had to be delivered. This mission was not over. The trailer had no handle to crank the landing gear down, and Mark had previously been a frequent, outspoken critic of both the landing gear problem and the communications problems. Now his frustration was brimming over.

"KBR may be pretty good at a lot of stuff," Mark says, "but when it comes to trucking operations, they would do well to read and adhere to the Federal Motor Carrier Safety Administration (FMCSA) regulations. Not being a licensed U.S. trucking company, KBR is not required to comply with those regulations. They should be." When Mark complains, it is because he cares about the mission, and the lives of the men and women, young and old, soldiers and civilians. "We are all Americans," he says, believing they should never lose sight of that common denominator.

Mark's after-action report reveals that from the time they rolled out of BIAP and into Rasheed, the Iron Pony Express had been outside the wire just fifty-one minutes. Like survivors of a bad car accident, in retrospect everything plays out in slow motion, but in actuality, the attack itself unfolded over the course of mere seconds. There were hours of preparation and fifty-one minutes of tension, terror, fear, concern, pride, camaraderie, and—most of all—professionalism. The young horseback riders from their namesake organization, the original Pony Express, would have been proud. Nearly 150 years later, Americans still risk their lives to deliver the U.S. mail.

It's not a perfect world nor a perfect war. Frustrations aside, Jeff sums up the evening: "Miraculously, we made it through the gates at Rasheed where Phil's truck promptly coughed, sputtered, and gave up the ghost. The trailer was transferred, and we went on to finish the mission the next night. And the night after that, and the night after that.... We will never give in to terror. Because, in my opinion, this is what it really is—a war on terror and evil."

III. Flaming Wheels

The Iron Pony Express was grounded. All mail runs for the 1544th were suspended. Sergeant Jessica Cawvey was just killed by an IED a day earlier. She was the fifth soldier from the 1544th to die, and more than thirty had been wounded in recent months. A senator from Illinois was demanding answers as to why this unit had experienced such a disproportionate number of casualties. A memorial ceremony was planned for 11 a.m. at BIAP's military welfare and recreation center (MWR). The KBR drivers, who normally operated at night and slept during the day, would not miss the memorial service. Every person rolled out of their cots and caught the bus to the MWR center.

Soldiers and drivers paid their last respects to Jessica, and the drivers boarded the bus back to the billeting area. The bus, which is normally noisy with banter, was silent. Each person was alone in his or her thoughts about the loss of Jessica and what would happen next. Ken McDonald recalls: "We had heard rumor that the 1544th was not going to be our escort unit any longer. Ironically, we were told that the army's solution to reduce enemy

exposure for the 1544th was to put them on fuel convoy escort."
Ken asks: "You call that a solution!" He continues, "Rumors were
flying and we had heard conflicting reports as to whether we
would be going back out on the mail run on this evening. As we
got back to the billeting area, word came down from KBR operations to catch whatever sleep we could, because in a few hours
we would be on the road headed for the Marine Corps base
Taqaddum. 'TQ,' as we called it, is about forty miles west of
Baghdad. They said that a Reserve Marine Corps unit from
Alabama would provide security escort for the trip."

The run from BIAP to TQ was usually a quick forty-mile trip
on a fairly direct route. In the last several months, convoys had
been hit by insurgents over and over again on this run. Now, in
an attempt to avoid insurgent activity, the trip is a circuitous 130
miles each way. The outgoing mail is stacked up, loaded into
trailers, and waiting. Ken recalls: "We were all a bit nervous about
making a trip with a new unit that didn't know how we
operated. We were used to the 1544th. With the 1544th, we all
knew we could count on each other when shit hit the fan. This
deal with the marines would be a new experience that we
weren't much excited about." The KBR drivers did what they
could to get some badly needed sleep, most just tossed and
turned. Around 6 p.m., they finished chow at the dining facility
and boarded the JMMT bus to the staging area to begin their
pretrip rituals.

Ken McDonald relates the Iron Pony team's experiences
over the next two nights: "When the marines rolled up, they had
eight gun trucks loaded for bear. In one sense, that was
comforting. We had often made these runs with only three or
four gun trucks. In another sense, the fact that they brought

eight trucks was scary. You think to yourself, *What in the hell do you expect we are going to run into that we need eight gun trucks?* We didn't know them and they didn't know us. It wasn't the usual joking around like we would do with the 1544th. These guys were all business.

"We had been accustomed to mission briefings where all the soldiers and drivers stood together and reviewed the night's mission. On this night, just three marines came over to where we were gathered. These marines all seemed to have that blend of a southern accent with a military formality: 'Y'all fall in, on the double!' They briefed the mission, situation, intelligence, and started to walk away. I shouted, 'Hey hold on a minute! We don't head out without a prayer.' The marine in charge looked at us for a long moment, 'You boys want a prayer?' he asked. 'OK, we got a guy that does that for a living back in the world.' The marine in charge hollered something like, 'Hey Schmidty, these boys need a prayer! You got one for 'em? Get over here.' A young marine cut across the staging area on the double. You could tell he was happy to be called. The young preacher from Alabama led us in a prayer. It wasn't the psalm we were used to saying, but it was a good prayer and the marine put in his best effort. We appreciated it." The Iron Pony saddled up and headed out for TQ.

"I'm sure all the drivers were still thinking about Jessica. It was especially hard not to think about her as we passed the scorched, blackened, and gouged-out section of highway where she had been killed. I know I couldn't get her off my mind. The trip to TQ went pretty well. We had a few sticky points as we began our standard procedure of reporting RPs and suspicious sightings. The marines, who were monitoring our radios hadn't expected that type of communication from us. They came up on the net [communications channel] and asked what that was all about. I gave them some 'on the road' education as to how the Iron Pony operates. They were surprised. As the trip went on, I think their respect for us increased. We pulled into the entry checkpoint at TQ without incident. We figured that we would be swapping out trailers and heading back to BIAP.

"The marines told us that those plans had changed and we would be spending the night at TQ. One of my many jobs, albeit an unwritten responsibility, was to always secure the hooches, cots, food, and shower situation for our soldiers and drivers. Oftentimes I was left to my own resources to work out the specifics. Sometimes I traded 'stuff' for other stuff to secure the best accommodations available. Sometimes the stuff was 80 proof. I enjoyed looking out for the team and had developed a reputation as the Iron Pony's scrounger. To my surprise the marines were as concerned about our welfare as I was. They offered to let us sleep in the same billets with them. I thought this was too much an imposition and hesitated. They thought it over, and then decided to clear out their MWR center and set up cots for us to sleep on. They made certain we had everything we needed and that the DFAC was prepared to feed us. They cared about us as they would have cared about their own men and women. This was a very encouraging sign.

"On the next evening, as we ran our pretrip inspections and got our mission brief, we learned through the rumor mill, and later at the briefing, that the enemy had been attacking convoys throughout the area. A lot of IEDs had blown up a lot of trucks. Everything had heated up. Our route would take us from TQ, around the outskirts of Fallujah, through the town of Abu Ghraib, and into BIAP. Due to insurgent activity, we had to clear Fallujah before 0300 hours. After that time, the Fallujah area would be off-limits for the convoy. The town of Abu Ghraib worried us too because that's where we had been hit several times recently. Our 'pucker factor' was up.

"For this run, we had seven mail trucks; a few of the trucks had empty mail containers and the rest were packed with letters to home. We also had two military trucks, an LMTV (light medium tactical vehicle) and an HET, and another seven or eight 'Haji' trucks and their drivers. All together, somewhere around eighteen big rigs, my bobtail, plus our eight gun-truck escorts and thirty-two heavily armed marines. The lineup was: KBR trucks, my bobtail, followed by the two military trucks, and the Hajis behind them. The marine gun trucks were integrated every third or fourth vehicle and one was a 'Rover.' Throughout the run, the Rover would alternate between passing the convoy on the left, and then crossing over to the right and letting the convoy pass him. In this manner, he could keep a constant vigil on every truck in the convoy. We also had air cover from an unmanned aerial vehicle (UAV) that was assigned to shadow our convoy.

"It's always an experience running with the Haji drivers. The American KBR drivers all knew the drill if we were attacked, but if we got hit when the Hajis were with us, God only knew what they would do. In addition to the language barrier, they didn't have the training we had. Sometimes they just stop, jump out, and run into the wilderness. Afterward, it was a real pain in the ass trying to round them up to continue the mission.

"I would be driving the bobtail tractor. I used to say that I was just your average coward and liked to bobtail because it made me a smaller target than a complete rig with trailer attached. Of course, that assumed that I wouldn't have to be recovering some blown-up hunk of metal in the middle of the night. If our convoy got hit with an IED and one of our trucks bit the dust, the rest of the group would go on a few klicks to a holding area. Then myself and a couple of gun trucks would have to try and salvage the load and hope that the insurgents weren't still hanging around.

"Our Marine Corps–appointed preacher of sorts was standing by and ready with a new prayer. He had probably worked on it all day; he had a new mission in life. Leading us in prayer was probably the best part on his entire tour in Iraq. We bowed our heads. After the prayer, everything was silent. The marine convoy commander looked at us and said, 'Ladies and gentlemen, put on your game face.' We took a deep breath and loaded up. A moment later I heard a marine's radio crackle, "Weapons status Red." The marines were locked and loaded. Once again, the Iron Pony rolled out the gate. The time was 8:30 p.m.

"I had barely wiggled my butt into a comfortable position when KBR truck 2 blew up. We had been on the road just seven minutes. KBR 2, driven by Craig Gambrel, struck a really dirty IED. By dirty, I mean one of those that isn't just a big flash-bang, but one that is loaded with lots of shrapnel and sends out a huge black cloud when it blows. Out of those black clouds, and flying in all directions, are thousands of steel shards. KBR 3, with Phil McCall, lost visibility and plowed into the back end of Craig's trailer. The two rigs lurched off the road and piled up a few yards down a gradual embankment. Unknown to me at the time, this attack was not a typical hit and run. This time, the insurgents were waiting for us to become ducks in their shooting gallery.

"I was behind KBR 7 and sped past them to get to the scene. I jumped out of my bobtail and yelled and motioned at the trucks behind me, 'Go, go, go, keep going, keep going.' The convoy needed to get out of the danger area or else we risked losing more trucks and getting bogged down in a possible attack. It was very dark now, and I ran toward the two stricken vehicles. Their engines were still running and lights were on, but there were no signs of life. I got to KBR 3 first. The door was open, the seat had broken off, the steering wheel collapsed into the dash, but there were no signs of Phil McCall. I shut off the engine and lights and bolted for KBR 2. Craig's truck was a mess: the door was closed, all the windows blown out, tires flattened, fuel tank leaking, shrapnel everywhere inside the cab, but again, no driver.

"I grabbed my small LED flashlight and began looking down the embankment for the drivers. I figured they must have been thrown or taken from the vehicles. I pushed the talk switch on my handheld radio and asked the marines, 'My drivers, the drivers, they aren't here, where the fuck are the drivers?' Just then a humvee gun truck rolled up with lights out. I heard over their radio one of the marines respond, 'We've got the drivers.' A marine jumped out of the humvee with two M16s in his hand; he tossed me one. The marine asked, 'Alright, what's gotta be done to get out of here?' I told him to hold on a minute and I ran to the KBR 3 and then to KBR 2 and took a look at the mail containers on the trailers. The marine asked, 'What the hell are you doing?' I said, 'Listen, the rear truck has no seal on the container; that means it's empty. The hell with it. The one in front has a seal. That's the one we have got to recover. It's loaded with mail!'

"I lowered the landing gear on KBR 2, disconnected the air lines, and disengaged the plate that locks in the trailer. I pulled my tractor around to the front of the crippled truck [and] hooked up a chain. It was going to be a challenge to get the damaged tractor out from under the trailer. The air lines were blown and the brakes had locked up. This was going to be a dead-weight pull. I remember saying to the marine, 'Here goes nothing!' I revved my engine, popped the clutch, damn near did a wheelie, and yanked that sucker out from under the trailer. I dragged it about forty yards away and came back and slid my tractor under the mail trailer. I was feeling pretty proud of myself and stepped out of my tractor and began to raise the landing gear. The marine was standing next to me.

"Just then, bullets began pinging off the mail containers, thumping into the ground, sparking across the pavement, and whizzing past my head. The marine literally knocked me to the ground and began returning fire. We could see muzzle flashes about a hundred and fifty yards at four o'clock. We had no protection and rounds were striking all around us. I'm an old elk hunter from Colorado, but I wasn't real familiar with M16s. It took me a moment, and what seemed like an eternity, of fumbling around before I got the safety off and was ready to fire. The marine was blocking my body. I asked him to move aside. He said, 'Sir, I ain't gonna let nothing happen to you!' I came back with, 'Who you calling Sir? Sir was my dad. My name's Ken.' Then the marine said something like, 'Well Ken, you see them muzzle flashes? You take the right and I'll take the left. Together, he and I began popping off rounds at the insurgents. I know that every time that we saw a muzzle flash, it wasn't but a split second later, one of us put several rounds on that exact spot.

"Now the humvee gun truck began to open up with their .50-caliber machine gun. I swear it just seemed to fire forever. That *thump-thump-thump* of the .50-caliber raining down on the enemy is every bit as sweet a sound as the sound of a bugle must have been when cavalry reinforcements were riding to the rescue. A second gun truck joined in and began popping flares into the night sky. The flares floated down from their miniature parachutes like lightbulbs dangling in the breeze. The firing had stopped. There was no movement coming from the berm where the insurgents had fired from. We lay frozen for a few minutes. It was only then that I realized my heart was pounding through my shirt. I was trembling, and sweat was pooling on the pavement beneath me. Later, I would learn that the UAV overhead had video of four dead insurgents. I can't say that I killed anyone, but then again, I can't say that I didn't.

"I finished the hookup of the crippled mail trailer and hopped up into my tractor. I turned to the marine and said, 'Let's go find us a convoy!' We began hauling ass with our lights off. About three miles up we found the convoy waiting for us. On the way I had been on the radio, alerting them we were coming and checking on the status of our drivers. Aside from a few minor shrapnel wounds, both Phil and Craig were physically fine. The military trucks had been alert enough to leave a space for me to slip into. I pulled into the lineup.

"I got on the radio and called our KBR convoy commander, Bob Garza, who was in KBR 1. 'Wait for me,' I said. 'I have to go back to the blown trucks. I'll be back in a few minutes.' At first, Garcia was incredulous, but then he understood when I reminded him that we had to recover the sensitive gear, like our Qualcomm satellite trackers and messaging systems, as well as the other radios. If those fell into enemy hands, the text messaging system could have been used by the insurgents who might try to deceive us with false messages.

"I climbed out of the tractor just as a marine gun truck pulled alongside. I got into the rear passenger side of the humvee and told the marines that we had to go back. The driver looked over his shoulder and said, 'You have got to be shitting me.' The vehicle commander, who was sitting shotgun, was the same marine [who] had been on the ground with me. He turned to the driver and said, 'Turn around. Do what he said.' We headed back down the road. My stomach was in knots. On the way back to the damaged trucks, Craig called on the radio and wanted to make sure I brought back his pocket watch. Then Phil called and asked me to make sure to bring back his hat. You'd thought I was just stopping at the neighbor's house or something.

"The idea of returning to the scene after we had left it unguarded was more than a little unnerving. The marines got on their radio and notified their headquarters that we were headed back to the ambush area. The UAV was circling the area watching the trucks. We crept up with lights off. The marines were using their night operating devices (NODs). They scanned the area. It looked clear so I jumped out, climbed up on the truck catwalk, pulled out my Gerber knife, and began cutting wires under the Qualcomm radome roof antennae. Then I went inside each cab, [then] cut the wires from behind the text messaging screens and the mobile UHF radios. I also grabbed the handhelds left behind and found both Craig's watch and Phil's hat. I tossed everything into a black plastic garbage bag. Almost as an afterthought, I grabbed the fire bottles and tossed them into the humvee also. We bolted back up to the convoy.

"When I first came to Iraq, whenever we were hit with small arms or a roadside explosive, I would take a deep breath, thank God I came through it OK, and have a sense that the threat was over for the day. I'd look forward to getting a good night's sleep at the next military base an hour or two up the road. Then one day we got hit and just a few miles later we got hit again. I knew then that the day was never over until it was over. Only when you were back *inside the wire* could you take that deep breath, count your fingers and toes, and go to sleep.

"During the time that I was back at the ambush site, the guys in the convoy inspected my rig for me. I had a couple of blown outside tires on the driver's side but it looked like I could run with it. We started rolling again. Around seventy miles from BIAP the tires started coming apart and wheels started sparking. In my side-view mirror, I could see sparks rooster-tailing out thirty yards behind my vehicle. We kept going. I knew we had to clear Fallujah. The split wheels started to completely disintegrate and come apart now. Rubber and metal were blowing out all over the road.

"The rover came alongside and radioed, 'Hey bobtail, you're starting to catch on fire. I think we need to address this situation.' The convoy slowed down and the rover pulled alongside of me and began spraying one of the fire bottles on the flames. We repeated this about seven or eight times until we had passed Fallujah and were winding into Abu Ghraib. I could see the glowing lights of the prison up ahead. The wheels were really flaming now and I was down to one tire on the rear axle. The whole trailer cantered to the left and was very hard to control. At one point, we had to stop at Abu Ghraib to put out the wheel fires, which were now burning the underside of the trailer.

"Finally I rolled, or should I say slid, the truck past the line of barrels and through entry checkpoint seven at Baghdad Airport. As I slid into the JMMT complex, flames and sparks trailed for fifty yards behind me. I brought the rig to a halt and climbed out. Dozens of marines and a whole bunch of guys from the KBR operations center came out to greet us. They had been monitoring our radio traffic all night and now they were pouring out of the makeshift buildings to greet our returning convoy. I remember some marine giving me a hug. And another one asking which we liked better now that we had run with both marines and the army. I told him the marines were good but jokingly asked, 'Hey, we still got hit. Didn't we?' An army captain walked over to me, stopped, looked at my smoldering vehicle, looked back at me, smiled, and said, 'Rough night?'

"You know, I was really proud that we completed the mission with all our drivers, all the critical equipment safe, and brought back all the mail. OK, so the mail was a little screwed up from bullets passing through a few boxes and envelopes, but at least the insurgents weren't reading it. I remember that when I got out of the truck at the JMMT, I was soaked with sweat and everyone around me was just saying over and over again, 'We did it, we did it!' "

Ken remembers one other poignant moment from that night: a marine approached him at the JMMT later on and handed him a note from the marine who had fought next to him earlier that evening. The note said, "Consider yourself an honorary marine." Ken looks back on that moment and says, "If I had been thinking, I should have written him a note: 'Consider yourself an honorary member of the Iron Pony Express.' "

IV. Malfunction Junction

On a typical muggy summer afternoon in June 2005, the town of Paris in east-central Illinois welcomes home the 1544th U.S. Army, Illinois National Guard Transportation Unit. Early that morning, scattered summer storms drenched the area. Tornados loomed in the weather report. Lightning flared and thunder crackled throughout the preceding night. The local high school gymnasium is decked out in red, white, and blue. In front of the stage, there are five lonely bayoneted rifles, stuck in the floor, with desert boots in front of each, a pair of dog tags dangling from the hand grip of each rifle, and helmets placed on their butt stocks. They stand as a silent tribute to the "kids" from Paris who didn't come home.

This little community in the U.S. heartland is welcoming back their farm boys, their grocery clerks, the pizza delivery boy, the girl from the Tastee-Freez, the local troublemaker, and the popular cheerleader. But they are no longer kids. They are not youngsters parading in uniform. They are young men and women who have watched their best friends die, seen their fellow soldiers scream in agonizing pain from burning shrapnel, picked themselves back up, and did what they had to do—over and over again, popular or not.

About a hundred soldiers in desert camouflage uniforms march into the gymnasium, line up in neat rows, and stand at attention. Many of the Iron Pony drivers are here too; they are mingled among the bystanders in the bleachers and watching their old friends from Iraq. The townspeople clearly all know one another and are chatting, shooting pictures, and hugging each other. The KBR drivers are an oddity in that no one recognizes them. No one pays them any attention. They just seem to be a bunch of middle-aged men who must have stumbled into town. The drivers are quiet, but proud, and keep to themselves. Everyone rises for the national anthem. There is hardly a dry eye in the place.

An Illinois Army National Guard officer, a major, begins the ceremony. Paraphrased: We are here today to honor the men and women from the 1544th Transportation Unit. They joined the National Guard for many different reasons. They did not choose this war. They did not ask to go to Iraq. They did not relish the thought of killing or dying. Yet, when they were ordered to go, they went. They performed their mission, and they come home now with honor and dignity. They have earned and deserve our respect. We hope that in some small way today's ceremony will demonstrate our admiration, respect, and lasting recognition of their accomplishments.

The major has said it all. Several other speeches from local politicians follow. The state deputy adjutant general is the presiding officer. He renders apologies for the fact that the Illinois adjutant general could not make the event. Short of a nuclear holocaust, his absence is hard to excuse to those in attendance. The deputy does his best to honor the 1544th. Dozens of medals, Purple Hearts, and symbolic tokens of appreciation are presented to the soldiers. Throughout it all, the KBR drivers grin from ear to ear. They whisper shared pieces of humor and recollections about this, that, him, or her. None of them shows the slightest evidence of jealousy. They are beyond such pettiness. Their satisfaction comes from simply knowing that they have been there, and done that. That's good enough for the truck drivers of the Iron Pony Express.

After the ceremony, dozens of soldiers head up into the surrounding stands. At times, a soldier and a KBR driver eye one another from across the gymnasium. They just point at each other and grin. The soldiers and KBR drivers exchange hugs. The soldiers introduce them to their moms and dads. A lot of comments abound like, "Remember when I told you about Ugly Puppy, well, this is him." Words can't describe the emotions. Parents don't know quite what to say. All they know is that this middle-aged man, a civilian and a stranger, was there with their son or daughter. And that makes this trucker important to them. It's that simple.

That evening, the town of Paris hosts a party for the soldiers of the 1544th. The location for the event is about three miles from the center of Paris, in a farm field with a couple of barns. The townspeople have erected a huge tent and a small stage for the evening's festivities. The soldiers have nicknamed this place "Malfunction Junction." Parents, township officials, soldiers, and KBR drivers all show up. The soldiers have changed into civilian clothing; the girls are dressed in jeans and halter tops. The guys are wearing their slogan T-shirts. Beer is pouring from several kegs. Mark and Renee Taylor are there. So, too, are Ken McDonald and Glenn Collins. The soldiers and drivers poke fun at each other and recollect the days and nights they ran the roads of Iraq together. Each one of them creates his or her own twist to the same story as to "how it really happened." Each finds an excuse to laugh at the other's antics during some operation in Iraq. Race, age, geographic, and occupational differences have long since disappeared.

During the evening, one soldier boasts, "We had the best looking girls in Iraq. We had to fend off other army units to keep them away from 'our women.' " The gathered soldiers nod and mumble in agreement. When he refers to 'our women,' he doesn't mean it in a sexual way. Rather, his exclamation is much more like a brother protecting his sister. Erin Hutchinson, a soldier from the 1544th, steps up on the small stage and picks up a microphone. She asks to sing a song she wrote while in Iraq. The crowd quiets down. The eclectic collection of moms and dads, sons and daughters, soldiers and war zone contractors stand side by side proudly watching one of their own. Erin sings a heartfelt and emotional rendition of a song she wrote herself, "Hero."

In this war, combat experience is neither gender nor job specific. On a summer night, in a farm field in the Midwest, the men and women of the Iron Pony Express have come together, as a group, perhaps for the last time: soldiers and truckers, bonded by their shared experience. They have witnessed the best and worst of humanity. For those who lived through it, they will always be proud of what they had the courage to do. Their sense of self is forever changed. Those who died would not have wanted it any other way.

Chapter 6

Training Contractors

I. An Overview

Dozens of PMCs offer training programs in military tactics and techniques. For most of these firms, training is one component of a multitude of *tactical* services they offer. Their training programs frequently include executive protection, marksmanship, close-quarters combat, and physical security. However, one company, MPRI, formerly known as Military Professional Resources Incorporated, differentiates itself from the myriad other PMCs that come and go. MPRI consciously avoids the "security service" business and all the associated negativity. When it comes to military tactics and training, few companies can come close to the expertise that MPRI brings to the table.

MPRI's different philosophy can be traced back to its origins. Unlike the many PMCs formed by a group of low- or mid-level ex-military officers and focused exclusively on tactical solutions, MPRI's focus is far more strategic. Begun by a handful of very senior officers drawn from the highest levels of the Pentagon, their vision imbued offering training and consulting at every level and every aspect of defense and law enforcement operations. With the exception of not offering security services, MPRI has become a total provider of defense-related requirements. MPRI's business plan and capabilities developed accordingly.

MPRI offers organization and force development planners; recruiting assistance; leader development; doctrine development; logistics planning; maritime, vehicle, and weapons marksmanship training; systems integration; democracy transition; and international security sector reform. With rare exception, MPRI contractors are unarmed, and that's the way MPRI prefers it. Any hint of mercenary-like appearance or conduct is shunned. The organization is run like military clockwork and with military discipline. There is no discerning MPRI employees from active-duty military personnel. MPRI's contact with every level of DoD keeps them in touch with the best military minds in the U.S. armed forces. Consequently, they attract the best former and retired military personnel available.

Most salaries are just slightly above what these men and women made while on active duty. The hourly wage breaks out to less than $20. Here again, the hours are long and hard, and the accumulation of wages when simply reflected as an annualized salary can be misleading. Also bear in mind that MPRI contractors were themselves senior officers and noncommissioned officers so their compensation was already in the upper echelons of military pay. Money is clearly not a primary incentive for joining their organization; professionalism is. MPRI's vetting process in hiring their contract employees is on a par with those found in the best U.S. corporations. In general, only the best applicants are hired as MPRI contractors. Those who are hired tend to stay with the organization for a long time.

MPRI has more than 1,500 full-time employees and thousands of contract personnel. They are currently conducting operations in Bosnia, Nigeria, Afghanistan, Iraq, Kuwait, and a dozen other countries. Every international operation requires

State Department clearance. At their headquarters in Alexandria, Virginia, they have a full-time staff dedicated to complying with State Department guidelines and approval processes.

In both Jordan and Iraq, civilian contractors operate police-training academies through a contract known as the International Criminal Investigation Police Training Program (ICIPTP). More than 380 current and former U.S. law enforcement officers are employed by MPRI in Jordan and Iraq. They conduct several different training programs ranging from four to ten weeks in length. The program offers basic police skills, correction-officer training, and senior leadership classes. The Jordanian location graduates about 1,600 students each quarter, and their Baghdad Police Academy is producing nearly four thousand new graduates every quarter. These programs are directed by the U.S. Department of Justice and are funded by the U.S. State Department.

An executive familiar with the program and affiliated with the Department of Justice analyzes the problems of establishing civil authority in Iraq: "When the U.S. invasion of Iraq was essentially over, U.S. forces were challenged to develop a law enforcement and a judicial system that would be capable of maintaining the peace. Military rule needed to give way to civilian authority. The two don't mix. Lack of understanding and planning for this transition resulted in a period of chaos and provided a window of opportunity for a plethora of criminal activity, including the creation and expansion of criminal organizations and quasi-insurgent groups. Sometimes, they're one in the same.

"This transition from the military to civil authority was, and still is, mired in complexities. Military police are good at temporary prisoner detention, convoy escorts, and static site security. They do not have the kind of skills or structure to recruit, train, develop, and deploy desperately needed civil law enforcement and judicial agencies. For a collection of reasons, the magnitude of the requirement was overwhelming, and the United States went through a lot of fumbling in an attempt to establish law and order among the Iraqi population. In fact, I personally believe, if trained correction officers had been introduced earlier, the whole Abu Ghraib prison scandal might never have occurred.

"A major faux pas in the process was that it was begun from the bottom up as opposed to from the top down. Naïvely, early efforts were aimed at putting large numbers of poorly trained police on the streets without a leadership structure, a judicial process, or court system in place. One day the police were being fired and the next day they were being rehired. What laws were being enforced, what procedures were in place, which agency had jurisdiction, in what area, and under whose authority were these police officers working? The transition was a 'Who's on first?' fiasco."

Police officers, on contract with DynCorp, SAIC, MPRI, or U.S. Investigations Services have stepped up to the plate and developed comprehensive law enforcement and criminal investigation training programs. In the end analysis, the only way to truly gauge the effectiveness of MPRI's police training will be to have personnel on the ground, in the local police stations, and accompanying Iraqi police on operations and patrols. By necessity, the job will clearly fall on the shoulders of civilian contractors. They are our only resource.

On a limited scale, some partnering is already taking place, however the danger for these contractors is enormous. The vetting process for hiring police recruits has been less than perfect. Insurgents have infiltrated their ranks. Iraqi police stations are attacked daily. Police training contractors working at isolated stations and checkpoints are terribly exposed. Many have been killed. By way of example, in June 2005, a retired county sheriff's deputy from Oregon, Deborah Klecker, in Iraq under a DynCorp contract to train police, was killed by a roadside bomb. She had been in Iraq just two months.

II. God's Will

"Enshalla, enshalla," the Iraqi police cadets respond. Translated from Arabic: "God's will." This isn't the response that Donna Kerns had hoped for when she asked her students, "Do you want to come home alive?" But this is the reality of training Muslims to become police officers in a war-torn country.

Kerns, a twenty-six-year veteran of the Memphis Police Department, has to deal with it every day. "Our Iraqi police cadets are fatalistic," she remarks. "Their religion, their culture, their history, and their life experience have conditioned them to be subservient. For most of them, it is simply, 'What will happen, will happen.'" She knows she has to change her students' mindset. She has to change centuries of ingrained cultural conditioning to deprivation, torture, and religious influence. She has big job, prays to her own God to make it doable. Still, she has moments of doubt.

This is the U.S.-run police academy in Amman, Jordan. It is here that most future Iraqi police officers come to be trained. This is where young and old Iraqi police cadets, 1,500 in each class, come to learn how to be a cop. To say that democratic concepts of law enforcement are foreign to the student body is an understatement. In fact, such concepts are contrary to nearly everything they've ever learned. The cadre has just eight weeks to turn out a product that can return to an active war zone and enforce some semblance of civil law, the kind U.S. citizens take for granted. Many of their students will be killed shortly after graduation. Some are notified of the killing of family members who preceded them at the academy while they themselves have yet to finish training. Yet the students somehow persevere, and the recruits keep coming.

Some cadets are nearly abducted off the streets by police recruiters, some are insurgents, some are criminals, and some just need the money. While many have selfish motives, many more hope to contribute and make a real difference in improving their country. Kerns admires those Iraqis who manage to hold on to this mindset while becoming police officers, despite all the forces and cultural barriers in their way.

When her cadets return to Iraq, they will find themselves working with many leaders who don't or won't share their concept of what a police officer ought to be. Many of their superiors have grown up with a ruthless dictatorship as their example of how to enforce the law. Those cadets who believe in a democratic cause and believe there is a better way to live will have a long, lonely, and painful road ahead. Kerns agrees with the program's director, Ted Weekely, when he says, "We are planting the seeds. Whether or not those seeds sprout in this lifetime or another remains to be seen . . . but they will sprout. Change is in the works."

During her time with the Memphis Police Department, Kerns spent about fifteen years as a uniformed police officer, four years in narcotics investigations, and eight years as a violent crimes investigator. In 1997, she was working the night shift known as the Dinosaur Squad because it always seemed to draw older officers with the seniority to bid on the shift over junior officers. Like a scene from the old sitcom *Barney Miller*, nearly every evening Kerns' police lieutenant would converse with her over coffee at the station. Night after night, he seemed to have a new idea about what he was going to do when he retired. No one ever seemed to take him seriously, but many of the officers wondered aloud about what he planned to do next.

The question always drew a few chuckles, some of the officers would roll their eyes, and others would say, "Oh, I don't believe you asked him that question!" Several officers would head straight for the door. "Time to roll," they would say. Everyone knew they were in for a long-winded story. Kerns never minded. She would just smile and say, "Let's hear it, Larry," and Larry always accommodated her. He had no delusions about the reaction of the other officers. He didn't much care. His good friend Kerns always lent an ear, and for that he was grateful.

So on one particular night, Kerns pops the standard question. She recalls, "Larry became excited and pulled out a mutilated, crumpled-up piece of paper. As he carefully unfolded it, he exclaimed, 'I'm gonna retire. I'm gonna fill out this application with DynCorp. I'm gonna make eighty grand a year, and I'm going to Bosnia to train those folks over there how to be good policemen.' "

For some reason this piqued her interest. "Where's Bosnia?" she asked. "Who are you going train? How do get a job like that? What are the qualifications? I sat up in my chair, walked over to the coffeepot for a refill, and strolled on over to get a closer listen to just what it was that Larry was up to this time.

"I had been mulling over retiring myself. Police work was getting old. Even with a perfect investigation and a mile of paperwork, too many criminals were just getting a walk, too many cops moving up the chain of command solely because they are [with] the in-crowd. Trying to be a good cop can just beat you to death after a while. I was tired and frankly felt I had been put out to pasture. It was getting awfully hard to look past the administrative murk and see anyone who cared. I looked over the qualifications and thought to myself, *I could do this*! Perhaps it was time for a change. I took that ratty piece of paper over to the copier, pressed out the creases as best I could, and made a reasonably ratty copy of the document.

"The idea was growing on me. By the end of my shift the next morning, I was excited to go home and have a sit-down conversation with my husband. If there was half a chance that DynCorp would accept me, the only real obstacle I could foresee would be the stress of being away from my husband for a year. We had been married eighteen years. He and I needed to seriously sound this out. We had many conversations over the next several days. I would look at my husband, Ken, in the eyes and ask him directly, 'If I go, will this be OK with us? I mean will you be OK? Can we handle the separation?' My husband, who was also a police officer, supported and encouraged me. I felt he could see that I was excited about the prospect, and he never once gave me reason to doubt that our marriage wouldn't hold together.

"I started faxing information and applications back and forth to DynCorp. The thought processes had started a ball rolling [that] was now irreversible. Over the next several days, I realized that I was retiring regardless of how the application to

DynCorp came out. I gave my notice, had a party, and retired all within a matter of days. I hadn't yet heard anything definite from DynCorp, but it didn't much matter. I was hanging up my police uniform.

"It was Thursday of that week and my husband and I planned a little celebration vacation. He and I were going to head out to California with my nephew and my mother to just kick everything loose for a couple of weeks. The decision to retire had lifted a huge load off me and I was really looking forward to the trip. We took our time en route to San Diego, arriving on a Monday, to a waiting message from DynCorp, telling me they wanted me in Ft. Worth the next Saturday morning for training prior to deployment to Bosnia. It was like a hot flash. I mean, reality struck like a lightning bolt. It's kind of one of those things: *Be careful what you ask for because you might just get it.* I flew out of California Thursday, spent one day packing for a year's absence from home, and flew to Dallas-Fort Worth Saturday morning. The rest of my family continued to the Grand Canyon, arriving back in Memphis after I had already departed for the Balkans.

"Well, I ended up in eastern Slavonia, near the Croatian-Serbian border along the Danube. I spent a year trying to keep the Croats from abusing the Serbs and vice versa. I became the regional civilian police human rights coordinator and had my hands full investigating allegations and counter-allegations between the two groups. I saw so many injustices and so many families destroyed and homeless. If Serbs had moved into a Croatian family's home while it was vacant during the war, many times the Croatian family was just SOL. It was there that I really started to realize how good we have it back in the States.

"A year later I came back to Tennessee. DynCorp soon wanted me to go to Kosovo. My husband told everyone how proud he was of me. He completely supported me taking another contract in eastern Europe. That should have been a clue that something was really wrong, but he just seemed to be so proud of me—more so than in several years. It wasn't until I served about four months in Kosovo, prior to the NATO involvement there and returned home for a few months, before the lightbulb went on and I realized he had hooked up with one of my 'friends.' So the marriage ended, and finding myself alone and needing to pay off some end-of-marriage debt, I returned to Kosovo for another six-month contract.

"On returning from Kosovo in 2000, I became an agent for the West Tennessee Judicial Violent Crime and Drug Task Force, directed by the Shelby County District Attorney General's Office. But I was never the same again. The quality of the people I had worked with overseas defied description. The bonding, the camaraderie, the mission, and the professionalism of the contractors was like something I had never felt before. I missed the excitement and the sense of purpose.

"If you have worked in the contracting business, you instantly have access to a network of contacts and people who know people. The people you have worked with become like family. They travel around the world. One may be in Idaho, another in Afghanistan, another in Kosovo. The network helps the network. I put my SOS out on the network in 2004. There was a lot of discussion about the U.S. building an Iraqi police academy in Hungary. We were all pretty excited. Hungary, compared to Bosnia or Kosovo, is a pretty nice place. When the Hungarian government balked at the idea, the U.S. government scrambled to find a new location. The Hashemite Kingdom of Jordan agreed to host the academy, and almost overnight Iraqi police applicants were pouring into Amman, Jordan, for eight weeks of police training." With a new sense of purpose, Kerns signed up with SAIC (Scientific Applications International Corporation) and headed to the Middle East.

Iraqi cadet police training consists of four weeks of general police/law enforcement subjects and four weeks of operational tactics. General subjects include such courses as policing in a democracy, gender issues, and antiterrorism. The last four weeks cover operational policing, which includes firearms, defensive tactics, tactical driving, and practical applications (i.e., officer survival). The class is broken into four color groups; black, white, green, and red. These are the colors of the Iraqi national flag. Classes in these last four weeks are independent subjects and the colored groups will rotate between instruction committees (i.e., the black group may go to firearms, and red may go to defensive tactics for their first week).

When Kerns arrived, about three months after the academy had opened, she was assigned to its practical applications unit. She was placed for the first introductory week with two other police officers, a Swedish and a British female who were responsible for officer survival training to a group of around forty Iraqi men. "Everyone thinks this would have been terribly complicated given the attitudes Arab men generally hold toward women," Kerns remarked. "Interestingly, I found that their attitude toward Arab women versus their attitude toward Western women is often very different. Watching a lot of U.S. movies has shaped their perceptions. U.S. women, especially U.S. policewomen, are frequently portrayed in movies as aggressive, take-no-prisoners, martial arts experts. As long as you don't start acting like some sort of 'girlie girl' and you take control of your class from the start, you can usually maintain good order and discipline.

"All our local contractors are tied one way or another with the Jordanian royal family. Tri-Services has the contract for base services." Kerns laments the problems: "Millions of American dollars are being spent here. The priority for facilities and equipment seems to be for administrative functions. Buildings have been finished for four months, but we are not allowed to use any of them for training purposes.

"Tri-Services is supposed to supply food, water, office supplies, uniforms, language assistants, and cleaning staff. The instructors here find themselves having to go into Amman and buy supplies out of their own pocket. We have all sorts of problems with the Jordanian contractors. For example, they provided pencils that break when you attempt to sharpen them and crates of pens that don't write. They put in cheap fifty-dollar desks and bill us for three hundred dollars. They charge thirteen dollars for a pair of foam earplugs that go for less than a buck in the States. We had about two hundred 'ghost' interpreters for the last six months. They were on the payroll but no one ever sees them. We're all pretty disgusted with this treatment.

"We are in desperate need of 'red guns' (the rubber ones that we use in training). We need vehicles for role-playing stop-and-search operations. Student uniforms are in short supply and many times a student has to go through the entire eight weeks in his sweatsuit and flip-flops. Cadets are told to bring no more than four changes of clothing. That's kind of comical, since many of them don't even own four changes of clothing. The age range is supposed to be between twenty and thirty-five, but we have many come here [who] are sixteen and I know I have taught a few [who] were pushing fifty. The younger ones, when we catch them, are sent back.

"Training these cadets is an experience I'll never forget," Kerns reflects. "The biggest challenge is getting them to take initiative. They are afraid to make decisions. Everything in their society, until now, was either given to them or they were directed what to do. Traditionally, taking initiative could get them tortured or killed by their superiors. They are afraid to speak up, afraid to ask questions, and afraid to assume responsibility. They are accustomed to simply taking orders and never questioning or clarifying directives. In a sense, they are like slaves who have just been freed and their newfound independence is uncomfortable. In order for a policeman to be effective, he *must* be able to make fast decisions and react in a rapid manner. Even more important is that he be proactive in his police work. Always waiting for another officer to tell him what to do won't work.

"When problems develop in training they are afraid to report it to anyone. One of the recruits shot himself one day as he was holstering his 9mm Glock. There was still firing going on so the sound didn't set off any alarms with the instructors. The guy continued on the firing line for probably an hour until one of the instructors near him noticed a pool of blood forming in the sand around his foot. When the instructor asked him what happened, he just calmly said, 'Oh, I'm sorry, I accidentally shot myself when I was putting the gun in my holster.' Fortunately it was a flesh wound in the thigh. The kid didn't want to stop shooting or get reprimanded, so I guess he was going to just try and pretend for the next three weeks that nothing had happened.

"We try to inculcate in our students that torture is never an acceptable form of interrogation. When we ask them, 'When can you use torture?' We have conditioned them, or so we think, to respond in chorus with, 'Never.' Of course, we never seem to get everyone to say, 'Never.' Inevitably several students will always seriously respond that torture can be used when you haven't gotten the answers you want. Sometimes, as instructors, we have to just shrug and laugh to ourselves, 'Well, at least torture is now a last resort and not the first option.' I guess that's progress.

"On another day, when I was teaching a class on setting up police checkpoints, I asked the class how many in the room had been stopped at checkpoints, and a dozen or so hands went up. I called on one of the students to describe his experience. So the student says, 'My friend and I were running guns out of Syria. I saw the checkpoint coming up and I got away but my friend got caught.' I thought to myself, *Oh, this is just great, and I'm training you to be a policeman.* On yet another occasion, I had a student ask if he could call his mother. He explained that when he was in Iraq, his mother had sent him to buy a loaf of bread. He bumped into a police recruiter and next thing he knew he was here in Jordan. He was concerned that maybe his mother would be worried and he should probably call her. Trust me, every day here brings a new surprise.

"Our training time is precious. These students have a whole lot to learn in a very short period of time. Most of our cadets will only get to practice a house search or vehicle search one time. After that they will be in a war zone doing it for real. We are hampered by the fact that everything we say has to be translated into Arabic and that eats away at our available time. Our Kurdish students understand Arabic but most of them don't read or write it. When we first started the academy, all the books and tests were in Arabic, and the Kurds really didn't say much of anything until it came to test time and they couldn't take the final exams.

"We have students whose relatives have come through an earlier class. Our graduates are being killed every day. Sometimes it is a family member of a student sitting in front of us. We had a cadet in my class this week [who] has two brothers that had come through our training and both were killed in a bombing at the beginning of the week. The family requested that we don't tell their son. They plan on telling him when he gets back home. I look at the student every day and ask myself, *What kind of homecoming for him is this going to be?*

"One of our newly graduated classes got off the plane in Iraq, boarded a bus, and was slaughtered by insurgents while on their way home. It was very hard to take. Many of these young men are so proud of what they have become at our academy. They are anxious to go home and show off their new stature to their family and friends. Many of them have so much optimism for the future of their country. As instructors I think we really understand, maybe more so than our students, the perils they will face when they return home.

"In one class, I was helping another instructor conduct training on building searches. I role-played the part of a sleeping person. I was a 'bad guy' laying on the sofa when the students entered the room. As one of the students found me lying there in the dark, he was just standing there. So I rolled off the sofa and attempted to ram him with my head—how ladylike of me! Unfortunately, and very much to my surprise, he did exactly what we trained him to do, he simply stepped aside. By that time, my body weight and momentum couldn't be stopped. I rammed my head into a metal wall—denting the wall—and knocking myself silly. I heard what sounded like several bones cracking in my neck and it scared me as I fell backward onto the ground. I just knew that I had broken my neck. After a day of ice packs, it turned out that I was OK, but I am still working out the kinks.

"During Ramadan, Muslims are required to not eat or drink anything from sunup to sundown. We're in the desert here so you can imagine what 'no water' all day is like. They eat breakfast before sunrise, which is about 4:20 a.m., and then they have nothing until after sundown, when they are served *iftar*, a small snack of dates, water, juice, or soup before prayer. After the fasting period, everyone eats and drinks until they are about to blow up. They stay up late into the night, just partying in general. This lasts for four weeks and is tied to the phases of the moon. During the fast, they are also not allowed to have any physical contact with the opposite sex—no touching, no holding hands, and, of course, no kissing."

Kerns writes home about the impact of Ramadan at the police academy, "It has been six days since the beginning of Ramadan and already it is an eye-opener. People are mad at each other all the time. There are fights in the streets and arguments everywhere. At the camp the local staff is about 98 percent Muslim. Muslims who don't fast infuriate those who do. It is against the law in Amman for a Muslim to smoke in the street, or to eat in public before sundown. If they do eat or smoke they are expected to do it in private so as to not offend those who are observing the traditions of Ramadan.

"The Jordanian police officers who work at the camp see it as their personal mission to punish violators. They have threatened language assistants who have not been fasting. They intimidate them with ruses of how they will be reported as 'security risks' and not permitted to enter the camp or return to their jobs. The language assistants are not flaunting their eating or smoking and really try to be private about it, but the Jordanian police tenaciously go after them. . . . Supposedly, Jordan advocates freedom of religion, but the reality is that this freedom seems to be meant for Westerners [who] happen to work in Jordan. They want to make sure that no Muslim drifts too far away from Islam.

"All of this is really troubling because we are trying to instill religious freedom in Iraq. We are teaching our students to be tolerant of other religions, but right here at our camp, the cadets can see that it is not practiced. Even within the various sects of the Muslim religion, the sect that is in power enforces its beliefs and traditions on the rest of the population. So much of the violence and subjugation that we see in here is Muslim against Muslim." Kerns sums up her feelings: "I will not stand by and allow people in power, who are supposed to have the best interest of their citizens, victimize the powerless. As far as I am concerned, this is why I am here.

"The cadets were allowed to vote here at the camp and they were so proud of their right index fingers, which were all stained with red ink proving that they had voted. Every one of them that I saw had that mark of their future. One of my students told me that he would never wash his finger, because it meant he was a free man at last. Things like this are encouraging but they must be really strong and make it come together when they get home. I want so badly for the U.S. to be able to leave Iraq. I don't see it happening anytime soon, but at least there seems to be some progress. . . . I can see a difference in their attitudes and the way they have started to carry themselves. Maybe it's starting to sink in.

"When our students get on the job back in Iraq, many of them will have commanding officers who are from the 'old school' of the Iraqi police force. Effectively, they will be told to sit down and shut up. They will face insurgents and criminals every day. They will face an Iraqi military that opposes their authority. Our cadets will have to deal with cultural and religious beliefs that fly in the face of democratic processes.

"They will have to overcome the long-held belief that if they try too hard to stay alive or they mourn too much over someone's death, they are questioning the will of Allah. In fact, it is this reason that Muslim men often deter women from coming to the grave site of a deceased relative. They say that women are too emotional and it could appear that they are questioning the will of God. I hope we have taught them a sense of self-preservation. I hope that they will want to live and become the hunters and not the hunted. Once they leave our academy and return to Iraq, ironically, I guess all that I can say is enshalla."

III. Iraqi Boot Camp

MPRI is also engaged in training military units around the world. In Kuwait, MPRI operates and manages training bases in both Kuwait and Iraq. The Kuwait facility, Camp Yankee, is a predeployment training center for coalition forces. In Iraq, they operate Butler Range, about forty miles east of Baghdad. Butler is a former Iraqi republican guard base and MPRI's in-country centralized training facility for Iraqi and U.S. military units. Throughout Iraq, MPRI employs civilian military trainers that are co-located with Iraqi forces on Iraqi army bases.

There is no doubt that the MPRI trainers working with coalition forces have contributed immeasurably to the combat effectiveness of coalition units and have subsequently saved the lives of coalition soldiers. There is, however, far greater skepticism concerning the effectiveness and relative value of preparing Iraqi army units to assume responsibility for stabilization operations in their own country. Many critics fault the trainers. The problem is not the lack of contractor effectiveness in training Iraqi recruits, but the abundance of cultural, tribal, ethnic, political, and religious impediments to the effective application of that training. In short, the trainees remain unconvinced that the cause is worth shedding their blood.

To a lesser extent, we experienced this problem in Vietnam. In that war, rural people found it difficult to relate to the established government in Saigon. In fact, many South Vietnamese peasant farmers felt a much greater cultural relationship with the North Vietnamese leader, Ho Chi Minh, than they did with their ownpresident, Thieu. When left without U.S. counterparts, many local militia units weren't willing to fight and die for their government. Placing soldiers and/or contractor advisors with these units in Iraq might help temporarily, but it will not solve the problem. At this time, it's merely a Band-Aid on a hemorrhaging chest wound.

Iraq is far more fragmented than Vietnam was. The divisions among the Shiites, Sunnis, and Kurds are only the tip of the iceberg. Within these groups there are yet further divisions. Surrounding nations complicate matters by encouraging the chaos. Probably one of the few saving graces in this whole mess is that the insurgents haven't come up with an alternative proposal. At least Ho Chi Minh had a plan—the unification of the country. That was attractive to many Vietnamese. In Iraq, the insurgents seem to kill just to kill. They have no specific agenda to bring to the Iraqi people except defeating U.S. efforts at democratization, which doesn't do much good for the people of Iraq.

Only time will tell if Iraq can create a government that has the support of all of its people. Until then, how much support can we really expect from Iraqi soldiers? Are PMCs creating well-trained, unmotivated soldiers? Undoubtedly some are picking up the ball and running with it. But as to the bulk of the Iraqi military, how aggressive will they be in seeking out and exposing insurgents? They are, after all, a microcosm of the population.

Iraqi army basic training units are a mix of both Arabic and Kurdish recruits. Placing these historical enemies into the same geographical area, let alone the same work space and sleeping quarters, creates unique challenges. Just a few years ago, one could never have imagined men from these archrival cultures in the same space, especially with guns. Conversely, keeping them separated would indirectly support centuries-old racist attitudes and be counterproductive to the developing government in Iraq.

As the coalition forces are engaged in ferreting out insurgents and maintaining stability, the task of training and equipping the one-hundred-thousand-man Iraqi army has fallen largely on the shoulders of civilian contractors. At the same time, predeployment training for more than 115,000 coalition forces each year has also become a major responsibility of private military contractors. Perhaps if this war lasts long enough, the expedient solution of employing civilian contractors will no longer be necessary. Over time, the military might gradually assume most of those responsibilities. Let's hope these longer-term solutions are never required.

Meanwhile, the Department of Defense continues to use private contractors to conduct military training over active-duty instructors. It is not as much of a stretch as some might think. Private contractors in the role of trainers, a.k.a. observer-controllers (OCs), have as much, if not more, experience than many senior soldiers. MPRI's OCs are all former soldiers or marines, most with twenty or more years of military service. Nearly all have fought in the first, and some in the second, Gulf conflict. In many cases, their retirement was driven by the military's up-or-out policy. The military employment pyramid gets very narrow at the top of the senior enlisted and officer ranks. Droves of otherwise highly qualified soldiers are forced into retirement every year. Civilian contracting opportunities aren't the reason most of MPRI's trainers left the service. Rather, most find that being a civilian contract trainer is as close as they can get to doing what they do best.

MPRI is able to amass highly skilled men and women for nearly any worldwide training mission on a moment's notice. The company maintains a huge database of available personnel. They can quickly acquire contract employees with rare skill sets that the military doesn't have or can't cut loose from other critical missions. It is not politically or economically feasible for the army to be recalling soldiers to active duty to meet these significant, but temporary, training requirements. Department of Defense outsourcing to civilian contractors is an efficient short-term solution. Finally, contractors have more time in country than most of the soldiers they train. This provides continuity, an invaluable commodity considering the frequent rotation and deployment of often inexperienced troops to the war zone.

* * *

John Karuza's son reported the news with some excitement in his voice: "Dad, my unit's deploying to Iraq."

Karuza paused for a moment to digest what his son had just said, then responded, "I'll see you there."

His son had recently completed basic and advanced individual training, and graduated from parachute training (Airborne School) at Fort Benning, Georgia. His new assignment was with the army's elite 82nd Airborne Division.

It satisfied his parental protector instinct to know that at least they would both be in the same hemisphere. A month or so earlier, a contracting firm recruiter from Group IV had called Karuza from Ireland and offered him a security contractor position in Kosovo. It was crazy to think that they would ever cross paths in Iraq.

But having retired from twenty years of infantry duty with the army, Karuza's skills were in high demand. While in Kosovo, he got a call from Bob Meley, an MPRI recruiter, offering him a position as a military trainer in Iraq. Group IV was empathetic and agreed to let him out of his Kosovo contract. The way everything came together could hardly be believed, like a Hollywood script or something from the pages of *The Celestine Prophecy*. But it was happening—both dad and son were going to Iraq, one as a civilian, the other as a soldier.

John jumped the next flight to the States and reported to MPRI. As the 82nd Airborne prepared for deployment to war, Karuza began his predeployment orientation with MPRI. He arrived with a dozen other contractor applicants at the company's Virginia headquarters for two weeks of orientation. They put him up in a first-class hotel and gave him ample time to get his personal affairs in order. Karuza relates: "They were very professional and strongly encouraged us to have family members visit during our weekends and time off. They did not glamorize the job we were about to do. The MPRI staff went to great lengths to provide a shameless exit for anyone not comfortable with the job. The days were filled with videos and briefings on the environment in Iraq, the enemy tactics, and the Iraqi culture, and completing administrative paperwork.

Next, the entire group of contractors flew to Fort Benning, Georgia. This army post was, coincidentally, the same location, at the same time, that his son was attending Airborne school. Now, in twist of fate, John Karuza would be able to attend his son's graduation.

The MPRI contractors remained at Fort Benning for three days of orientation, vaccinations, and equipment issue. "It was like being back in the army [all over again]," said Karuza. "We moved through the line at the supply depot and one by one the pieces of equipment were handed out: flak vests, helmets, pistol belts, sleeping bags, boots, and canteens. More than ever before, the reality of what we were doing was sinking in. This was for real. We were going to Iraq."

By now, the personal bonding of Karuza's contractor group was starting to take hold. Nights were a mix of reflection, introspection, apprehension, and a thinly veiled pretense to be casual about things—to think that they had undertaken such an audacious and terrifying adventure by choice.

The collection of civilian contractors boarded a plane back to Virginia. MPRI provided two last opportunities to their new employees: the first was to give them another chance to back out, and the second was to provide a few more days to see their loved ones one last time. As the moment of departure approached, some men had a change of heart. As Karuza puts it: "From afar, these jobs seem like a great adventure, but as you get closer and closer to going, the adventure can begin to look pretty unattractive. We boarded a commercial flight to Kuwait with an intermediate stopover in Amsterdam. I've heard stories that some contractors have been known to turn around in Amsterdam and head back to the States."

After a couple of days in Kuwait adjusting to the hot, arid climate, Karuza and his fellow contractors were on a C-130 cargo plane headed for Baghdad. From the airport they traveled through the city streets to one of Saddam Hussein's grand palaces where they bunked out in ornate splendor. To Karuza, the mix of people, clubs, bars, blown-out buildings, palaces, tanks, armored personnel carriers, traffic jams, strange-looking characters with weapons, and soldiers doing PT on city streets seemed surreal to him, like being dropped into a scene from *Apocalypse Now*.

Three days later, his team of contractors and their convoy escorts had finalized preparations to make the journey about sixty miles northeast to the town of Kirkush, near the Iranian border. There, at an Iraqi army base, Karuza would settle into his new home for the next year.

"We packed onto something like a Greyhound bus. We were wearing our flak vests, load-bearing equipment, canteens—the whole nine yards. We had everything except a gun. A 'cherry' [inexperienced] army lieutenant was in charge of the movement. Most of us were experienced soldiers or marines having served many years in the service. Many of us onboard had seen extensive combat action. Having no control or influence over the lieutenant and his security detail was unnerving. The lieutenant put a gun truck in front of the bus and one behind it. As we plowed through bad neighborhoods and got stuck in traffic jams we found ourselves developing a plan in case the shit hit the fan. We even planned on what we would do if the bus driver cut and run during an attack. This was a tense drive through Baghdad. I doubt that there was a single contractor on board that bus [who] wasn't asking himself, 'What did I get into?'

"Eventually we left the urban sprawl behind us and traveled for hours across the barren desert landscape. From time to time we approached some isolated town. You could see it ahead from miles away. The towns were surprisingly green with vegetation sprung from a network of irrigation canals. People watched us with curiosity and sometimes warm smiles and greetings."

But the sight of waving children, curious men, and women in their burkas was hardly a reason to relax. "We were wary of everyone and everything. Finally we closed in on our Iraqi army training camp in Kirkush.

"It was a desolate place, construction by the Yugoslavians having been halted when it was only half complete. We passed by the makeshift dilapidated buildings housing U.S. military personnel. Soldiers had placed blankets in the windows to block out the searing sun. The convoy came to stop at our quarters. Our buildings were prefab structures called PODs and were laid out in circular formations of five to a group. We referred to them as donuts. All in all, they were in a lot better shape than those we saw the army living in. Everything's relative, so we really had no complaints.

"We got two hot meals a day, one in the morning and then [another] in the evening. Our noon meal was always meals ready to eat (MREs), sometimes referred to as rat feces. For the most part, the soldiers ate MREs three times a day. That's a pretty rough diet. I felt bad for them, but I also remembered operations during my time in the army when I was in the same boat. Evidently, contract trainers, at least in regard to food, were a higher priority than the soldiers: a phenomenon that may have [stuck] in the craw of some. But, they had guns and we didn't. We felt pretty naked without a weapon. If I'd had a choice between a rifle or a hot meal, over there, I'd take the rifle. I don't think that the soldiers would have traded places with us.

"We began training the Iraqi recruits following a basic program of instruction torn from the pages of the U.S. Army's basic combat training program. Our instructor group was mostly American but we had a mix of cadre from other countries like Australia and Great Britain. We were known as the coalition military training team. The Aussies insisted on formation drills and marching in a manner reflective of their British heritage. They contended that since Iraqi history was heavily influenced by the Brits, they were on solid ground with their program. So they won that argument, but we insisted that all cadence calling and running songs would be from the U.S. military. You gotta know when to hold 'em and know when to fold 'em. I'll never forget hearing Iraqi soldiers with their Arabic accents trying to sing, 'C-130 rolling down the strip, Airborne daddy gonna take a little trip.'

"Our camp was covered in gravel. It is kind of like volcanic ash. Everywhere you walk you can hear the sound of gravel crushing beneath your feet. At night, you can hear a person walking across that gravel a hundred yards away. Sometimes, I would lay awake listening to the crushing sound of someone walking outside my hooch. I would test myself to figure out which way they were walking. I will always think of Iraq whenever I hear that sound. It's just one of those things that sticks with you.

"Everything in Iraq is called 'Haji' this or 'Haji' that. I never figured out exactly what that word means. I guess we just used the term to describe any collection of people or stuff that we didn't know what else to call it. Hell, we even called insurgents Hajis. Anyway, the Haji shop inside the camp sold Iraqi junk food and trinkets. The shops just outside the gate sold *everything*: prayer beads, prayer rugs, alcohol, food, guns, watches, jewelry, motorcycles, and even women. Some of our contractors bought Russian motorcycles from them. Of course, they were no substitute for a good Harley but you gotta have some fun. You can buy *anything* at a Haji shop. All you gotta do is ask for it.

"The Iraqi recruits bonded with us, and we with them. We trained hard and played hard. They love to dance and invite you to join at every chance. The dancing turns competitive and by dawn you can barely walk. They are good at it, really good. At night everyone would watch Arabic television. This was a problem in that we were also training Kurdish soldiers from northern Iraq and the Kurds resented that all the TV programming promoted Arab adventures. In a compromise to solve the problem, the Kurds procured some VHS tapes featuring Kurdish themes and actors. TV night alternated between Kurdish and Arabic movies.

"One night the movie was about a Kurdish battle that portrayed the Kurds as defeating incompetent, bungling Iraqi soldiers. You can imagine how that went over! The Iraqi soldiers went ballistic. Verbal expletives were flying through the air. Our MPRI guys had to jump into the middle of this to keep the two sides from slicing each other's throats. I remember saying over and over again, 'Hey calm down, it's just a movie. It's only a movie!' After that night, we never left the Kurds and Iraqis in the movie room alone. Every night, among us contractors, we would say, 'OK, who's got movie duty tonight?'

"Close to graduation from our training program, the Iraqi soldiers received information that they would be deployed to the Iranian border. This went over like a lead balloon. They had joined the military to protect their hometowns, to ferret out the insurgents, to keep their communities and families safe. Now, not only were they not going to be doing what it is they had joined the army to do, but they also discovered that their pay was far less than the compensation of Iraqi police and National Guard.

"That evening after the training day had come to an end, we returned to our quarters and were startled by the loud din of chanting soldiers. We stepped out of our buildings and saw over six hundred armed Iraqi soldiers shouting angry slogans about Americans. The mob was moving toward us. As the group approached our building, several of the demonstrators peeled off to talk with us and our Iraqi translators. Evidently they were not coming to confront us. They made clear that their 'teachers' were not the object of their anger. The unruly mob made a sharp left turn and headed toward the coalition headquarters that housed the American soldiers.

"Our camp had about a hundred unarmed civilian contract instructors and around ninety U.S. Army military police. The base had over one thousand three hundred Iraqi army recruits. The odds were definitely not in our favor. The U.S. soldiers scrambled to get their weapons. This had all the earmarks of a showdown at the O.K. Corral. It was small comfort that the mob wasn't specifically after us. All of us contractors knew that if the Iraqis began attacking Americans, we couldn't be casual observers. Quietly, among ourselves, we began sorting out how we would respond if this protest turned violent. Like it or not, this was our problem too.

"The mob circled around the Coalition Force headquarters building. A U.S. Army major stepped out of the building and met the protesters. Shouts, chants, and Arabic slurs continued for quite some time. Some chants were in English, 'Bad Bush, bad Americans, bad pay.' We watched as the major over and over again tried to quell the crowd. Several times they moved closer toward him. They were shaking rifles and clenched fists in the air. It sure looked like it was going to go ugly. I thought for certain the major was a dead man. He deserved a medal for his composure through it all. After several tense hours, the hostility level was diffused. The major made some promises and convinced everyone to go to bed. I suspect, afterward, that he went back into his building, had a shot of Jack Daniel's from some secret stash, and collapsed.

"More than ever, that night, I realized that we had a very special relationship with our students. They revered us as teachers and friends. We were invested in each other. We woke up every day with these Iraqi recruits. We ate with them, trained with them, ran with them, sang with them, and even danced with them. We had crossed some barrier that had stood between our cultures for centuries. Although the angry Iraqis had differentiated us from the U.S. soldiers, bridges are crossed one at a time.

I think, just the fact that the bridges can be crossed at all gives me some hope. Our behavior had changed their attitude. I was proud of that. I felt I had made a difference in the world."

IV. Team Viper

In the middle of the desert, an hour-and-a-half drive from the nearest highway, and just a few miles south of the Kuwait-Iraq border, is Camp Yankee. Surrounded by barbed wire, guard towers, and a classic zigzag entry checkpoint known as "dragon's teeth," this isolated facility could easily be mistaken for an army base. But it isn't. Camp Yankee is operated by civilian training contractors from MPRI. They are known as Team Viper. Skeet Charlton turns to Paul Collins and asks, "You got the coffee?" Paul holds up a thermos. Charlton glances at Collins. "We've got less than an hour to clear the camels out," he says. "We go live at five. Let's hit it." It's four in the morning. The sun hasn't yet broken over the surface of the desert floor. For the last hour, the two men have been loading their humvee with water, radios, MREs, ammunition, smoke grenades, and artillery simulators. Now dressed in their desert cammies and full battle rattle, they climb into their vehicle and make a final radio check with Curtis Acton back in the ops shack. A retired master sergeant and old army cavalry soldier, Acton is the MPRI operations center manager. He makes some quip over the radio like, "Oh, good morning sleeping beauties, I thought I wouldn't hear from you guys until noon!"

Paul and Skeet smirk at one another. Paul chides back, "Hey, Curtis did you sleep with your radio again last night? Your wife's going to be jealous!" The humvee begins to roll toward the gate. Tariq, the Pakistani guard, steps out of the guard shack and raises

153

the gate. As always, he smiles from ear to ear and renders a salute. Watching Tariq, one can quickly conclude that he likes Americans and he does his job well. His family is back home in the eastern Pakistani town of Punjab. From his meager paycheck, he covers some minimal living expenses, and pays the Kuwaiti royal family $5,000 a year for the right to work in Kuwait. After doling out that cash, he has just a couple of hundred dollars a year left over to send home. He works long hours in sweltering heat, in the middle of nowhere. For Tariq, this is still better than any job opportunity he could find in Pakistan.

A Wisconsin Army National Guard heavy equipment transport unit is en route to the ranges northwest of Camp Yankee. This unit has already been in Iraq several months, and now their commander has requested some refresher training from MPRI. Skeet Charlton is MPRI's chief of convoy training operations. Today, Skeet, Paul, and several other contractors will be conducting live-fire convoy training. Their contract requires them to further prepare coalition force units for their deployment into Iraq. They have trained U.S. Army soldiers, marines, Navy Seals, Australians, Japanese, Koreans, British, and police contractors. In fact, nearly all army units stop here for a week or so of training before crossing the Berm. The area around Camp Yankee is surrounded with dirt roads and ranges designed to simulate the Iraqi war zone. Most of the training on the ranges and road networks will be live fire. In the wee hours of the morning, Viper OCs scour the area looking for stray camels or sheep that might have wandered into the area overnight. They talk with the Bedouins, living in tents scattered miles apart in the desert. The Bedouins are usually Egyptians tending to the camel herds of wealthy Kuwaitis. The Viper OCs have made friends with them and sometimes bring them a snack or soda and spend a few minutes. This is a valuable friendship. The Bedouins are very observant and frequently inform the Viper team about strange sightings of men or vehicles in this desolate area along the Iraqi border.

Living conditions for Team Viper are harsh. They have one hot meal in the evening, otherwise it's cold cereal and fruit for breakfast, and MREs or whatever they can scrounge together for lunch. The thermometer outside their operations building seems stuck at 120 degrees Fahrenheit. That is as high as it can register. The actual temperatures at Camp Yankee have been known to exceed 140 degrees on occasion. The OCs start their day well before dawn and are often at the ranges late into the night. Their quarters have improved recently from tents to small prefab buildings. Between the rows of buildings are concrete and sandbag-covered bunkers. Although they are in Kuwait, being this close to the Iraqi border is still a dangerous area. There have been several instances of insurgent attacks against Kuwaiti police checkpoints in the area.

Many military units deploying into Iraq perform combat-related duties that were not originally part of their unit's primary mission. The conflict in Iraq doesn't require large field artillery units or chemical decontamination units. It does require lots of convoy escorts, military checkpoints, and soldiers to conduct house-to-house searches. Every unit has to understand the basics of urban combat. There are no "relatively safe" areas. Everyone is at high risk of being caught up in street fighting. There are not enough of the appropriate types of military units to accomplish these missions. Thousands of soldiers, airmen, and marines require refresher training.

The training is realistic and incorporates the most current lessons from combat actions in Iraq. MPRI instructors on Team Viper are good at what they do. Skeet Charlton, Bill Bratten, Paul Collins, Curtis Acton, Dave Judah, Jack Strickland, Larry Word, Ron Jones, Toby Tobias, and a half dozen other full-timers at Camp Yankee may be graying at the temples, but woe to the person who would underestimate the skills they bring to the table. They are all retired soldiers and marines who are totally committed to providing outstanding military training for the units deploying into Iraq. The team's convoy trainers are tank and Bradley crewmen and have a career's worth of experience with battlefield maneuver, crew-served machine guns, and tactical communications. The checkpoint trainers are infantry and cavalry NCOs who have extensive experience with road-blocks and screening operations. MPRI's urban-combat trainers are all former Rangers or special forces NCOs. On top of these skills and added to this "learning environment" is the "location." Somehow, the whole idea of being in the desert along the Kuwait-Iraq border, knowing you'll be in Iraq in a day or so, has a way of getting your attention.

Team Viper is led by Larry Word, a sixty-seven-year-old retired army colonel, whose physical condition would be wishful thinking for many a thirty-year-old man. Technically, Larry is the program manager. He also acts as base commander and director of training. Aside from a few wrinkles and gray hairs, he and his staff are fit and trim and could easily be mistaken for active-duty military personnel as they wear standard military-issue desert-camouflage uniforms (DCU), and all their gear is standard army equipment. They drive military humvees equipped with military radios and military weapons systems. Only the letters *M-P-R-I* spelled out in black-and-gold tape above their shirt pockets give away their status as civilian contractors.

Nearly every aspect of Larry Word's military career and subsequent civilian positions prepared him for this job. During his nearly thirty years in the army, he commanded the army's Joint Readiness Training Center at Fort Polk, Louisiana, and was a senior observer controller at the army's National Training Center at Fort Irwin, California. After retirement, he worked as a military trainer for several defense contractors and was the senior trainer in Bosnia at the Federation Army Combat Training Center. It is not a stretch to say that few men or women walking the face of the earth could match Word's background for leading the type of mission that Team Viper performs.

Larry is a no-nonsense professional—not one to openly discuss his accomplishments nor one to accept any special privileges of position. Although not a big man, he still manages to cut an imposing figure. His short, closely cropped (high and tight) haircut, square-jawed, tanned, weather-beaten face, and military bearing give the appearance of a rock-hard soldier. Through heat, cold, sandstorms, and rain, in the middle of the day, or at two o'clock in the morning, he is personally involved in every aspect of training. Each morning at about 4 a.m., Larry goes for a three-mile run in the middle of the desert. His team of a dozen permanent contractors and fifty to seventy temporary contractors holds him in the highest regard. He is somewhat of a legend among them. Quietly, among themselves, the team likes to joke that someday they will find a mummified Larry sitting in his humvee, peering through his binoculars in one hand, a radio mike in the other. They plan on burying him undisturbed in his humvee, although he'll likely outlive them all.

The sun is beginning to rise. Skeet and Paul have cleared the area of stray animals and Bedouins. The operations center thermometer has already passed 100 degrees Fahrenheit. In the distance, a huge cloud of sand is being churned up as the line of twenty or so eighty-six 1,000-pound heavy equipment transports (HETs) from the Wisconsin National Guard cut a swath across the desert. As the convoy draws near, several humvee gun trucks can be seen interspersed like baby calves among a herd of elephants. The convoy comes to a halt and young soldiers, most in their teens, climb down from the gargantuan up-armored trucks. HETs are designed to haul tanks and aircraft engines. The sight of a five-foot-tall blonde female soldier jumping off the running board with an M16 rifle in hand is incongruous to your senses.

The soldiers gather around in a semicircle. Ronald Jones, another MPRI OC, is teaching a class on convoy ambush reaction. All the soldiers are listening intensely. Remembering that these soldiers have already experienced attacks in Iraq, the casual observer might have expected cynicism from the soldiers such as "What can these old guys possibly teach us?" There is not a hint of that attitude. To the contrary, they seem to really appreciate the opportunity to refine their skills in a less-threatening environment. They ask good questions. They relate stories from recent experiences. The OCs pick their brains about each event. They solicit input and consider every piece of new information. There are no wrong answers. There are no perfect solutions. The OCs take the attitude: "If it works, do it!"

Ron briefs the soldiers: "The first couple of runs we'll make this morning will be dry fire. You will have to respond to enemy fire, treat and evacuate casualties, call for and coordinate aerial medical evacuations, and recover downed vehicles under fire. When we have perfected the application of those tactics, techniques, and procedures, we'll go hot [use live fire]." He continues: "You'll be exposed to simulated IEDs and different levels of simulated enemy fire that closely resemble the most current information from Iraq. Some of these attack methods you may have already experienced, many, you may not have seen yet. Keep your eyes open." The OCs review safety procedures and direct the soldiers to load up.

The convoy begins lumbering along a sandy road. They drive through an artificial city, pass under overpasses, buildings, and berms, and cross over bridges. Suddenly, a vehicle on a rail system comes charging toward the convoy on a 90-degree angle. The gun trucks fire warning shots followed by direct engagement. The convoy picks up speed. The trucks are smothered in a cloud of sand. Then, several silhouettes pop up from behind a berm. Through the dust cloud, flashes and sounds of gunfire emanate from the berm. The OCs signal that a vehicle has been hit and has casualties. The designated truck manages to drive past the kill zone and comes to a halt. Several gun trucks and one of the HETs begin a hasty recovery of the wounded and the downed vehicle.

Both men inside the truck are casualties. The cab of an HET is way too high in the air to simply pull the wounded men out. Another HET pulls up alongside the downed vehicle. A stretcher team stations itself between and below the two trucks. Soldiers then straddle the narrow space between the two trucks and begin removing and lowering the casualties to the stretcher team. The trucks have formed a box and the casualties are placed on the ground in the center of the box. Medics immediately begin diagnosing and treating the wounded. The convoy commander calls for a medical evacuation helicopter. The gun trucks traverse the area to secure a hasty helipad. Another team sets out marker panels for the helicopter.

The soldier on the ground radios the evacuation helicopter. "I've thrown smoke," he says. "Identify—over."

"Roger," the pilot responds. "I see purple smoke—over."

"That's affirmative."

This method of requiring the helicopter crew to identify the color of the smoke helps prevent deceptions by the enemy. The enemy wouldn't know what color smoke grenade to throw. If the chopper pilot had said that he sees some other color, the deception would be exposed. After the correct identification is rendered, the chopper pilot can be reasonably certain that he is coming into the right location.

The soldiers take up positions surrounding the landing zone. Time is critical and each soldier must perform instinctively. It's like watching a professional football team pull off a complex play; only this play has life-and-death consequences. As the chopper approaches, dust billows up everywhere. A soldier uses arm and hand signals to guide the chopper into the hasty helipad. A litter team dashes across the open space with the wounded. As the chopper touches down, there is a quick exchange of medical information between the onboard medics and the transportation unit personnel. This is another dangerous moment for everyone. The helicopter on the ground is a huge and prized enemy target. This transfer of the casualties must be accomplished quickly and flawlessly. This phase of the training exercise wraps up and the Viper OCs have a lot of observations. The soldiers are listening intently. They want to learn. They want to survive. They want to come home someday in one piece. In this environment, there is no one taking training casually.

Paul Collins points out that the wounded soldiers were evacuated with their body armor, rifles, and ammo magazines. "Why would you do this?" he asks. "What do you suppose these casualties are going to do with their rifles and body armor. You are still in the fight. You may need an extra rifle, ammunition, or body armor. The casualties have no need for this equipment anymore. You have to take it. The hospital doesn't want it and the wounded don't need it."

During battle, equipment changes hands between soldiers on an as-needed basis. This is hardly second nature. In fact, soldiers in training are punished for losing any part of their gear and may have to pay to replace it. It is a lesson so deeply ingrained, paratroopers conducting combat jumps have been known to risk their lives to roll up and store their parachutes for later use, despite a hail of bullets all around them.

Skeet gets on the radio to Viper Operations Center. "Range status red," he says. "We're going hot."

Curtis Acton, back at the operations center, has finally gone to catch a few hours of sleep, and Bill Bratten, another MPRI contractor and former marine, has taken over the watch at the operations center. Bill checks his logs of other units scheduled to come into the area. "Roger copy," he responds. "Range status red. You have until 1100 hours before we have an Aussie unit coming onto the range. Make certain that all safety measures are in place. Call back in when weapons status is green. The convoy will be driving many miles of open desert engaging targets with live ammunition." Several humvees from the Viper team are sent out to designated intersections several miles away where they will block all traffic attempting to enter the training area.

The Wisconsin guardsmen lock and load. Every M16, squad automatic rifle, and .50-caliber machine gun is loaded with live rounds. The convoy rolls again. Fifteen minutes into the trip, metallic silhouettes of insurgents attack from multiple directions, simulated IEDs blow off on guardrails, and vehicles on rail systems charge into the convoy. Explosions are detonating on both the right and left of the convoy. Bullets fly in every direction; chaos and the "fog of war" are introduced into the scenario. Vehicles are separated, communications are disrupted, and simulated casualties mount. Skills are tested to the maximum degree.

The event is eventually stopped. Everyone dismounts and gathers around in a semicircle. An OC picks up a stick and draws figures in the sand, then places rocks representing the location of every vehicle in an after-action review (AAR). The soldiers relate who was where and what they were thinking as events unfolded. The group discussion lasts nearly an hour, with analysis, analysis, and more analysis. Everyone with an opinion is heard, with no criticism. Every unique perspective is valid and offers something to the discussion. Nothing is left out, as one person's observation during this exercise could mean the difference between life and death in the days and weeks ahead. In fact, tomorrow these young soldiers will be in combat, and Viper's primary objective is to get them back alive.

Paul and Skeet head out to link up with the Australian unit that has just arrived. "Unlike most military operations," Paul explains, "every soldier in a convoy becomes an independent decision maker. The individual soldier driving a truck may be the only person who spots an insurgent, a VBIED, or an explosive device hidden on the road. He has only seconds to make a decision. There is no time for consulting with his commander. The wrong decision could cost him his life or the life of an innocent person . . . or the lives of the soldiers in his unit." Paradoxically, many of the soldiers encountering frequent enemy contact are service and support troops that had, once upon a time, assumed they wouldn't be on the front lines. Paul continues, "Never before in the history of combat, have so many soldiers shouldered alone, so many life-and-death decisions, so frequently. It's asking a lot of a nineteen year old."

Checkpoints (CP) and entry checkpoints (ECP) have been constructed, and soldiers learn the right and wrong way to manage the complications of establishing and maintaining them. Kuwaiti civilians: men, women, and children participate in the training by being role players attempting to pass through these checkpoints. The role players are also trained on how to replicate events that will confront the soldiers in Iraq. Soldiers are challenged with myriad scenarios that they must successfully work through. Aviation units are afforded mock cities and targets where they must learn control and accuracy over their application of firepower. Following an incident in Iraq, where an Italian journalist was shot and her bodyguard killed, Camp Yankee was flooded with military units requiring updated and improved training on how to establish and run a checkpoint. There's no doubt that some of this training is part of the unit's predeployment activities back in the States, but the changing information from the war zone filters into this base daily. Unlike the weeks or months it may take to cause a change in training curricula back at home, new information on insurgent tactics is updated and incorporated every day into the training at Camp Yankee.

Very few army support units have opportunities to develop their close-quarters combat skills. MPRI plays a major role in helping these types of soldiers perfect their skills in house-to-house fighting. House-to-house fighting is very complex. Soldiers must protect themselves and avoid shooting their comrades under very stressful conditions. The paradox of protecting innocent civilians while engaging insurgents with lethal force is a major training challenge. As the size and scope of urban-clearing operations expand through an insurgent-infested neighborhood, the possibilities for mistakes, fratricide, and the death of innocent civilians exponentially increase from block to block.

Camp Yankee's urban ranges replicate close-quarters combat (CQC), house-to-house fighting. These ranges, also known as military operations in urban terrain (MOUT) sites, are full-scale mock towns that accommodate live-fire training for teams, platoons, and company-sized units. Viper's close-quarters combat (CQC) and close-quarters marksmanship (CQM) training begins with "glasshouse drills." Initially, all training is dry fire until the tactics and procedures are fully understood. In the glass house, soldiers practice entering a sandbag replication of a building in four-man stacks and are exposed to corner-fed and center-fed rooms. They study fire control, points of domination, and the path of travel. The training focuses on footwork and movement within a room.

Next they will enter a corral, an enclosure with four-foot-high walls with catwalks, upon which Viper OCs can move around and observe each soldier's movements and techniques. A corral has the additional challenge of introducing hallways. Training progresses to squad-sized "shoot houses" where they rehearse dry firing (meaning without live rounds or projectiles) in both day and night scenarios. Shoot houses have all the components of an actual building except that there are no ceilings. The rooms contain silhouettes of both enemy and noncombatants. Some of the rooms have furniture.

Live-fire training is the final phase. The walls of the rooms in each building are three-feet thick and filled with sand. Bullets will not pass through these walls. However, in an actual house entry, soldiers must be aware that bullets will frequently penetrate a wall, and their movement must take this into account. Shooting inside a twelve-foot-by-twelve-foot room is a unique experience, especially in darkness. The noise level, the brilliant muzzle flashes, the sound of bullets flying around a room, and the difficulty communicating above the din, is a new experience for them. Despite all the safety precautions, CQC is dangerous training, but absolutely necessary to get the soldiers used to a type of combat they will experience in Iraq.

Larry Word recalls a visit to Camp Yankee by an active-duty general in the First Cavalry Division. "The general was back in Kuwait observing a National Guard brigade training up to join the division," he says. "He told me to not change a thing about our urban operations instruction. He said that his soldiers, who all trained with us, dominated the enemy in room clearing. In six months of house-to-house fighting to include the tombs of Najaf (where they expected heavy casualties), the division did not incur a single soldier killed in action."

Paul Collins relates another self-congratulatory moment for the Viper OCs: "An army convoy in Iraq was ambushed. A female buck sergeant, Lee Ann Hester, and several other soldiers were caught in the kill zone of an insurgent ambush. She maneuvered her humvee onto the flanks of the attackers and began delivering withering machine-gun fire. She and her crew then dismounted, closed off the enemy escape route, and began attacking the enemy with hand grenades and grenade launchers. As the battle continued, she picked up her rifle and personally killed several enemy soldiers. Many of the insurgents were carrying handcuffs. They had intended to destroy the convoy and take U.S. prisoners.

"When the battle ended, Sergeant Hester and her small team of fellow soldiers had killed twenty-seven insurgents, wounded six, and captured one. Sergeant Hester became the first woman since World War II to be awarded the Silver Star. When asked about her heroism, she commented: 'Your training kicks in, your soldier kicks in. It's your life or theirs . . . you've got a job to do protecting yourself and your fellow comrades.' "

Team Viper had conducted convoy ambush reaction training for Sergeant Hester and her unit just a few months earlier. Her unit's reaction to the attack was a page out of Viper's training manual. The report of her actions in combat had the OCs grinning ear to ear with pride.

Their job satisfaction is best summed up by Viper Team Operations Chief Curtis Acton: "Every day we know that someone, some American soldier in Iraq, has lived through an enemy engagement because of what we do here."

Chapter 7

Security Contractors

I. An Overview

During an attack on a headquarters in Najaf, Iraq, eight Blackwater security contractors found themselves facing hundreds of Iraqi militia fighters. While urgently calling for U.S. military reinforcements, in the middle of the firefight, Blackwater's own helicopters brought in ammunition and supplies to the besieged contractors. They also coordinated an aerial medical evacuation of a wounded marine. At the same time, near the city of Kut, UN forces assigned to protect coalition administrators abandoned them, leaving their fate to the enemy. While the UN forces continued their retreat, a group of security contractors fought for three days in a heroic attempt to save the administrators.

Hart Security, a British firm, was on contract to protect a local construction project. A UN military unit was responsible for securing the area. The UN unit abandoned them, and the contractors found themselves alone and in an intense firefight with the enemy. Under intense enemy fire, they were eventually evacuated and forced to leave one of their own dead behind. It's no small wonder that security contractors are demanding more and more sophisticated weapons and greater flexibility in their response.

Civilian security personnel are not contracted to attack people while in Iraq. They are not directed to conduct operations against insurgent forces. Contrary to the movie stereotypes, they are not hired to conduct covert assassinations. They are contracted by private companies and coalition governments to provide security for people, vehicles, buildings, construction sites, energy facilities, and water-treatment plants. Enemy tactics targeting these people and the facilities they guard have created circumstances beyond the contractors' control.

The complexity of this new kind of war has rendered international law obsolete in many ways. Attempts to enforce definitions of combatants and noncombatants are muddled. Private military contractors are caught in the catch-22 situation of trying to conform to laws and regulations regarding civilian conduct in a war zone and dealing with the realities of the jobs they are asked to perform. In at least one instance where the military disarmed four private contractors, a few hours later the contractors were captured by insurgents, tortured, and killed. On whose hands is their blood?

In broad terms, there are two types of security contractors operating in Iraq: those contracted by the U.S. State Department, and those providing security for dozens of other coalition operations. Some contracting firms, like Blackwater, execute both types of contracts with different teams. The composition, personnel, equipment, and operating policies for State Department contracts are very specific and highly regulated. Ostensibly, all firms are under the control of the Coalition Provisional Authority—in other words, the U.S. military. State Department contracts are awarded to U.S. firms and require that all personnel be U.S. citizens. The teams are equipped with U.S. weapons, protective gear, and vehicles.

In contrast, contracts to private security companies by independent businesses or contracts awarded by government agencies other than the State Department such as the Army Corps of Engineers contract with Erinys Security and allow for any composition of personnel from most any country. It's not uncommon to see teams from companies like Erinys, Custer Battle, DynCorp, and Triple Canopy comprised of personnel from the United States, Australia, South Africa, and Britain. Additionally, due to the complications of bringing weapons into Iraq, these firms often resort to acquiring their weaponry on the thriving arms black market inside Iraq.

There is much controversy over how security contractors should dress, appear, and conduct themselves in a war zone. One covert technique, widely used by armed contractors in the days immediately following the initial occupation, includes driving standard Iraqi vehicles, such as Mazdas or Toyotas. They immerse themselves in the local population, hiring local civilians to work with them and develop contacts and friendships in the area. To fit in with the locals, they drive with their windows up and air conditioning on, hair unkempt, mustaches and beards grown out. Women contractors wear head scarves, while men wear loose-fitting shirts and sandals.

Low-profile techniques afford access to greater intelligence on enemy activity. The indigenous workers will frequently tip off contractors to impeding enemy activity, either by their sudden absence from work or by directly furnishing information. Blending into the community reduces their visibility as foreigners as well as the number of attacks against them. These techniques have the added benefit of much greater acceptance in the local, national, and international community.

The downside to the low-profile concept is that military and police personnel may be wary of these disguised contractors and in the heat of the moment become highly suspicious. If they are spotted with hidden weapons, they can be mistaken for insurgents and subsequently fired upon by coalition forces. Hiring local Iraqis has major benefits, but one never knows when an Iraqi employee has sold out to the enemy. If just one of their indigenous employees begins leaking information on planned operations to the enemy, or worse, becomes a suicide bomber, the contractors are as good as dead. Last but not least, concealing weapons and driving with windows up, if identified, make the occupants easy nonthreatening targets.

Contrast this with contractors who have adopted a high-profile approach. These contractors drive around in black Suburbans, Yukons, and Avalanches; windows are down and guns are pointed out in every direction. In the open back of the Chevy Avalanches are mounted machine guns with a gunner on the ready. They wear black body armor and have a pistol strapped to their thigh. They carry an assortment of rifles, machine pistols, and submachine guns. Most have high and tight military-style haircuts. They carry enough ammunition to wage a five-hour battle. To a man, they look like they would shoot to kill in the blink of an eye.

While parts of the world consider this look to be that of the quintessential "arrogant American," security contractors consider it part of *security through intimidation* and an important aspect of their safety. An imposing and confident appearance is more likely to give insurgents pause. They are, after all, human, and want to live—at least for a few more days. It might be politically incorrect, and it doesn't win many friends in international circles, but contractors swear by it. In their view, it gets the job done.

In practice, many U.S. security contractors have tried to reduce the problems associated with both extremes. More and more, security contractors consciously go out of their way to avoid pointing weapons at civilians. While most security contractors maintain the basic concepts of aggressive posturing, many have hired teams of armed Iraqis who work with and dress identical to their U.S. counterparts. These are called hybrid teams and have proven to be a very effective deterrent to enemy attacks.

Construction of buildings, pipelines, power-generation facilities, and communications infrastructures is taking place on a daily basis throughout Iraq. But the fact remains that no U.S. citizen is safe working or driving anywhere in Iraq. Unfortunately, neither the U.S. military nor UN forces are able to provide the necessary level of protection for workers and convoys. Construction companies are forced to solve their own security issues.

Most security contractors have considerable military special operations or specialized civilian law enforcement backgrounds and training. Soldiers in Iraq, with an average of eighteen months of military service, are not sufficiently trained and do not possess the depth of experience required to assume the independent nature of security operations. Civilian security contractors must be capable of fighting against overwhelming odds using complicated and efficiently coordinated tactics honed from years of experience. Finally, soldiers on active duty with special operations skills are needed for offensive operations against the insurgents. It would not be the best use of their talent or organizational capabilities to assign them to security duties.

On any given evening, Blackwater contractors stationed in Baghdad's International Zone (a.k.a. the Green Zone) assemble to review the following day's security operations. Blackwater is on State Department contract to protect U.S. diplomats visiting and traveling around Iraq. Their assignments include protecting high-level officials from the U.S. Embassy and State Department, like Paul Bremer and John Negroponte. They also routinely escort mid-level U.S. government executives and employees. It is not uncommon for a Blackwater contractor to run three to five missions a day.

Blackwater security teams consist of two primary elements—a personal security detail (PSD) and a combat assault team (CAT). The PSD has responsibility for remaining with and securing their "principal" or "package" throughout the scheduled visit. The CAT is responsible for ensuring that the principal and the PSD team travel safely to each destination on the itinerary. Although many of the trips are relatively short, six to ten miles, the drives are extremely hazardous. Insurgents would love nothing more than to kill or capture a senior U.S. government official. Clearly, there are limitations on the number of routes that can be chosen, and insurgents lie in wait on all of them. There are no safe routes.

Each morning, Blackwater teams roll out of the IZ and head to the airport. At BIAP, they will meet and greet their usually "nervous" principal and his staff. The officials will be loaded into armored Chevy Suburbans. The CAT will position its heavily armored humvees with huge "pushers" mounted on the front bumpers, and the team will head out to the first destination of the day. As they traverse the streets of Baghdad, they will see insurgents with movie cameras filming them. They will see men on rooftops releasing pigeons or waving flags signaling to insurgents farther up the road that the U.S. diplomatic convoy is coming. The Blackwater contractors will make decisions as circumstances unfold. The best-case scenario, plan A, is that they will outfox the insurgents in this shell game of what roads they will travel on and at which intersections they will turn.

Insurgents proliferate the area with vehicle car bombs that may approach the convoy at any moment from any direction. If a vehicle approaches the convoy, the contractors will immediately go through a quick warning sequence. If it keeps coming, they will open fire, first to disable and then—if necessary—to kill the driver. If a man is standing on an overpass seemingly waiting, they will first attempt to avoid him, but if that's not possible, they will fire warning shots in his direction. If a vehicle turns suddenly into their lane, they will plow it out of their way without so much as slowing down.

Getting stuck in a traffic jam is more than a nuisance—it is life-threatening. Some traffic backups are artificially created by insurgents for the sole purpose of attacking U.S. diplomatic convoys. In September 2005, Stephen Sullivan, a U.S. State Department employee, and three Blackwater contractors were killed when a suicide car bomber simply drove up alongside their SUV in the left lane. The insurgent slowed down, and when he was parallel to them, he detonated his bomb. The explosion was so large that, in addition to killing the occupants in the adjacent vehicle, several contractors in a following vehicle were severely injured.

At times the suicide bombers will drive cars marked covertly with a swatch of duct tape on the roof or a brightly colored stuffed animal on the front dashboard. The markings are constantly changing, so security contractors have to be especially observant. Any unusual marker might indicate a VBIED.

The insurgents know that their bomber may not successfully make it to his intended target or that he might even lose his nerve to carry out the detonation. They will often position a lookout on a rooftop or nearby street corner with a remote-control detonator to blow up the marked car if the driver is unable or unwilling to do so.

When encountering a suspicious vehicle, contractors follow a warning sequence dictated by the rules of engagement. First, they issue a warning hand signal. If the intruding person or vehicle continues to approach, they will point their weapons at them. This is followed by engaging the vehicle to disable it, and then engaging the occupants if required. Some security contractors, after initiating the hand signal with a verbal warning, have developed the unofficial practice of tossing a plastic water bottle in front of an approaching vehicle as an additional step in getting the driver's attention.

Contractors view visiting diplomats and U.S. government employees in two ways: those who are scared speechless and those who second-guess everything they say or do. On a recent trip, a high-level USAID worker, visiting Baghdad, couldn't resist commenting on everything the Blackwater contractors did or failed to do. The visitor's negative opinion had evidently been formed by a slanted article or two he'd read about private contractors. The principal suggested that the water-bottle toss was inconsiderate and terribly offensive to the Iraqi people. The critique continued for some time. Rather than arguing with a principal, the contractors shrugged, skipped that step, and simply aimed their weapons and opened fire on the approaching vehicles sooner. That settled that—at least for now they appeased their passenger.

If left to their own devices, many security contractors would try to incorporate even more warning measures, time permitting. Several have commented that they would like to use (and some have) "flash bangs," a relatively harmless large firecracker to ward off intruders. This is strictly prohibited by the State Department rules of engagement.

II. The Fog of War

In the dark early morning hours, a Crescent Security team of five U.S. citizens, one Gurkha, and two Iraqis loaded up their three SUVs and departed their home base in Kuwait for the 450-mile drive to Camp Anaconda in northern Iraq. The Coalition Provisional Authority (CPA) had directed them to pick up an army officer named Major Van Elkin and a second passenger and transport them one hundred miles south to Baghdad International Airport. Everyone knew that the last stretch between Anaconda and Baghdad would be especially hairy. It would be well into the next night before this mission was complete, and they were well aware that insurgents ran that area of the country after sunset. Even though this wouldn't be a walk in the park, the team felt like they had their act together.

The contractors in the Toyota Prada who led the way were all experienced and confident. Jake Guevarra rode shotgun. About twenty-five years old, Jake was a clean-cut, combat-experienced former infantry marine and was in top physical condition. He spent some time in the war as a scout sniper. He was a voracious reader of military history, quiet, and not prone to macho displays. You might call him the intellectual of the group. For

Jake, this job was not about the money. Some unknown, elusive force drove him. Jake was very much a realist about the dangers he would face, and he had no thought of making a career out of this line of work. Experience told him that if he stayed at it too long, one day his number was bound to come up. He hoped that today was not that day.

Dee, the trusted Iraqi member of the team, occupied the back seat. He was a counterpart to team leader Wolf Weiss and supervised the Iraqi members of the team. In addition to being a shooter on missions, he was responsible for identifying and screening Iraqi job applicants, and collecting the Iraqi team members together every morning for Crescent's daily operations. Dee proved his courage, tenacity, street savvy, and skill in his countless contacts with the insurgents and bandits.

Wolf Weiss drove. A former member of the Marine Corps' elite Force Recon, Wolf was thirty-six years old, stocky, muscular, and an all-around colorful character. Whether sporting the traditional high-and-tight haircut or a ponytail, he was no cookie-cutter marine. After leaving the Corps, Wolf spent a few years in Los Angeles as a heavy metal guitarist, even recording a few CDs. He traded in his guitar for a rifle when the war erupted and headed back to the Middle East as a contractor. While still in country, *Rolling Stone* interviewed him for an article titled "Heavy Metal Mercenary." "There's only a few things in this world I can do really, really well," he told the magazine. "War is one."

As the Toyota rolled north, conversation was lively and spirits were high. Jake liked riding with Wolf, who was quite the storyteller. His brazen life-and-death tales were always entertaining. "I just felt safe when I was around him," Jake remarked.

"Wolf had this air about him. You just knew the guy had it together." Wolf's running dialogue helped the time pass, and Jake always learned something new that he thought might save his life one day. Wolf was his friend, his boss, his mentor, and in Jake's eyes, the consummate warrior. But as each team member in that vehicle would soon learn, combat skills will only get you so far; after that, it's up to luck, fate, or God. By the end of the day, everyone in the vehicle would be dead or wounded.

The second vehicle was a heavily armored Chevy Suburban, designated to transport the eventual "package" back to the airport. Kedar, a Gurkha who had been with the team from the beginning, sat in the passenger seat. The Gurkha tribesmen from Nepal, a small country sandwiched between India and China, were legendary stealth fighters who decimated the British army in the nineteenth century and later joined its ranks in the trenches of World War I. In Iraq, they got off to a rough start working as contractors. After a dozen fellow Gurkha fighters were beheaded by insurgents, Kedar was one of the few who chose to remain.

The team's number two man, Scott Schneider, drove the trail vehicle, a GMC Yukon. A former army combat engineer with fourteen years of military experience, Schneider's frame was shaped a lot like Wolf. He was in his mid-thirties, with cropped blonde hair, blue eyes, and a weather-beaten mug.

Dustin Benson, a former marine grunt and friend of Jake's, rode shotgun. He was about five-foot seven, mid-twenties, slim, and freckle-faced. He joined the team that very week, and this was his first mission as a security contractor. Although new to the team, he was not new to battle. As a marine during the initial stages of Operation Iraqi Freedom, he was involved in some of the most intense fighting of the war in the Ramadi region. Dustin's platoon sergeant and platoon leader had both been killed. He had assumed command of the platoon until replacements arrived.

In the back of the Yukon was the team's highly skilled tail gunner, an Iraqi by the name of Alowi. One would think that the highly exposed tail gunner would be the least desirable position, but you couldn't pay Alowi enough to give up his job. He was a good-natured guy and was always smiling about everything, especially when locking and loading his machine gun.

Jordan Hind, who drove, was the only team member without a military background. A former cage fighter and martial arts expert, he was trained by the team on weapons, military tactics, and techniques. Jordan had demonstrated his abilities in a number of scrapes.

The men had a standard uniform: a black Crescent T-shirt; a black body-armor vest with multiple pockets loaded with ammo magazines; a bayonet-length knife; a handheld radio clipped to the right vest shoulder; a collapsible-stock Russian AK-47 assault rifle; a Glock .45-caliber pistol strapped to the right thigh; and other essentials.

As for the vehicles, antipersonnel hand grenades were stacked in the center console. A half-dozen loaded thirty-round banana clips sat over the transmission hump in a curved container. Every vehicle had at least one light antitank weapon (LAW). A Russian 7.62 PKM was mounted on a special rotating bracket modified to fit the back of the Yukon.

On the trip north, Schneider schooled Dustin on the team's operating procedures and quick-reaction drills. His pupil asked all the right questions and proved to be a quick study. Every 150 miles or so, the team stopped at military installations to refuel, eat, check weapons, and reload.

Jake was particularly happy to have his old friend Dustin on the team. He thought to himself, *This is a good day, a good team. We've got our shit together.*

The three SUVs made it through Baghdad without a problem. At Camp Cook in Taji, about twenty miles northwest of Baghdad, they stopped at their last refueling point. The next stop after that would be Camp Anaconda, where they would load up their precious cargo and return to Baghdad International Airport.

After a bite to eat, and some smoking and joking, the team rolls out of Camp Cook. Darkness has fallen, and with the night has come a heightened sense of seriousness. A steady, increasingly intense rain begins. The road is slick as ice. Bugs pelt the windshield like a locust swarm on a Mississippi summer night. The wiper blades only smear the bug juice and make visibility worse. Wolf, Jordan, and Schneider squint through the goo hoping to see just far enough ahead to stay on the road. Wolf reluctantly reduces his speed to avoid the possibility of plowing into a military armored vehicle. The army's Bradley fighting vehicles frequently drive this stretch of road at night with only their tiny blackout cat-eye drive lights on.

As they round a curve, they spot two civilian vehicles blocking the road about fifty yards ahead. The three drivers can barely make out the brake lights. They have just seconds to react. Wolf Weiss shouts into his radio, "Brake hard, brake hard!" Jordan's SUV swerves right. Wolf swerves left, and both vehicles skid to a halt on opposite flanks of the stopped cars. For a moment there is an eerie silence as Wolf tries to figure out if the two vehicles are a threat. He covers them with his AK-47.

Jake, in the meantime, is scanning the surrounding area for a possible ambush. Wolf realizes they are in a choke point and this could be a trap. He begins to move the vehicle forward. Jake thinks he sees something dead ahead. He leans into the windshield trying to discern the object. "Wolf, hold up. I think I see something in front of us at about fifty meters," Jake remarks.

"We're taking fire, we're taking fire," Jordan repeatedly shrieks into his radio.

Schneider could also be heard shouting in response, "Back up, back up."

Wolf was on the radio too. He started to say, "Good job, Jor—" but was cut off mid-sentence.

In the seconds preceding all this radio traffic, Jake recalls hearing nothing—not a sound. He remembers: "Just as I made the comment to Wolf that I thought I saw something, there were a bunch of muzzle flashes directly in front of us. I didn't hear a sound, nothing. I just saw those flashes firing directly at us and instinctively went into my immediate action drill.

"I swung my AK-47 around from where I had been pointing out the right-side window and leveled it at twelve o'clock just above the dashboard. I had no choice but to begin shooting right through the windshield. I was dumping my entire clip through the glass. All I could think of was pumping out enough bullets to get some kind of fire superiority and buy us some time. Out of the corner of my left eye, I could see rounds coming through the windshield and they just seemed to be walking in slow motion across the glass toward me. Only a few seconds had passed since I had seen the muzzle flashes—just the time it takes for twenty-seven rounds to leave my AK on full auto. Then I felt a burning sensation on my face and I went down. I figured I'd been shot, and I remember thinking that I hoped I would die quickly. I slumped over and began fading in and out of consciousness."

Wolf's SUV wasn't moving. Bullets glanced off the car like sparks from a welder's torch. Jordan began to swing his armored vehicle around to try and block the bullets pouring into Wolf's car, but the attackers pulverized Jordan's vehicle with bullets and disabled it. Jordan and Kedar leaped from their vehicle and used it to shield them as they returned fire. Schneider and Dustin began shooting out their side windows. In the mayhem of the moment, Schneider and Dustin had completely forgotten about their tail gunner with the PKM machine gun. Now Dustin shouted at Schneider, "Get the PKM firing!" Schneider did a 180 with the Yukon so that Alowi could get a clear field of fire. Alowi's machine gun began pumping out lead. Dustin was now facing rearward with his head out the window. He was shouting out fire adjustments: "Shift right, shift right, drop, drop, drop, lower." Dustin was determined to get Alowi's gun firing directly into the attackers' center of mass.

Bullets ricocheted off of the car door and blasted apart the side-view mirror. Dustin ducked his head back inside, probably not a second too soon. He and Schneider decided to make a break from the Yukon. Schneider would go left and Dustin right. Dustin saw a tree about ten meters away and figured it was his only chance. He jumped from the Yukon. As he stepped out of the vehicle, in the mud and muck, he immediately fell flat on his face. It was at that moment, in that quirk of a fall and twist of fate that happens in the heat of battle, that Dustin had an epiphany. He realized that there was a chance to end this horrific firefight. Lying face down in the mud, Dustin Benson lifted his head, and from his very low vantage point, with the headlights of his

Yukon still beaming, he could make out the silhouettes of a humvee, and the boots of U.S. Army soldiers. His shocking observation: they were in a firefight with U.S. soldiers.

Dustin tried to crawl on his belly across the slick road, but there were too many bullets flying within feet of him, so he got up and bolted for the tree. The hail of bullets followed him. Instinctively, and out of self-preservation, he continued to shoot back. Behind the tree, he tried to get a grip on himself. Exhausted and trembling, he sporadically returned fire. The terrifying sound of bullets thumping into the tree vibrated and resonated through his body. Bullets ricocheted off the ground beside him and tree bark flew off like wood passing through a shredder. Red-hot tracers streaked by like speeding fireflies, and some struck the tree. The smell of gunpowder and burning wood drifted into Dustin's nostrils. Real or imagined, it seemed a certainty that at any moment a round would pass clear through the tree.

Dustin's brain raced at mach speed. He second-guessed what he had seen while he had been lying in the muck. With his heart pounding through his body armor and gasping for air, he asked himself, "What the fuck was I looking at? Were those really Americans? Or am I just seeing shit?" Once again he moved his face as low as possible to the ground and attempted to view the attackers against the dark sky. There was no error in his original observation, the black ghostly images of boots, human figures, and vehicles in front of him were unmistakably Americans. He knew that at any moment they could begin shooting far greater quantities of explosive ordnance at him and his team members, all of whom were still heavily engaged in fighting for their lives. He had to make a decision. He felt very much alone. He knew what his teammates didn't know. There was no one to consult on the merits of what he had to do to stop the insanity. The entire burden was on him. Dustin Benson stood up.

Covered in mud, and struggling with the overwhelming sensations of terror, Dustin laid his rifle down and found the intestinal fortitude and presence of mind to extend his arms skyward, exposing himself to the withering fire. The headlights of the three Crescent SUVs were still shining directly into the eyes of the attackers. To the U.S. soldiers, he was just a dark figure walking toward them. He shouted "Coalition, coalition." Bullets continued to fly into the mud around him. He could feel the air slice next to his face, as rounds came within inches of ending his life.

Dustin had committed to this action as the team's only chance to come out alive. There was no turning back now. The soldiers were shocked to see a surrendering figure approaching them, and it was nothing short of a miracle that they suddenly stopped firing. A soldier hollered out, "Lay down your weapons." Dustin, with his hands still in the air, was reluctant to reach for the Glock strapped to his thigh. One misinterpreted move would mean certain death. He opted instead to yell back, "I have no weapon except for the sidearm holstered on my leg. I'm an American."

Around the same time that Dustin stood up, Schneider had gotten a similar perspective on the images firing at them. He could make out an outline of a humvee and had begun shouting at his men to cease fire. Everything was quiet now except for the commanding voice of the soldier directing Dustin. He moved cautiously forward toward the approaching soldiers.

Then, without comment, without warning, without any apparent cause, Jordan leveled his AK-47 in the direction of the approaching soldiers and opened fire on them. Perhaps the unfolding events were unclear to him. He may have thought that insurgents were taking Dustin as a prisoner. Maybe Jordan just hadn't been able to digest that the battle was over. Was he still in survival mode like a dog in a fight that bites his owner in the fury that lingers after the threat has subsided? Did he have a violent knee-jerk reaction to now seeing his two friends slumped over in the Toyota? It has never been clear why Jordan began shooting, not even to Jordan himself.

Once again, both sides let loose a torrent of bullets in fierce exchange. Dustin, still standing there with his hands in the air, was torn between diving for cover and continuing to stand there with bullets now passing him in both directions. He mustered whatever courage and energy that was left in him. "Cease fire," he implored. "Cease fire."

Even for a seasoned combat veteran like Dustin Benson, to passively stand in the middle of a hail of gunfire was an extraordinary test of self-control. Like playing dead while being mauled by a bear, it may be the textbook response, but every instinct in his body opposed it.

Again, the shooting stopped. Schneider had been crawling toward Wolf and Jake's SUV. Schneider made it to the driver-side door. In the darkness he reached in to pull Wolf from the car. With one hand cradling Wolf's head, he could feel his hand immersed in the warm, wet matter he realized was Wolf's brain. Schneider, holding the lifeless body of his friend, incredulous and torn with grief, bellowed an anguished cry, "You blew his *fucking* head off!" His tortured voice permeated the night air and pierced every soul for a hundred yards around. A U.S. soldier's bullet had passed through Wolf's temple and exited out the back of his skull. Everyone on both sides of the firefight just froze in disbelief and horror at what had just happened. They realized this mistake could not be undone.

To Schneider, the last words of this valiant and compassionate leader were indicative of how he had lived his life, cared about his men, and led his team. In his final utterance before a scorching bullet ripped into him, Wolf Weiss had tried to say, "Good job, Jordan."

Dustin was now back at the passenger door of Wolf's vehicle. Jake lay slumped over in the passenger seat. Dee, in the back seat, was moaning and writhing in pain from a gaping gunshot wound to his arm. Dustin reached for his friend Jake. Jake recalls: "I could hear Dustin calling my name and I don't know why, but I just couldn't talk when I first heard him. I was aware of my surroundings as if I were someone else watching everything going on. I had heard Schneider scream out about Wolf and I wasn't at all surprised because as I had laid there in the car next to Wolf, I remember hearing sickening noises from his side of the car; a gurgling discharge, like water trickling from a garden hose on concrete. I'm not sure how or why I knew it, but I did have a realization that the sound was coming from Wolf's body.

"I guess I was just busy trying to die," Jake reflects. "While I had been drifting in and out of semi-consciousness, I had visualized a big hole in my face and I knew that the back of my head was bleeding. So my image was that the hole went clear through. It wasn't a very pretty thought and I was in no particular rush to live that way. When Dustin saw the back of my head, he thought I was dead. I was bleeding heavy and pretty well covered with blood. He kept repeating my name, 'Jake, Jake, Jake, talk to me, buddy.' So as he was dragging me out of the SUV, I discovered that my vocal cords still worked and finally said something to him. I don't remember what I said, but the fact that words came out of me at all stunned Dustin. I think he damn near dropped me. It was kind of like Dustin was thinking, 'What the hell was that?' It took him a second or two to adjust to the fact that I was alive.

"He laid me down on the pavement alongside the car. Of course, I still figured I was dying. All in all, I was pretty calm about my fate. I guess when you really think you have bit the bullet and it's all over, you don't get too terribly excited about that shit. Of course, I still had that thing about the hole through my face, so the first words I remember saying were, "How do I look?" That was a dumb question because I got the stock answer, 'You look good. You're going to be alright.' So I thought, *So much for that bullshit, of course he's going to say that. A lot of good asking that did!*

"For some reason, I couldn't stop moving my legs. Dustin was trying to access my wounds, and I couldn't get used to the idea of just laying there helpless. Then I heard someone say something about me lying in a pool of gasoline. Well, that did it! Survival instincts must run deep. I mean dying is one thing, but frying is another! I asked Dustin in a panic, 'Pull me out of this, pull me out of this.' Dustin began pulling me by my body armor; I tried to help him by kicking at the pavement. It was a rough go. In the struggle to get away from all the leaking gas, Dustin asked if I could stand up. To my surprise, I did. One side of me thought, *Gee, I must be OK. I'm walking around.* Then, being the fatalist I am, I recalled stories of guys shot in combat [who] walk around and talk a few minutes like everything's normal, and then just plop over and die. It wasn't like the thought scared me, or that I dwelled on it. It was just a matter-of-fact thought.

"Dustin took care of me. He took off my body armor, cut open my shirt. He applied some pressure bandages and started an IV on me. I had a non-life-threatening shrapnel wound to the back of my head. Jordan had a few shrapnel wounds; Dee had a bullet wound in the arm. The army medic on the scene wasn't much help. In fact, our guys knew a lot more about how to treat and evacuate wounded than this 'green' army unit knew. Dustin even had to coordinate and safely direct the landing of a medevac chopper.

"The Blackhawk helicopter touched down. The wounded and the dead were loaded onto the same chopper. Wolf, Jake, Jordan, and Dee lifted off into the raining black abyss. En route to the military base at Balad, they looked at one another inside the dimly lit confines of the Blackhawk. No one spoke. They just blankly stared at nothing in particular. Each man was alone with his thoughts; far louder than the whir of the blades, the roar of the engine turbines, or the seemingly distant voices of crew members communicating on the radio."

They will forever carry with them the surreal memories of this night. With the passage of time, the human coping mechanisms will naturally and gradually push these events to the recesses of their minds. But throughout their lives, again and again, and at times when they least expect it, the memories of this night will be played out, always in slow motion, always in excruciating detail, and always painful.

III. The Knife Fighter

Fifteen days after the friendly fire incident, Jordan, Dee, and Jake rejoined the team. Schneider moved into Wolf's old position as Crescent's director of security operations. He listens intently and is well spoken. On the rare occasion that he cusses, it is clearly a moment chosen for effect and not the product of uncontrolled emotions. He doesn't drink or smoke. He addressed these vices years ago and banished them from his life, yet he passes no judgment on those who do. Schneider expresses only two emotions with regularity: he either smiles like a school kid with his blue eyes twinkling and a mischievous grin or he is deadly serious, and few men or women would challenge his rock-hard appearance. He has that look that instantly makes the observer feel that he could break you like a pretzel. This is not someone you disrespect in a bar. Yet he is polite and courteous almost to a fault.

A street kid from Sacramento, Schneider joined the army as a teenager and trained as a combat engineer. He was fortunate enough to land some great assignments with good military units so he could hone his skills along the way. He traveled through Europe and felt lucky, as a back-alley kid, to experience the people and cultures of other countries. Restless for a change after fourteen years, he left the service to live with his wife, Belinda, in Adrian, Michigan. His decision meant that he would forego a retirement check just six years away. This decision was not unlike his original decision to join the army; it was time for a change. He would figure out his new direction later. For now, he just wanted time with his family.

The transition was difficult. Employment opportunities for former army combat engineers were rare. He enrolled in a truck-driver training program and picked up a big-rig license. Somewhere along the line, he learned that KBR was hiring truck drivers in Iraq. He and Belinda discussed it intensely. The money would solve a lot of problems. They decided that he would try it for a year and sack away the income. Schneider contacted a KBR recruiter who wanted him on a plane the next week. He and Belinda got their affairs in order and he left a few days later. Schneider remarks: "In the beginning you come here for the money, in the end you stay here for the mission."

On arrival in Iraq, KBR reassigned Schneider to a fuel point in the middle of the country. Wolf Weiss, who was at the time managing just one three-man security team, periodically stopped in, so Schneider and Wolf developed a friendship. As is Schneider's personality, he always made certain that Wolf's men were well taken care of. He would frequently give them additional water or food to take along on the dangerous road trips through the Iraqi countryside. One day, after a couple of months in country, Wolf asked Schneider what he'd like to do. Schneider responded, "I'd like your job." Wolf said he'd keep it in mind. A week later, Wolf lost a man and Schneider was offered a spot on the team. Schneider gave notice to KBR, and within two days was headed south to Kuwait to join Crescent Security.

Crescent Security, like the dozens of other security firms operating in Iraq, did not originally go into business to take advantage of the financial benefits offered to war zone security contractors. The intent of their development was to protect their own logistics assets, not to be hired guns for other companies. Crescent was the brainchild of Franco Pecco, an Italian businessman who was raised in South Africa and who has operational oversight responsibilities for a half-dozen businesses, including several trucking operations. His trucks in Iraq required security, and that was both expensive and unreliable. Franco

189

reasoned that it made more sense in terms of cost and quality control to create a security company. Based on his own military experience with the South African army in Angola, he began looking for a few good men. He found Wolf Weiss and hired him to begin Crescent Security.

Crescent has developed a written manual of standard operating procedures, and all of their contractors are required to know it by heart. They observe the military's rules of engagement and are quick to go through the required procedures before opening fire. Although Crescent's team exercises a great deal of self-control and fire discipline, when circumstances dictate they will not hesitate to open fire. And circumstances require it frequently. Schneider is known to say, "I'd rather be judged by twelve than carried by six. Iraq is all about the quick and the dead."

Schneider, Danny, Jake, and Justin roll out of bed in their Kuwait villa, the headquarters for Crescent Security. The contrast between where the team is now and where they'll be just a few hours from now is striking. Although some contractors would envy their living conditions, many would find it a struggle each day to leave the relative safety and opulence of Kuwait for the harrowing mission that will take them four hundred miles into Iraq and back to Kuwait in just thirty-six hours. The experience is somewhat like a strategic bomber pilot leaving Whitman Air Force Base in Missouri to attack targets in the Gulf and coming home to dinner the next night. In such short periods of time, the human mind has to struggle with rapid cycles of mental preparation, tension, terror, and subsequent decompression.

Everyone is in the standard uniform: desert boots, khaki pants, a black T-shirt, and a black Crescent Security baseball cap. Their vehicles are lined up in front of the villa. Engines are running. They hook up satellite trackers, load cases of water, check body armor, and tighten gun holsters onto their right legs. With the exception of a quick radio check, there is very little conversation. They are still waking up and each knows exactly what has to be done.

Still wearing her robe and a cup of coffee in hand, Belinda is standing on the steps, about ten yards away. She's watching her husband and the team get ready for work. Jake, Danny, and Justin climb into their Chevy Avalanche. Schneider glances back at his wife, and they move toward each other for a quick kiss and a few words. Then Schneider turns and climbs into his Yukon. The four vehicles begin to roll through the streets of Kuwait City and head north, toward the Iraqi border.

Belinda will be working in Crescent's operations center. Along with Paul, Franco, and a British operations manager, she will track every movement and every vehicle location while the team is on the road. As always, they will experience intense apprehension when unplanned events unfold and will endure painful frustration when radios and cell and satellite phones fail. Communication is their lifeblood. God willing, Belinda will see her husband and his team drive up tomorrow night. She won't be surprised to see a few new bullet holes in the Yukon. This is what Schneider and Belinda bought into when he signed on to be a security contractor.

On the highway to the border, the team rolls by Mutlah Ranch, where the Kuwaiti government has posted several signs leading to the Mutlah Ranch exit. Above each sign is another. It says, "God Bless U.S. Troops." Some Kuwaitis still remember the brutal and savage treatment received at the hands of the Iraqis during the 1991 invasion. It warms the hearts of today's U.S.

soldiers to be remembered and appreciated by the Kuwaitis, who see them in the same light as those who fought and died to free them from Saddam Hussein's tyranny.

About ten miles south of the Iraq-Kuwait border, a few hundred yards short of a Kuwaiti police checkpoint, is the last truck stop. This is Kuwait's version of a greasy spoon. Truckers from around the world return to this small café and convenience store to stock up on water and grab a quick breakfast or a cup of coffee. The atmosphere is friendly and jovial. The shouting of food orders sounds like the Arabic version of Chicago's Billy Goat Inn. Lively conversation and laughter abound. One would never guess that these truck drivers are headed north to Iraq and that an hour from now they may be getting shot at, hijacked, and executed. They live for the moment, and at the moment they're a happy group.

Schneider buys a couple of cases of Red Bull for his team and gets back on the road again. The four Crescent SUVs cruise past hundreds of trucks creeping through the last Kuwaiti police checkpoint prior to reaching the Iraqi border. There are trucks of every conceivable dimension and size. Some are just homemade flatbed trailers with furniture and miscellaneous junk piled twenty feet into the air. Some are old SUVs with eight feet of stuff piled on top of the roof. A few miles up, on the left side of the road, are a cluster of forty or fifty damaged and deserted homes, stores, and buildings. This was once a thriving Kuwaiti border town. The trees that were once carefully maintained and manicured are now dried stumps with naked branches. When the Iraqis invaded Kuwait, they killed nearly everyone and destroyed everything in this town. It was never rebuilt. The sand dunes have reclaimed the decrepit buildings. This is a ghost town.

The border crossing is just ahead. Off to the right is the sprawling U.S. Army compound known as NAVISTAR. Barbed wire, blast walls, and armed guards are everywhere. This is the staging area for all military and contractor convoys headed north. The Crescent SUVs turn into NAVISTAR and move slowly through the checkpoint maze. Just short of a sign that reads "Welcome to NAVISTAR, Major Thomas Palermo, Commanding," the vehicles are halted and searched. After they're cleared into the compound, they go to an area with a half-dozen lanes leading up to fuel points. No one begins a trip into Iraq without a full tank of gas.

Gassed up, they move over to a prefab building, which is the NAVISTAR northbound movement control center. Dave Bowman, a big, burly KBR employee, is the operations manager. He's got a half-dozen people milling around his office waiting for one thing or another. Dave has a phone in each hand and he seems to be holding three different conversations at the same time. Behind him is a rack of M16 rifles. He looks up at Schneider and asks, "What can I do you for?" Schneider gives him some paperwork on the trucks he's taking north. At the same time, Captain Waldman, a young, stressed-out military counterpart to Bowman is also trying to sort out what to do with all the gun trucks that are ready to roll.

Schneider glances through a copy of today's *Road Warrior*, a daily intelligence report that covers enemy activity along major Iraqi highways during the last twenty-four hours. He turns to Jake, Danny, and Justin. "Take a look," he comments. "The usual stuff up north, but the Italians lost a couple of guys down south." Schneider continues, "Remember that guy on the overpass yesterday, a few klicks north of Cedar II? We shoulda taken him out. I'll bet anything that he's the one [who] hit them." They browse through the report, make a few comments to each other, leave the building, and head back to their SUVs. Each of them is silently committing to memory the locations of yesterday's attacks. It's good to have information, but who knows where the enemy will strike today?

The Crescent team walks across the huge sandy staging area where row after row of trucks are lined up. A thirty-truck convoy with an army escort is in the middle of rolling out of NAVISTAR. Several up-armored humvees are standing by, ready to slip into position in the departing convoy. Their mounted .50-caliber machine guns are pointed at a 45-degree angle skyward. A young lieutenant, obviously the convoy commander, stands off to the side of his humvee. He is using arm and hand signals to control the flow and placement of vehicles in his convoy. Except for his desert camouflage uniform, he looks a lot like a New York City traffic cop going through his motions. This is a typical morning at the Iraqi border.

Crescent will be providing protection for eight trucks this morning. A couple of the trucks are carrying food for the Italian army. Those will be dropped off at Tallil Air Base north of Basra. Several others are DHL mail trucks, and a couple of trucks are loaded with construction materials headed for a military base just south of Baghdad near the town of Karbala, called Scania.

Crescent's truck drivers are waiting. A couple of them are Pakistani, several are Syrian, one is from Egypt, and another is Jordanian. As Schneider and his crew approach, they are greeted with warm handshakes and big smiles. Everyone is ready to roll, and Schneider leads his convoy out the gate and across the Berm. The Kuwaiti border guards don't much care what cargo is leaving their country and just wave the northbound trucks past. They will be far more thorough when the convoy returns.

As the convoy slowly approaches the Iraqi border station, they pull over to the side and let a couple of trucks they call gauntlet runners cut ahead. The gauntlet runners are the poorest of the poor drivers and are working for themselves or for trucking companies that do not provide security. Independent truckers trying to deliver supplies in Iraq are often the victims of extortion, robbery, and executions. Corrupt local Iraqi militia units, police, and bandits frequently intercept these loner trucks and hold them hostage for some extraordinary toll that amounts to ransom. If they don't pay, the truck and driver are taken a few miles into the desert, where the driver is killed and the cargo is looted. Mile-long stretches in the desert are littered with the remains of such unfortunate encounters. As the gauntlet runners pass by, Schneider and Jake exchange looks, shaking their heads in disbelief.

About a quarter of a mile into Iraq, the four Crescent vehicles pull into a small storage compound. This is nothing more than a sandpit and some scattered concertina wire guarded by a dozen or so Iraqi soldiers. A Bosnian civilian seems to be running the storage yard and is barking out directions to several men of mixed nationality. In the sandpit are a handful of prefab metal buildings and some scattered trucks. The Crescent convoy's trucks pull off to the side of the main road and wait.

Jake, Danny, and Justin pull over to one of the buildings. A moment later, the trio emerges from the metal shack carrying armfuls of Russian AK-47 automatic rifles. Then come the PKM machine guns, Glock .45-caliber pistols, and dozens of metal boxes of bullet-loaded magazines. There are even a couple of light antitank weapons (LAWs) in the mix. Schneider is talking with Dee about who is going on which missions today. Dee, dressed in a traditional white robe and headdress, is not going on this mission. He will remain behind today and manage Crescent's Iraqi contingent of contractors as subsequent Crescent convoys depart and return throughout the day. Behind Dee are a dozen or so Iraqis driving up in two pickup trucks. Dee has rounded them up this morning and brought them to work. They are in various states of dress as they change into their khaki pants and black Crescent T-shirts.

The U.S. contractors and Iraqis greet one another like long-lost cousins. They shake hands, high-five, and slap each other on the back. Schneider passes out a few bottles of cold water. One of the Iraqis, nicknamed Mongo, is encouraged by his friends to share some pictures with Schneider and the U.S. crew. Mongo is a world-class weightlifter who was once on the Iraqi national weightlifting team. After a few gentle ribs and nudges, he pulls out several color snapshots of himself in the classic muscleman poses. Everyone gathers around to look. Mongo grins sheepishly. The whole team starts chiding him to show off his biceps. Mongo, both proud and embarrassed by all the attention, pulls back the sleeve of his T-shirt and flexes his muscles. Everyone breaks out in a combination of laughter and good-humored chiding. Like the drivers at the truck stop, one would never guess that these men will confront grave danger today.

Most security contractors are not allowed to possess firearms in Kuwait. Consequently, each morning the U.S. Crescent guys link up with their Iraqi counterparts here at the storage yard on the Iraq side of the border. They distribute the hardware, discuss the missions, and tell a few stories before heading north. On their return trip, and before entering Kuwait, the weapons are returned to the shed. From this point, the Iraqis head back to their homes in the Basra region, and the U.S. contractors cross the border into Kuwait and back to their villa. For security reasons, before heading home, the Iraqis will change out of their Crescent uniforms and back into street clothes. Assassinations of Iraqis working for U.S. contractors occur all too frequently.

A pall of seriousness comes over everyone now. Jake, Danny, and Justin begin passing out weapons. The machine guns are hoisted up onto the rear of the trucks and fastened to their mounts. A pile of AK-47 rifles and fully loaded magazines is passed out to the group. Glock .45-caliber pistols are locked and loaded and slid into thigh holsters. Schneider inspects a couple of LAWs and makes certain that each of the four security vehicles has at least one LAW on board. The gunners in the back of the trucks attach a metal ammo can to the side of their machine guns and feed the ammo belt into the gun's chamber from the can.

Iraqi gunners take their positions sitting in the open back of the SUVs. They pull ski masks down over their faces. The masks will protect them from the brutal blowing sand that would otherwise scrape their faces raw as they travel at fifty to ninety miles an hour. They rotate and swivel the machine guns to ensure that the range of travel on the gun mounts isn't impaired. Now everyone looks at Schneider. They're ready. Schneider doesn't say it, but you can guess that he is thinking one of his favorite slogans: "Locked, cocked, and ready to rock." He climbs into his Yukon and leads the four SUVs back onto the main road to the waiting trucks. Each truck begins to roll as the SUVs fall into place in the convoy.

Schneider takes his AK-47 and slides it into a prerigged sling dangling just above the driver's window. The butt of his weapon rides against his left rib cage. He knows that if he has to fire while driving, his fire won't be accurate, but he gambles on the fact that any bullets bouncing around an insurgent could provide a second or two of distraction. A couple of seconds of distraction may mean the difference between life and death—Schneider's life and death. The convoy begins to pick up speed. They drive past the town of Safwan and head toward MSR Tampa, the main route to Baghdad. On the sides of the road, groups of Iraqis are watching the convoy. As usual, the kids are begging and the adults are just staring. A couple of Iraqi soldiers wave as the convoy passes.

They drive through large tracts of barren desert. There are no vehicles, animals, or people in sight. Schneider picks up the mike on his Motorola radio, "Is everyone ready for test fire?"

Danny, Jake, and Justin each respond in the affirmative.

He then directs, "Go ahead and test fire. When you're done, report back on weapons status." The machine gunners burst out ten or so rounds. Dust tracks kick up on the desert floor as each round strikes. The AK-47s fire off one or two short three-round bursts. Brass pings off the inside of the windshield and bounces around the vehicle like corn in a hot-air popper. All weapons systems are functional. All shooters are ready. All vehicle gauges read normal. All radios are working.

A few miles farther up the road, they approach the entrance to the main highway. Two of the three SUVs accelerate forward and take up positions blocking traffic. The men inside jump out with rifles in hand and position themselves on the road a few feet from their SUV. The third SUV scurries up a slope to get a clear view of the overpass and the road ahead. The rear gunners scan the area and traverse their machine guns as they survey the surroundings. Part of the overpass is destroyed from a previous bomb attack. The convoy will have to bypass the normal entrance ramp.

Schneider leads the convoy through a short detour and around the caved-in overpass and toward the highway. He keeps a safe distance from fallen concrete and rubble, because new explosives may be hidden in the debris piles. Everyone quickly loads back in the SUVs and the convoy continues to roll. The SUVs speed back into their positions among the big rigs. The whole process is part of Crescent's standard operating procedures, and the entire event is executed like clockwork without much comment. This action will be repeated a couple of dozen times today at intersections and danger spots until the trucks, cargo, and drivers, are once again safe inside the wire.

As the convoy rolls, the Crescent radios crackle. Justin, in the rear SUV reports, "Chevy with tinted windows coming in about two hundred meters at six o'clock."

"Roger, copy," Schneider responds, "I see him, keep him outside."

Jake in the lead SUV reports, "Debris on the right shoulder, I'm shifting left." A moment later he continues, "Southbound British convoy ahead."

"Copy," responds Schneider.

"Red truck on overpass, man outside of vehicle," reports Danny who has sped ahead to recon the highway.

Schneider comes back, "Stop short . . . if he doesn't clear, warn first and then light him up." And the alerts go on and on. The radio chatter is continuous as each SUV spots different potential threats and notifies the rest of the team. Nothing, and no one, is taken for granted.

Coming off the main highway and onto a secondary road, the convoy has had to slow down to about ten miles per hour. Schneider spots a dark-brown pickup racing toward the convoy. At nearly the same time, Danny and Jake report seeing the vehicle. Schneider responds, "I got it." He positions his SUV between the charging pickup and the main body of the convoy. He throws a water bottle in the direction of the intruder. The truck keeps coming. Now, one of the SUVs has pulled alongside. Both trucks fire warning shots, and when the vehicle doesn't slow down, they both open with bullets walking up the desert floor toward the charging pickup. The pickup careens off the road and makes a swooping 180-degree turn. Apparently undamaged, it heads back into the desert and quickly disappears over the next hill.

Schneider comments, "I don't know what that was about. He knew better than to be speeding at us like that. The only person in Iraq who doesn't know the rules of engagement is a wet newborn baby. He should have backed off. It was clear he wasn't going to." Schneider grins, "That's what I call muzzle phonetics!" and he laughs for a moment and explains, "I swear you can scream stop, halt, or throw water bottles all day long but it falls on deaf ears. They only seem to respond to the sound of those bullets leaving the muzzle. That seems to be the only thing that gets their attention. These people only respect power. Anything less, and they'll walk all over you. It's their culture. It's centuries of subjugation under dictators and tyrants. That's what they've come to know. That's all they respect."

Schneider goes on: "These people laugh at Americans trying

to enforce rule and order through negotiations and common sense. Most of these Iraqis think we are pretty timid.

"I know that we could have blown that pickup off the face of the earth. He's lucky we shot in front of him first. Another second or two of that, and he'd have been history." This event is no big deal to the contractors. Having to ward off approaching vehicles is a daily occurrence, but the one time they don't may be their last road trip in Iraq.

They pass by the town of Nasiriyah. Schneider points out a small bridge, where during the initial fighting in Iraq, a U.S. supply convoy was ambushed. This is the place that a U.S. soldier had been wounded and captured. She was later rescued by special operations forces. "Now how the hell could they have missed the main road here and wandered back and forth in that town?" Schneider remarks. "They were totally screwed up. Worse yet, they actually went back over that bridge twice! It was like they were hanging around just asking to be fired up!"

The first stop is Cedar II (Tallil Air Base), north of Basra and about a hundred and fifty miles into Iraq. It's just about noon, and the temperature is now close to 120 degrees Fahrenheit. Given that the day started at 4 a.m., everyone has worked up an appetite. The convoy pulls into the base. Two of the trucks will remain at Tallil. The rest of the convoy will head up to Scania, just south of Baghdad. The group parks in a sandlot. They leave their weapons in the vehicles and head over to the dining facility. Hundreds of soldiers are lined up at the entrance to the DFAC, clearing weapons before they enter. A couple of soldiers are inspecting identification and checking to ensure that weapons are clear. Schneider shows his contractor ID and vouches for the Iraqi men on his team.

The dining facility is huge, with several serving areas. One is a short-order line for sandwiches, hamburgers, and hot dogs, and another features full-course meals. This is quite a smorgasbord and one wonders what is passing through the minds of the Iraqi team members who are, like everyone else, loading up their food trays. Scattered throughout the giant facility and on the periphery are drink dispensers and refrigerators with double-wide glass doors, stacked with bottled water, Gatorade, soda pop, and desserts. Seated in row after row of long tables are soldiers, sailors, airmen, marines, and contractors from around the world; rifles slung across their backs, pistols dangling against their chests from shoulder holsters. The casualness of the entire scene takes a moment to digest. This is quite an eclectic collection of humanity, each person with his or her own unique job. They are all here for one purpose, to stabilize, secure, and rebuild a war-ravaged country. Everyone chows down.

Relaxed, stomachs full, thirst quenched, the U.S. and Iraqi Crescent team leave the dining facility and heads back toward the parking lot. Jake is talking with Danny, Justin, and Schneider about a Stephen Pressfield book, *Gates of Fire*. Jake reflects, "In 500 B.C., thousands of fine Spartan warriors died to save Greece from Persian invaders at the Gates of Thermopylae."

Almost rhetorically, one of them asks, "Do you think war is just nature's way of managing human population growth?" Danny and Justin smirk.

At first no one comments, but then one of them asks, "What are you doing here, Jake?" Jake thinks over the question.

"After working this job, I just don't know what else I would ever be content doing. I haven't been able to figure that out. I work on that question every day."

The team climbs aboard their SUVs. Some of the vehicles have to make a quick pit stop to gas up again. Now the convoy rolls out the gate, past the same guards that meticulously checked them in an hour ago. This time they just wave to each other. Winding toward the highway, they drive by kids scattered in ones and twos every hundred feet on both sides of the narrow, sandy, potholed road. All of them are begging.

Although the children seem innocent enough, the contractors cautiously eye each of them. The slightest sign of aberrant behavior by any of them will require immediate evasive action. The wind is blowing hard, and the trucks are kicking up large dust trails that make it difficult to see ten yards ahead. Now and then, the team spots the faint image of a child darting across the road between the slow-moving vehicles. Tension sets back in as they merge onto the main highway and head north to Scania. It will be at least four more hours before anyone can relax again.

As they drive north, signs of recent enemy activity become more frequent. They drive past burned-out trucks here and there. Every ten or twenty miles they encounter blackened sections of road and twisted guardrails that attest to an earlier IED detonation. A long sand berm runs on the right side parallel to the road. This would seem like an ideal spot for insurgents to hide. But Schneider knows that it's unlikely that they'll be attacked from that side. He remarks, "If they hit from the right, they will have to escape toward coalition forces behind them in that direction. No, around here they are much more likely to hit us from the left, when we're on the way back, because they have plenty of desert over there to disappear into." Then he adds as an afterthought, "Well, that's what they've done in the past, but if someone pops his head over that berm and he's pointing an AK at us, don't hesitate to light him up."

About an hour into this second segment of the road trip and fifty miles north of Cedar II, Schneider spots a wisp of smoke on the right side and shouts into the radio mike, "RPG 3 o'clock!" The Crescent shooters on the right side of all the SUVs open fire with AK-47s on full automatic. Shooters on the left scour their side to make sure it's clear. The left-side shooters are ready to hand off ammunition magazines to the men engaged on the right side. Hot brass is pinging all over the inside of the vehicles.

The PKM machine gunners in the Avalanches open fire on the same general spot. Bullets by the thousand are striking a sand mound about two hundred yards off the road like a bucket of pebbles being tossed into a still pond. Every vehicle in the convoy has gone into maximum acceleration. As the last SUV passes the RPG location, the sound of rifle shooting diminishes. Schneider pushes the talk switch on the radio mike, "Is everyone clear?"

The report comes back from each of the SUVs, "Clear."

"Give me a status report," Schneider directs.

The convoy is gradually returning to normal speed. The SUVs speed up alongside the big rigs. They make a visual inspection and get a thumbs-up from their drivers. Danny and Jake report back that everyone is OK. The entire event is over in less than a minute.

Schneider is back on the radio again: "Keep a sharp eye out; remember the last time we were hit less than five minutes after the first attack. Everyone watch their gauges. Make sure you are not losing oil, fuel, or water." He sets the radio mike down, "You know, if you put out enough firepower quick enough, the bad guys lose their concentration." Then he adds, "I shouldn't laugh just yet. The last time we ran through one of these, I thought we had made it by unscathed. When we got to Scania, we saw that an RPG round had gone clean through a prefab metal building that we were hauling on a flatbed. The damn thing never exploded. And then, to make matters worse, we noticed that one of our SUVs had several new bullet holes. We'll take a closer look at everything when we stop."

On the way to Scania, Schneider calls Franco at the Kuwait Crescent operations center to report the attack. During the conversation, Franco asks Schneider if he can pick up a package in Sadr City and deliver it to the Green Zone. Schneider glances at his watch. "Yeah, but aren't there any Blackwater or TDL guys that could do it?" he asks. "OK," he tells Franco, "it will be late before we get there. Tell them to expect us around 1900 hours." Crescent gets requests for unplanned additional missions nearly every day. The coalition forces are constantly scrambling to find available security escorts. Sometimes Crescent will have to turn around from heading south and go all the way north to Mosul to pick up some informant or provide security for some Iraqi politicians having to go back down to Baghdad. Before the conversation ends, Belinda exchanges small talk with her husband, who ends with, "I love you, too."

While driving, Schneider tells a story about one of his "arms runs" to Samarra, which is northwest of Baghdad. "We were expanding our teams and needed some more guns. A couple of us drove into Samarra late one afternoon to make contact with a dealer there. We got the weapons we needed, but the transaction took longer than we expected and it was getting dark before we could leave. Samarra is not a fun place to hang around at any time, let alone at night. We were getting lost on some back streets and side roads. A lot of Iraqis were looking at us like we were a meal. Some were just standing in front of our vehicles and not anxious to move. Other times, vehicles would just stall in front of us for no apparent reason.

"We were traveling in a pair of SUVs and were crossing over a highway bridge when suddenly to my front a couple of pickup trucks at the far end of the overpass pulled in from opposite directions and blocked our path. I stopped and slammed the car in reverse. Then, just as I glanced back, I saw two huge dump trucks doing the same thing behind us. We were being boxed in. It was clearly a trap. Our only option was to throw the cars back into drive and hit the gas. I spotted a gap behind one of the two pickups and at the last minute swerved behind the truck and through the gap. There wasn't an inch of clearance on either side but at that point, it wouldn't have mattered if I had hit them. There was no other choice.

"As we raced through Samarra, we were chased by a half-dozen vehicles. They tried to cut us off at intersections. They blocked off side streets to try and channel us into another trap. They were even clever enough to have a chase vehicle behind us turn off and replace it with a different chase vehicle. One moment we were going a hundred miles an hour and the next moment we were slamming on the brakes. I went into controlled skids, or maybe not so controlled, at turn after turn. Sometimes I slid sideways all the way across the road. In what seemed like a Hollywood movie, the chase lasted for several hours. At different times, I actually pulled into, and through, five Iraqi police stations. There were no police in sight, so we were off and running again. Eventually, we shook them off. You can imagine my surprise when the next day three out of those five police stations were blown up by VBIEDs."

The Crescent team pulls into Scania and drops off their trucks. The vehicles are inspected and everyone shares their version of events when the RPG was fired. There's a lot of smiles and clowning around. No one is worse for the wear. The truck drivers remain at Scania, and one of the Crescent guys gets them fed and bedded down. The team has one more mission to complete. They gas up, lock and load, and roll out the gate headed for Sadr City, a very dangerous area of Baghdad. The trip has a few scary moments when vehicles slow and stop in front of them in a traffic circle. Schneider comments that he has a thirty-second rule for this: "Thirty seconds and we warn them, forty-five seconds and that vehicle will be moved one way or another." The front ends of the SUVs are all equipped with large steel pushers for just this purpose.

"We can't sit here exposed. I have an obligation to keep my guys alive, and indecision or hesitation in a situation like this is how people get killed," Schneider comments in a tense voice. "At one point, when we got backed up in traffic, several of the contractors step outside of their vehicles. They are watching every car and truck and every person standing on the sides of the roadway; guns are at the ready." The trip goes without incident and they pick up and deliver the package to the Green Zone. Later that evening, they bed down for the night at Scania. By morning, the trucks will have been emptied and reloaded with cargo and DHL mail bound for Kuwait.

The return trip south is the reverse of the previous day, except that there are no RPG attacks this time. Evidence of fresh

IED attacks has increased, and the team passes several smoldering vehicles surrounded by U.S. Army soldiers who are working with an explosive ordinance demolitions (EOD) team. The EOD guys are in the process of rigging to blow some secondary bombs that did not detonate during this attack. Two helicopter gunships can be seen circling overhead. About fifty soldiers are searching some buildings and homes in the surrounding area. As the convoy passes through the cloud of acrid smoke, a few soldiers glance at the Crescent security team. The whole scene has an uncanny similarity to passing a road-construction crew on a U.S. highway in the heat of a summer day. They nod at one another—nothing more.

Finally, the SUVs and trucks roll off the main highway and back past the town of Safwan. The border is just ahead and the trucks pull over while the SUVs, needing to drop off their weapons, pull up to the gate at the sandpit storage yard. A couple of Crescent's Iraqi team members, tired and thirsty, get out of their vehicles and start to climb over a sand berm surrounding the storage yard. They are in a hurry to get to the vehicles they left there yesterday and just want to head home. Suddenly, Arabic voices are shouting, followed by several bursts of automatic-rifle fire. Bullets are whizzing past everyone. Dirt flies as bullets strike within inches of the men who just jumped the berm. A bunch of Iraqi soldiers have surrounded Crescent's Iraqi team members. Schneider, Danny, Jake, and Justin jump from their vehicles and rush over. Everyone has guns, and everyone is pointing them at everyone else in a classic Mexican standoff worthy of Hollywood.

About fifteen Iraqi soldiers and several Iraqi civilian security personnel form a semicircle around the Crescent team. They are

Charles "Chazz" Rudolph: "The Welcome Committee."

After some light-hearted encouragement from the team, Mongo,
one of Crescent's Iraqi operators, shows off his biceps. He is a
world-class weightlifter and former member of the Iraqi Olympic
team. Mongo is now a shooter/operator with Crescent.

↑ Jake Guevarra sucks in some air and controls his breathing as he gets ready to run another convoy mission on the roads of Iraq.

↓ Dee, Crescent's Iraqi team leader, shows off the scars from the bullet wound he received during one of the team's engagements.

↑ A scruffy-faced Scott Schneider, director of Crescent Security, supervises unloading weapons at the "sandpit" storage yard in Safwan, Iraq.

↓ On MSR Tampa, the Crescent team passes a burning fuel tanker that was hit by an insurgent IED just moments before.

↑ At day's end and having spent the last twelve hours running the roads in Iraq, Scott and his wife, Belinda, get ready to go out to dinner in Kuwait. Just another day at the office.

↓ Paul Chapman (sitting) and Belinda Schneider at Crescent's operations center track the movement of their vehicles on the roads in Iraq.

Dustin Benson (left) and Scott Schneider wait
for their Iraqi team members to arrive for another
trip north through Iraq. Scott is holding a light
antitank weapon (LAW).

Dustin Benson stands by for the daily
mission brief.

↑ Security team on the road in Iraq with guns protruding out of every window.

↓ Left to right: Scott Schneider, Staff Sergeant Stouffer, Captain Waldman, and Franco Pecco. Captain Waldman is the "gatekeeper" at the Kuwait border. His job is to control the movement of convoys into Iraq.

↑ On the streets of Baghdad, David Carlton (left), Jason Stanford, and Stanford's bomb-sniffing dog, Enroll, search for bombs following another IED attack.

↓ The Crescent security team with UN inspectors and an Iraqi informant at an Iraqi mass grave site. The Iraqi informant and his family were assassinated after he returned home later that evening.

Left to right: Louie, Alowi, Basim, Chazz, and
Jason B. (kneeling).

Major General Peterson, David Carlton, and
Blek in front of the Al Sadeer Hotel, known to
those who reside there as the Pink Flamingo.

Interior of Scott's Yukon with extra 30-round AK-47 banana clips stacked on the transmission hump. When having to fire while inside the SUV, the collapsible-stock AK-47 is easier to manage than a fixed wooden stock.

Chazz and Mickey's Chevy Avalanche after an Iraqi
dump truck plowed into and toppled over on top of
it, with them inside.

↑ Danny, the author, and Jake on their last break before crossing the Kuwaiti border and heading into Iraq.

↓ Dee (left) and Jake Guevarra display an interior chest plate from Jake's body armor. The indentation on the plate is from an insurgent's bullet that struck Jake but narrowly missed entering his body.

Wolf and one of his men return from
the area of an IED attack.

Wolf and Jake's SUV after the firefight in "The Fog of War" (Chapter 7). Wolf had been on the radio directing his team when he took a fatal bullet to the head. "I could see the bullets, like in slow motion, just walking across the windshield toward me," Jake recalls.

Wolf Weiss sports the tattoo of a panther on his left bicep and the grim reaper playing a guitar on his right. His hair is braided and pulled back in a ponytail. Inked into his back is a full-color image of a wolf preparing to attack; in one of the wolf's eyes is the reflection of a hunter with his hands in the air. Weiss sees himself as that wolf. He is not your typical military-looking contractor. As he is known to remark, "There's only a few things in this world I can do really, really well. War is one of them"

standing less than ten feet apart. It's about 5 p.m. The 130-degree heat and the tension are taking a toll on everyone. Every face and forehead is dripping with sweat. A few men rub their eyes to clear the salty sweat obscuring their vision. It's like two street gangs in a neighborhood showdown. Somebody has violated somebody's turf rules. The Bosnian, who seems to run this hellhole, is screaming at Dee and poking him in the chest. Evidently, the storage yard had come under attack by insurgents the night before and the Iraqi soldiers there were pretty rattled.

The Iraqi contractors who had jumped the berm were clearly wrong. Schneider tries to apologize and calm the situation down, but the Bosnian guy will have none of it, and he continues to verbally abuse and poke Dee in the chest. Schneider momentarily loses his temper. He swings the Bosnian around and starts poking *him* in the chest. Schneider exclaims, "So how do you like being poked in the chest, uh, uh! You like it . . . do you?" Shit hits the fan.

In Iraq, guns are fired into the air in celebration, and into the ground to intimidate an adversary or express rage. The way the dust is flying all around the storage yard leaves no doubt what everyone is feeling. Schneider instinctively goes for his Glock pistol. He yanks the Bosnian around in front of him and puts his Glock at the guy's head. Schneider blurts out, "Everybody, calm down." The shooting tapers off and stops. Schneider says again, but this time very calmly, "Everybody just . . . let's all calm down and talk."

Schneider holsters his weapon. Everyone lowers their rifles. The Bosnian is visibly shaken, breathing hard, sweating profusely, and red faced. Again, Schneider apologizes. He begins to explain how jumping the berm was a mistake and it won't happen again. Suddenly, as if this nightmare were never going to end, a screaming knife-wielding Iraqi civilian charges from one of the storage shacks toward the U.S. contractors. As he shouts and curses in Arabic, he viciously swings the twelve-inch blade within inches of their faces. From the way he is holding the knife, it's evident that he is well practiced in the art of knife fighting, but he has clearly lost his composure. This guy's not playing with a full deck.

The Iraqi with the knife gets more and more dramatic, whipping the knife through the air in mock stabbing motions and running in circles. In his frenzy, he inadvertently runs the huge blade right through his own thigh. He must have severed his femoral artery. His right leg and the crotch of his pants turn bright red, blood pouring down his leg and onto his sandal. The lunatic looks at his leg like *How in the hell did that happen?* He falls to the ground behind the soldiers in the semicircle.

Now the Bosnian is back in the act. He grabs an AK from one of the Iraqi soldiers. Bullets are flying again. Schneider goes for his gun—too late. The Bosnian has the AK in Schneider's face. As if on cue, the firing stops instantly. Everything is quiet. Schneider breaks the silence. He is speaking to his team, "Everyone, slowly raise your hands above your heads. Don't anyone fire." All the Crescent guys raise their hands. With the AK still stuck in his face, Schneider again attempts to resume a civil discussion. The lunatic is about fifteen yards away and on the ground. He starts to shake as pools of blood turn the sand by his leg rusty red. No one seems to be paying any attention to the wounded man. Schneider asks, "Would you like us to give medical attention to your guy over there?" The Bosnian glances over at the injured man, who now appears to be going into shock. Several of the Iraqi soldiers look puzzled and then look back at the bleeding man. It's almost as if they were thinking, *Oh yes, that's right, where is our guy who stabbed himself?*

The Bosnian thinks for moment, then looks back at Schneider. "Sure," he says, and lowers his weapon. Danny and Jake run back to the SUV and get a medical bag. They apply a pressure bandage and begin treating the injured Iraqi for shock. They grab an IV, and one of them comments that the IV fluid is about 130 degrees Fahrenheit. The Iraqi soldiers intervene; they say they will take care of him. Schneider and his crew back off. He and the Bosnian agree to meet in Kuwait later that evening to discuss procedures for preventing this in the future. The team stores their weapons. The Iraqi contractors change back into their street clothing. The Crescent Iraqi and U.S. teams say good-bye to each other and set the time to meet the next morning.

The U.S. contractors lead their trucks through the Kuwaiti checkpoint and into a temporary holding area where the trucks and their cargo can be searched. Sometimes returning trucks have hidden contraband such as weapons and drugs. Smugglers have been caught concealing contraband in fuel cans and inside tires. At times in Iraq, when one of these smugglers has hit an IED, opium or hashish is scattered all over the highway. Under Kuwaiti law, drug smugglers are punished severely.

Schneider knows that if he leaves now, his truck drivers could be hung up here for hours waiting to end their day. He tells Danny, Jake, and Justin that he'll meet them back at the villa. Schneider enters the border-guard shack and speaks with a stern and somewhat unfriendly Kuwaiti army officer. After twenty minutes of schmoozing with the bearded officer, sometimes referred to as a Mullah, the paperwork gets stamped. Schneider's trucks are cleared to move out of the holding pen and into Kuwait where they'll pull into NAVISTAR. The big-rig drivers say good-bye 'til tomorrow and head home. Schneider hits the road headed for Kuwait City. He says, "Ya know, this hour drive up to the border in the morning always seems to fly by. But this last hour to get home just seems to take forever. More than once, I've nearly fallen asleep at the wheel on this stretch of highway between the border and Kuwait City."

It's about 6 p.m. now, and Schneider's SUV traverses through the heavy traffic of Kuwait City. In Kuwait, people hibernate from the heat of the day and come out in droves every night of the week. He turns off the main highway and rolls up to the Crescent villa. Belinda had just called on the cell and she's now standing in front as he pulls up. He gets out of the SUV, brushes off some dust, and gives her a hug. Franco is standing in the background grinning. He's happy to see his final team member back home, even if it's only for tonight. The three of them talk for a moment. Schneider says to his wife, "Let's go out for dinner at that new restaurant we've been meaning to hit."

"Great," Belinda says. "What time?"

"Let's make it around 8 p.m. I've got to head over for a quick meeting with a Bosnian from the storage yard, and then I'll get cleaned up and we'll head out to eat."

Belinda smiles. "Sounds like a plan."

IV. The Ransom

Battlefield demands sometimes dictate actions that might be considered unethical outside the context of war. But this story takes place in the fog of a war zone, where reality gets turned upside down and judgment gets skewed in less than a moment's notice. Although all events in this account are factual, the names of the trucking company and all security contractors have been changed.

You might say that Iraq is controlled by private interest groups. These may take the form of tribal unions, family affiliations, religious organizations, ethnic associations, and a number of criminal subcultures that may or may not be linked to the preceding groups. Some gangs are so well entrenched that they could be considered organized crime. They are exploiting the chaos and lawlessness of this developing country. Victims of their tyranny are generally helpless. Law enforcement agencies are incapable of coping with the myriad demands placed on them. Police agencies are infested with co-conspirators and informants. Nearly anyone can be bought for a price. Those who can't be bought live in fear. Those who live in fear have to look over their shoulder every moment. It's a real challenge to do the right thing in Iraq.

In this country, poverty is abundant and hunger is commonplace. Having two arms and two legs is a plus. Nearly every family has been personally affected by war. Hope is a vague concept. Only life after death has any real promise. Against the backdrop of this existence, it's no surprise that so many are willing to risk so much to get so little.

"Jeff, I just had two trucks and my drivers hijacked by the Abu Hyder gang," said Bill Schmidt, director of security for SIMCO Trucking, to Jeff Katz, his old friend at Paradigm Security. "They've demanded one hundred thousand dollars and we had the money delivered to the bastards. The problem is that when we delivered the money to their guy at the border, they said we'd be contacted on where and when to pick up the trucks. I've gotta get my drivers and trucks back. Would your guys be willing to go and get 'em? You know I don't have the guys to do this." SIMCO doesn't have an internal security team; they depend solely on the U.S. military to provide security for convoy operations through Iraq. When SIMCO's two trucks were hijacked, the military basically said that recovering them wasn't their problem. Both Bill and Jeff know that reporting this to the police is a ridiculous option. The extended Hyder family "business operations" have a lot of clout and a lot of contacts. No one would dare prosecute them. Abu Hyder is the notorious top dog in the clan. In Iraq, when a man has children, his name is expanded to signify an acquired level of respect. People still use the man's given name, but in a gesture of respect they also frequently refer to him as "father of." In this case, Abu Hyder translates to mean, father of Hyder. It's common knowledge that Abu Hyder's raw materials originate from hijacked trucks. Jeff had long anticipated that it was just a matter of time before one of his own trucks would be hijacked by Hyder's thugs. A chance to actually recover the trucks and drivers is an unexpected opportunity. Jeff's only disappointment is that SIMCO had paid Abu Hyder. Jeff didn't believe in paying ransom to these guys. It just perpetuated the problem.

Jeff is a burly, no-nonsense, seasoned combat veteran with a special operations background. He is sick and tired of hearing about the abuse of U.S. citizens. His blood boils whenever he hears the stories about U.S. civilians and military units exploited and laughed at by Hyder's bandits. He knows that many Iraqis looked at the U.S. methods of handling crimes as weak and inefficient. This country is accustomed to believing that real power comes from the point of a rifle or at the entry scoop of a wood chopper. Abu Hyder knows that Americans won't do much of anything of consequence to counter his operations. But Abu Hyder never met Jeff Katz.

Jeff doesn't need to think twice. He isn't the kind of guy who would ever say no to a friend in need. If the truth be known, Jeff Katz was probably quite pumped. This is the kind of stuff he was born to do. "Tell me about it," he responds to Bill. The operation seems easy enough: make phone contact with the hijackers, link up with their contact in Nasiriyah, and pick up the trucks and drivers. This is just your run-of-the-mill hijacking. These people just want money. With any luck, the drivers will still be alive. Obviously, the truck cargo wasn't that interesting to them. Had it been, they would have just killed the drivers and taken the cargo.

That evening, as everyone is winding down from an earlier convoy run, Jeff waits for the right moment. He calls four team members into a room and closes the door. Everyone senses that something unusual is brewing. The guys in the room know that it is no accident that they have been invited to this informal get-together. Jeff starts off, "I got a call from Bill Schmidt earlier today. Two of his trucks were hijacked and both drivers are unaccounted for. SIMCO delivered a hundred grand ransom to Hyder's man at the border, but the trucks weren't anywhere to be found. Bill's asked us to recover the trucks and drivers. We're going to work out the details to recover the trucks tomorrow. This is strictly unofficial. None of you needs to go, but I need to know who's in."

Jeff looks around the room. The question is rhetorical. The team is family. If one goes, they all go—and they know it. Jeff's question is really just a pointless courtesy. Brad, Ryan, Kato, and David all nod and mumble their consent. Jeff continues, "We'll take three vehicles and put one Iraqi in each vehicle. We'll need them as shooters and translators. In the morning, we'll stage at NAVISTAR and from there we'll call the contact number for Abu Hyder. He's supposed to tell us where to meet him in Nasiriyah. They say that the trucks and drivers are somewhere in the Nasiriyah area and they'll take us to them. Then we'll head south to the Kuwaiti border and return SIMCO's trucks and drivers to Bill Schmidt. Granted, this is a vague plan right now, so on the way to Nasiriyah, we'll stop about two hundred klicks north at Tallil Air Base and try and collect more intelligence and refine the plan."

Jeff stops talking. He looks around the room. Brad is the first to speak: "What time do we roll?" "We load out at 0400," Jeff responds. David adds, "I'll get ahold of Mohammed and have him round up a couple of the Iraqis. Jeff responds, "Mohammed already knows. He'll be at the border at 0600. He's making some contacts tonight to see what he can learn about Hyder's pukes. Mohammed will be bringing Khalid and Saadoun."

The four men think about that for a moment. Then, Ryan tosses out a question, "Why Khalid? You know he's a Sunni and this whole thing could get ugly." "Hey, Khalid's been with me since I started this company," Jeff responds. "I've got no reason to believe he would turn on us. Hell, I trust him more than some of our Shiites. Besides, he hates Abu Hyder, and since Abu Hyder is a Shiite it probably works in our favor. He'll be fine." The fact that Jeff had Mohammed already putting plans in the works is interesting. It tells everyone in the room that their participation was really a foregone conclusion. Then again, maybe not, Jeff would have run this mission alone if he had to.

At 6 a.m. the team leaves NAVISTAR and crosses the border headed north. Just across the border they link up with Mohammed, Khalid, and Saadoun. Jeff gives the three Iraqi men a quick briefing. They actually seem excited about the operation, but they laughingly remark about Jeff being nuts. He says, "We'll talk more when we get to Tallil." Everyone locks and loads. The three Iraqis separate and each one jumps into one of the three SUVs. Jeff, Brad, and Mohammed are in the lead. Ryan, Kato, and Khalid are in the center vehicle, and David and Saadoun are bringing up the rear.

About a hundred miles into Iraq, Jeff's cell phone rings. The Iraqi contact says, "Oh no. Big mix-up. Not Nasiriyah. You must meet me in Safwan at the border. You come Safwan now. I wait for you." Now the team has to turn around and drive a hundred miles south back to the border. Frustrated, angered, and apprehensive, the team cuts across the highway median strip and heads back south.

Brad tells the rest of the story: "We get all the way back down to the border and we meet this guy who works for Hyder alongside the road on the outskirts of Safwan. He tells us, 'No, you must go to Nasiriyah.' By now it's clear that were getting jerked around. So Jeff says to this guy, 'I've had enough of this bullshit! We're not going anywhere. You tell Abu Hyder to meet us right here.' So the guy is all shook up and makes several phone calls. Finally the guy says, 'OK, you meet Abu Hyder's cousin at the office in Safwan. I take you there.' This was the hijackers' first mistake. Until then, we had never seen Hyder's office. So we get to Hyder's office in Safwan and meet the cousin. The cousin climbs into the car with Jeff, me, and our Iraqi interpreter, Mohammed.

"We start working everything out with the cousin. The cousin says that this is all a big mix-up and that he will call Abu Hyder and fix it. Everything seems to be coming together. After several more phone calls, the cousin says, 'You must go to Nasiriyah.' Jeff was the kind of guy who just had infinite patience. If you pushed him over the edge, he could burst out and make his point felt like you wouldn't believe. But I never saw him blow up with anyone on the team. To my surprise, Jeff just smiled and said, 'OK, we'll go to Nasiriyah.' Once again, the plan was to stop at Tallil Air Base, make contact with Hyder's group, and finalize our procedures. So we drove 150 miles back north to Tallil.

"It was about lunch time now, and we were having problems getting a good cell phone connection, so we headed over to the Italian army part of the base, Camp Mittica. They have a great pizza place. I can't say much about their soldiering but they're a lot fun to party with. When you're with the Italians they seem a lot more relaxed than the U.S. soldiers. I guess they don't take anything too seriously. Whenever one of their convoy trucks breaks down on the highway, they usually just blow it up and drive on. It's too much trouble for them to hang around and try to recover their vehicle.

"While we were wolfing down some food, Jeff continued trying to contact Hyder's group. Finally, he got through to them. The guy on the other end of the phone call says, 'It's too dangerous for you to take your vehicles to where the trucks are. You will be noticed and you will probably get ambushed on the way there.' So Jeff tells this guy OK, and they set up a time to meet us at a spot just a few miles from Tallil.

"Jeff quickly outlines a hasty plan. Jeff, David, myself, and one of our Iraqis would put on traditional Iraqi headdress. It was a pretty weak disguise, but since it would be starting to get dark by the time we did this, it might just work. We would link up with Hyder's man and get in the car with him. The rest of the team would stand by in a quick reaction force mode. We would be able to track our vehicles through a satellite tracking system and cell phone communication. The three of us would also have red star clusters as an emergency backup signal. The QRF would locate as close as possible without compromising the operation. It was a dangerous plan, but we believed that it was unlikely that Hyder was planning on killing Americans. Committing crimes and killing foreign truck drivers is one thing, but killing an American would bring down some real grief on his operation. Hyder knew it, so we decided to chance the mission.

"I took as many ammo magazines as I could stash in my gear. Then I grabbed a day pack and loaded it with another ten thirty-round mags and some additional water. We clipped on as many hand grenades as we could and brought along several light antitank weapons. We reviewed every possible scenario that could be imagined. The plan had to be flexible. There were a lot of unknowns outside of the basic objective of recovering the trucks and drivers. We headed out for the link-up point. Our plan was to arrive at the link-up point at the exact agreed-upon time. It was important that we weren't seen loitering around some intersection. Insurgents might be quick to take advantage of us as a target of opportunity.

"A half hour passed. An hour passed. Two hours passed. We called and called the phone number we had for the contact—no answer. After about two-and-a-half hours the phone rang. It was Hyder's man. The guy beat around the bush. We couldn't get any direct answers from him. Finally, Hyder's guy laid down the hammer. He wanted forty thousand dollars more, or no trucks!

"Jeff is now in a controlled rage. With pursed lips, he tells the hijackers that we will call them back. Jeff paces a moment, takes a deep breath, and calls Bill Schmidt. During the conversation with Bill, it turns out that the two SIMCO drivers had turned up somewhere unharmed. Now the only remaining issue was the trucks.

"Bill and Jeff talk. Tempers are high. They are both in agreement that forty thousand dollars more is just throwing good money after bad. This game could continue forever, and the trucks may never be recovered. Negotiations are over. The two men determine that driving around Nasiriyah in the middle of the night looking for two trucks is not a sound idea. Jeff tells Bill that we know where Hyder's offices are in Safwan and that he has an idea about how we might recover the trucks. Bill Schmidt is exasperated. His exact words are, 'Hit the motherfuckers and hit 'em hard.' At this point, that's all Jeff needs to hear." Jeff Katz had been pushed over the edge of his tolerance level. As far as Jeff is concerned, Abu Hyder is never going to take U.S. citizens for granted again.

"We all loaded up and headed back to Tallil Air Base. It was dark now and we drove over to the Tomb of Abraham, a massive pyramid-like structure at the south end of the base. I don't know if Abraham is really buried there. It seems to be a point of some contention, but it was a good spot for us to regroup and consider our next move. We decided we were going to raid Abu Hyder's offices in Safwan. We figured we'd confiscate all his documents and records that might help point the finger at his rampage of corruption. And while we were at it, if the opportunity presented itself, we'd take one or more of his relatives hostage. We didn't want to kill anyone but we knew that it was a risk. We counted on the element of surprise. Abu would never expect this.

"So, there in the sand at the base of Abraham's tomb, using our vehicle headlights, we began constructing a terrain model of the town of Safwan and Hyder's headquarters.

"The entire team participated in recollecting the town layout and the interior of the office building. It's what we call a Chinese parliament: Jeff outlined the basic plan, and each one of us threw in our two cents. Jeff and I would comprise the assault team that would actually enter Hyder's offices.

"We found an empty building nearby and rehearsed our room-clearing procedures. We did a slow walk-through at first, and then just kept repeating the procedures until we could move swiftly from room to room covering each other. Jeff and I had never cleared rooms together, but we had both been to military schools that taught essentially the same principles.

"Eventually we did full dress rehearsals at mock speed. Our guiding concept was speed and intensity. The practice runs incorporated prisoner detention and questioning. We assigned our security elements and identified each man's responsibilities for blocking all possible exits. We identified a final staging area just north of Safwan where we would wait until the right moment. By the time we finished rehearsals, it was 1 a.m. We were all in agreement; the raid would take place just before dawn.

"We redistributed ammunition, locked and loaded, and drove one hundred forty miles south through Iraq in the middle of the night. None of us could sleep. We were wound pretty tight. By the time we pulled off into the staging area twenty-five miles north of Safwan, we had all been up over twenty-four hours. Everyone had plenty of time to think about the plan. Surprisingly, there were no major changes suggested. Just a few comments to fine tune what we already knew. Jeff, being the perfectionist warrior he is, made each one of us brief him again on our individual actions at the objective. He wasn't going to leave anything to chance.

"We were running the risk of getting into a firefight with everyone: police, Iraqi army soldiers, insurgents, local militia, Hyder's security guards, and even armed neighbors [who] might think we were Ali Babas or insurgents. Our hope was to be fast and efficient. It was too risky to run a reconnaissance of the objective. We decided that about fifty yards from the building we would turn on our police light bars, headlights, and roof lights. This would hopefully deter some people from opening fire on us, but once we exposed ourselves we would have just seconds to control the entire building and its occupants. We were ready."

There is no bravado at a moment like this. There is no whining. In fact, there isn't much discussion at all. What can be planned for has been planned for. What can't be known will be discovered soon enough. This is the moment of commitment. This is the point of no return. In the history of men and women going into battle, this is the point and time that one comes to know who he or she is and what he or she is made of. This is when cowards quibble and brave men and women just nod and say, "Let's do it." And that is all Jeff Katz needed to say: "Let's do it."

The Paradigm security team and their three SUVs roll into Safwan just as the sky is starting to show signs of first light. The point vehicle and the first to arrive at the building will be Ryan and Kato. They will seal the back exit. Jeff and Brad, the assault team in the second vehicle, will enter through the main door and clear each room. David, in the trail vehicle, will provide security for the road network. He has the additional responsibility for building containment. Mohammed, Khalid, and Saadoun are now in David's vehicle. They will cover the office building windows to intercept anyone attempting to burst out. David's rear-mounted PKM machine gun, manned by Khalid, will be trained on the approach roads to greet any outsiders [who] might try to interfere.

Brad continues, "According to plan, our three vehicles stop in the center of town, at what we call the four corners. We are about five hundred meters short of Hyder's offices. Nothing is moving: no vehicles, no people, no animals, no birds. With the exception of the low rumble of our engines, everything is silent."

The team takes it all in. They visually scan the war-ravaged, dilapidated ruins that pass for buildings and homes—nothing unusual. The sand table back at the tomb had reflected the town layout quite well. At least it was close enough. From their vantage point, they can see Hyder's office. The wait is unnerving. Without anyone speaking a word, you can hear the metallic sound of rifle safeties being clicked off and into the fire position. Unconsciously, forefingers normally extended parallel to the rifle barrel begin to move onto the triggers. Finally, Jeff picks up the mike on his radio, "Execute now."

All three drivers in the SUVs hit their accelerators. They reach speeds of seventy-five miles per hour screaming down the two-lane road headed toward Hyder's building. About fifty yards from the objective, the drivers turn on their flashing red, white, and blue police light bars, roof lights, and headlights. As Ryan and Kato's vehicle peels off the road headed for the building's back door, a dust plume envelops Jeff and Brad's SUV. Jeff veers through the dust cloud, and a rooster tail of dust trails behind him. He skids to a halt just a few yards in front of the main entrance. David slams on his brakes while still on the road in front of the building. His Iraqi team leaps from the vehicle taking up firing positions. Through the now massive, billowing dust cloud, the flashing lights give the entire scene a surreal effect. Just like we had planned, everything is going like clockwork.

Even the best battle plan survives only the first five minutes of contact. After that, the side that demonstrates the greatest flexibility wins. This plan begins to unravel in the first five seconds.

Jeff and Brad jump from the car, just off to their right flank. Brad spots two human forms lying on a flatbed trailer and shouts to Jeff, "I'm taking 'em."

He runs toward the flatbed. As the two waking guards begin to rise, and as their blankets fall off them, he can see them reaching for their AK-47s lying next to where they had slept. Brad has covered the distance to the flatbed and is now just a few feet from them. He shouts at them in no uncertain terms to put their hands up and freeze. The guards are staring down Brad's gun barrel. His finger is on the trigger, and he looks pretty damn intense. The two Iraqis think better of reaching for their guns. Brad has won this draw. The men surrender.

Hyder's guards are handcuffed with zip ties. David's security team scrambles to take control of the prisoners. Jeff and Brad still have to clear the building, but now the element of surprise is gone. In a raid like this, every second counts. Any men inside the building might now be awake and waiting for them. Both men know that they could be greeted by a hail of bullets the moment the door is opened. Still, they hoped for some advantage if they could move quickly. Jeff stood to the side and kicked open the door.

"The building was really too large for a two-man clearing team, but we managed to sweep through the rooms and complete the operation in a matter of minutes," Brad reflects. "There were no people inside. Jeff and I began collecting every file and record book we could find. We stashed them into our vehicle. Heads were beginning to peer out of windows from surrounding buildings but no one approached us. We were a pretty intimidating-looking group. We had counted on that. Jeff and I, with Mohammed's help as a translator, began interrogating the prisoners.

"We tried to find out where the SIMCO trucks were. We tried to get the location of Abu Hyder's home. The guards were either lying or really didn't know. They probably knew where Hyder's home was, but it was doubtful that they knew the whereabouts of the trucks. Jeff asked them for their weapon permits. They didn't have any. Then Jeff came up with another hasty plan: we would leave one guard there to communicate back to Hyder and we would take the other with us. We had separated the two prisoners. We told the guard [who] would be left behind that if the trucks weren't returned we would turn over all of Hyder's documents and the other guard to the U.S. military. We said that the coalition will be told that the guards carry guns without permits and that Hyder's business is really a front for terrorists.

"We told the other prisoner that he was coming with us and that he would be executed by noon if the trucks weren't returned. To tell you the truth, the prisoner we were taking really took the threat lightly. He damn near laughed at us. He knew the reputation of Americans. Sure, we could kick ass, but he knew that we didn't run around executing people. This guy just wasn't gonna take us seriously. We loaded him, now blindfolded, into our SUVs and headed back north to our last staging area. During the drive, we interrogated the prisoner and tried to sound really tough. In rapid fire, Mohammed translated our comments into Arabic. At times, even I had a hard time not laughing.

"We never slapped him, kicked him, or beat him in any way. We were careful that he didn't hit his head getting in the car. We checked the zip-tie handcuffs to make sure that his circulation was OK. We gave him water whenever he was thirsty. Since our actions didn't support our words, it was getting pretty difficult to convince our prisoner that we were bad. We knew we could turn this guy into the military for carrying a weapon without a permit, but the surrounding questions could get pretty sticky. So we get to the staging area and we are all just exhausted, but now we gotta *really* figure out what we are going to do with our prisoner.

"Jeff tries to contact Abu Hyder again but with no success. So Jeff figured that a little time and some sleep might be a good idea. Hyder probably doesn't even know what happened yet. Jeff assigns watch duty, and a few minutes later most of the guys are snoring, including our prisoner. I couldn't sleep. I'm still pumped with adrenaline. I was proud of the team and reflecting on how well we had executed the raid. Besides, I was still on edge about what might happen next. Shit, this is the kind of stuff I had only dreamed about, and I wasn't going to miss any of it. Jeff and I stayed awake. Around 8 a.m., Jeff made phone contact with Hyder.

"We woke up Mohammed and he translated on the phone for Jeff. As the conversation developed, everyone was beginning to stir and collect together. Jeff shouted his threats. Mohammed translated the 'smack' into Arabic and shouted it to Abu. Abu shouted into the phone in Arabic. Mohammed shouted the translation of Abu's terse and heated remarks back to us. This went on for ten minutes. It would have made quite a show for *Saturday Night Live*.

"Jeff said we would turn over the guard and all the documents to the U.S. Army. The shouting continued. He said the army would rip Hyder's corrupt business apart. Jeff continued with threats like Hyder and his family would be broke and in jail. Hyder didn't take kindly to the verbal assault. Arabs can be quite prideful, especially if they are men of stature. Abu Hyder hung up on us. We all looked at each other. Well, shit, now what? That wasn't supposed to happen!

"On the one side of things, we had underestimated Abu Hyder. On the other side, Abu had underestimated Jeff Katz. This standoff was now ratcheted up to the next level. Jeff dialed the phone again. Abu Hyder had been steaming and still was. Hyder's anger had developed into a rage. This time Abu just laid into him. It was now Jeff who was taking the brunt of the verbal abuse. Finally, Jeff says in a relatively calm voice, 'Here's the deal: We were wrong in threatening to turn over your man and all the documents to the army. We won't do that.' Of course, all of us are watching Jeff apologetically make these remarks. We're like, huh? That's when Jeff really blew into Hyder.

"We're going to kill your man!" Jeff shouts, and it sounds believable.

"Now Mohammed is getting better and better at communicating Jeff's level of anger," Brad said. "Except for the fact that he was speaking to Abu in Arabic, he even sounded like Jeff! You really gotta hand it to these Iraqis on our team. I mean, hell, they live in the community. They'll still be there long after we're gone. I mean, talk about loyalty to us. It takes some real balls to be helping us like this!

"Jeff doesn't stop there; he's really on a roll now. He's yelling at the top of his lungs: 'I'm not *only* going to kill this guy, but before I do, he will tell me where you live. Then I'll rocket your fucking office and level it to the ground. Next, I'm coming to your house. When I'm done, there will be nothing left of your home, and I don't give a shit who's inside when I do it! I'll blow up your neighbors' homes, too, and I'll tell them this was done because Abu Hyder has stolen from Americans and you are a thief. We'll tell them that Abu Hyder is responsible for this.' Jeff suddenly spins around and jerks the prisoner to his feet. The prisoner's hands are still tied and the hood is still over his face. Jeff yells at Mohammed, who still has Hyder on the phone, 'Tell this guy that I'm not fucking around. If we don't get the trucks back, I will kill him!' Mohammed is in mid-sentence with the translation when Jeff pulls out his Glock 21, levels it on the guard's head, and pops off two rounds.

"Whoa, that got everyone's attention. I was stunned. The team was stunned. Abu Hyder's ranting on the phone stopped. Mohammed's mouth was wide open. Everyone was just frozen. That is, everyone except for the Iraqi prisoner. Jeff had fired the two rounds a few inches off to the side of his head. Our Iraqi prisoner was fine, but it was clear that he had the shit scared out of him. The guy started babbling in Arabic. His voice was cracking. He began uncontrollably shuffling his feet. To tell you the truth, I felt bad for him. This guy wasn't a terrorist. He was just some unlucky bastard [who] happened to work for the wrong person. I wasn't happy about watching someone stripped of their dignity. It was humbling. Don't get me wrong, if he had been a terrorist, I could've worked on him for days and not missed a wink of sleep. But this was different.

"Like I said earlier, if Jeff wanted to, he could really make his point felt, and he wasn't through yet. He grabbed the cell phone from Mohammed and put it up to the prisoner's mouth. All the while Jeff is yelling, 'Tell your boss we're not fooling around, you're gonna be a dead man if we don't get those trucks!' While the prisoner is shaking, stuttering, and trying to talk to Hyder, Jeff fires a couple more shots. Now the guy is just talking a million miles an hour. The whole time, Jeff's got the barrel of this .45-caliber gun pressed against the guard's head and the shots are going off right next to the guy's ear. I don't think anyone could remain stoic under those conditions. I mean, Christ, this was some heavy-duty shit going down.

"I think this guy finally believed us. It was clear that he no longer thinks that being taken prisoner by Americans is all a big joke. Now even Hyder is convinced that we're 'crazy,' and he begs us not to kill his guard. Someone said the guy was related to Hyder, but I don't know about that. Hyder pleads on the phone, 'Please, please, stop this madness. Don't kill him. I give you your trucks. Don't kill him.' Jeff calms down. He tells Hyder that we'll return the documents and his guard. We'll drop them somewhere near Safwan. Hyder says it will take a few hours to get the trucks down to the border. Jeff says, 'I'll take your word on it and we'll drop off your man shortly.' And then he adds, 'If there are no trucks, everything I said will happen.' Abu Hyder had no doubt that this crazy American would actually do it.

"We loaded up and headed south the twenty or so miles back to Safwan. We fully expected that Hyder's guys might be waiting for us with an ambush. As we approached Safwan, our three vehicles turned off the main road and we headed about seventy-five yards down a dirt road toward a farmhouse. We slowed down and stopped near a depression on the side of the road. Kids at the house saw us. As they always do, they started running toward us looking for a handout. We tossed out the documents and then rolled out the prisoner, legs and hands still tied, hood still over his head. The kids stopped in their tracks and immediately turned around. They didn't know what was going on, but when they saw the prisoner tumble out, they knew whatever it was, it wasn't good. We were crashing now. The up-and-down adrenaline rushes had taken everything out of us. Completely exhausted, we crossed the border into Kuwait. Four hours later, the trucks were delivered to the border, and, to our surprise, so was the money. We hadn't even asked for the money, but I guess Hyder must have just assumed we wouldn't be done with him until the money was back too!" Bill Schmidt's men picked up the trucks and the cash.

It was over. Paradigm Security still runs their convoys over those same roads every day. They drive through Safwan nearly every morning. At times they see Hyder's men, collected near an overpass or alongside the road. They're waiting for some unsuspecting truck to be their next catch. Not much has changed. Sometimes the Paradigm team sees the now-familiar faces of the two guards. When the two groups see one another, they wave and smile like long-lost friends, but the Paradigm convoys are never stopped. They are never harassed. SIMCO has never had another truck hijacked. The Hyder gang knows that Bill Schmidt knows a guy, and Abu Hyder never wants to meet that guy again.

V. Bomb Dogs

It's another hot day and Blek, the bomb dog, has been on guard at the front gate since early morning. He's thirsty and tired, but relaxing on the job is not in his constitution. At least a dozen times, Blek has caught insurgents trying to get in this compound. He will inspect every truck or car that attempts to enter. Lives depend on how well he does his job. He knows that sometime today an insurgent will probably try to come through this gate with a bomb-laden vehicle. At least he hopes so.

A gray Nissan approaches Blek's position and comes to a halt a few feet away. Blek studies the vehicle. The driver steps out and moves to the opposite side of the containment wall. He approaches the car. The unmistakable smell of Semtex wafts into the air. All his senses go on alert. He is clearly disturbed. His tail begins to wag furiously. Blek has hit pay dirt!

The black Dutch Shepherd from Indiana circles the back of the Nissan and begins to whimper and move excitedly. All the preliminary signs are rapidly developing. This is enough. David Carlton, Blek's handler, isn't going to wait for the dog to go down into the conclusive alert posture. He pulls on the lead and starts backing away from the car. The Iraqi guards at this entrance to the Al Sadeer complex instantly know that the driver, now standing on the other side of the containment wall, may be an insurgent. Blek is not known for false alerts.

The soldiers scramble to the safety of the containment wall, and one of them conducts a quick search of the driver. The driver is annoyed and argues with the guards. He says he works at one of the construction projects. He's got identification to prove it. Several Iraqi soldiers are designated to search the vehicle. First, they scan the surrounding area to determine if there may be an insurgent lurking nearby with a remote-control detonator. Several of the trucks and cars waiting in the line to enter the compound are about twenty-five yards behind at an earlier stop point. Without being directed, they begin to back up. Everyone knows what's going on, and it doesn't take much encouragement to get people to begin clearing the area. A couple of soldiers cautiously approach the Nissan. They study the car for trip wires. They use long-handled L-shaped mirrors to look at the underside of the vehicle. Then one of them opens the trunk.

Inside the trunk are an assortment of blankets, stuffed animals, water bottles, and other junk. An Iraqi guard carefully peels back a corner of one of the blankets. Underneath he can see a maze of wires and explosives. The bomb is ready to blow. Both guards now bolt for the safety of the containment wall. They slam the driver against the wall and yank both his arms behind his back. The insurgent knows the game is up. He is now blabbering Arabic slurs at the Iraqi guards. Blek pegged it right. This insurgent has failed. Dozens of people might otherwise be dead or maimed were it not for a dog. The irony is that most Muslims in Iraq hate dogs.

This isn't the first or the last time that David Carlton and his canine companion have found the bombs before the bombs found them. Carlton is a former deputy sheriff dog handler from Charlotte, North Carolina. He served on the Charlotte police force for more than twenty-two years. His father had been a career army soldier but David had never served, and the desire to serve his country in a combat environment had lingered with him for many years. At forty-one, Carlton was too old to enlist in the army, so he took advantage of an opportunity. A friend in the New York Police Department helped him link up with a DynCorp recruiter. David took a leave of absence from the police department and accepted a position as an explosive ordnance dog handler in Iraq.

In Iraq, David was assigned to provide security for the sprawling ten-square-block Al Sadeer military complex in Baghdad, known to those who reside there as the Pink Flamingo. The obscenely huge pink hotel, the compound's primary structure, dominates the landscape. Adjacent to the Al Sadeer compound is the Iraqi Department Of Agriculture complex. Dave comments on life inside the complex: "We live in the typical metal boxes and eat over at the hotel. Our food catering contract is with some East Indian company. Everything is curry, curry, and more curry. Every now and then, when the curry is just coming out our ears, the American contractors take over the mess hall. We cook up some American cuisine for all six hundred contractors living here.

"When I first got to Iraq, in early 2004, we routinely went on patrol in support of army operations. There was a time, early in my tour, where we would jump in an SUV, and myself and couple of buddies would ride downtown to the local shops. Not anymore! Now even a short trip to the airport requires at least four heavily armored cars and a bunch of shooters. It has gotten so much worse over the last year. No one goes outside the gate without being heavily armed and then only if you have to. Even a five-block drive has to be coordinated like a military operation."

David continues, "Blek is trained to 'alert' on fourteen different explosive components. As a very young puppy he was conditioned to distinguish these scents, and in training he is always rewarded with a tennis ball. Blek would die for his tennis ball. He loves that ball more than anything in the world. I swear, he would jump out the window of an eight-story building to get his tennis ball. When he begins to detect one of the correct scents, his tail begins wagging, he gets excited, and when he is certain of his discovery, he crouches down on all fours in the alert position. Once he is in that alert position, it damn near takes a bulldozer to budge him. When Blek knows he has found the right scent, he wants his reward!

"Part of my mission in Iraq includes conducting dog-handler training classes at the Baghdad Police Academy. Given that the Muslim culture views dogs as filthy and unclean, it is very difficult to find Iraqis [who] will even work near them. Sometimes we can find a couple of Christian police cadets [who] don't have a problem with dogs. The Iraqis treat dogs with disdain and often kick and throw rocks at them. Complicating this attitude is the fact that the sons of Saddam Hussein, Oday and Qusay, used dogs to punish errant police officers. They would chain up police officers, and then have attack dogs rip them apart. Most Iraqi people won't even look at a dog. I think our dogs don't much care for them either. Their hatred of dogs becomes a self-fulfilling prophecy. The dogs probably sense the hostility and are reacting in kind.

"While I can't prove this, I actually think that sometimes I am a lot safer *because* I'm with Blek. An insurgent suicide bomber takes one look at me and Blek, and he knows that if he detonates his explosives the dog remains will be all over him. I've heard that they believe that if they die spattered with dog parts, they will be considered unclean and unacceptable to enter heaven. Of course, I don't do anything to dissuade that line of thought. It works for me! I hardly go anywhere without Blek. Oh, and also my MP5 submachine gun, a 9mm Beretta, and a helluva lot of ammunition.

"When I first got to the Pink Flamingo, our group of contractors saw a lot of problems with the compound security. We began scrounging everything we could to build up obstacles and barriers to prevent entry of vehicle-borne IEDs. We begged, borrowed, and stole whatever we could get our hands on to build a large concrete containment wall. Eventually, we felt we had made some substantial improvements that probably would make us a real challenge for the insurgents. Some people thought we were overreacting.

"On the morning of March 9, 2005, a garbage truck with two insurgents, one driving and the other standing up and shooting, plowed into the containment wall. The wall was a major factor in the truck not getting too deep into our compound. But even at that, it was later determined that the truck was carrying over two thousand five hundred pounds of explosives—the largest vehicle bomb in Iraq that anyone had ever encountered. The blast knocked me out of bed. Seven of our guards were instantly killed, and it blew out every window in the complex. There were a lot of casualties. One of my friends lost an eye. I think we would have had a bunch more dead people if that wall hadn't been there.

"I check anywhere from one hundred to one hundred fifty vehicles entering our complex every day. The scariest moments for me are the few minutes leading up to an alert. When Blek begins to get excited my pucker factor goes way up. I have to quickly determine if he is going into an actual alert or if something else has simply stirred his senses. If a waiting insurgent were to see that my dog is about to alert, he is going to blow the load. I can't let the insurgent realize by the dog's behavior or my actions that we are on to him. The guards pretty much know that if I start backing away from the vehicle without giving it a clear, we are probably seconds away from being disintegrated. The dog handlers have a saying, 'We either have initial success, or we have total failure.' There's nothing in between.

"As I mentioned earlier, our bomb-sniffing dogs are trained to detect a lot of different components that are used in making explosives. One of those elements is diesel fuel. The problem in Iraq is that everyone uses diesel fuel for damn near everything. We have to untrain the dogs so that they stop alerting on the smell of diesel.

"Well, another dog handler and friend of mine, Gary Dodds from Tupelo, Mississippi, and his dog, Luke, were walking past a parked diesel tanker. Some U.S. soldiers were milling around the area, working on a couple of other trucks. Luke got excited and just locked up in the alert position. Gary couldn't get the dog to move. He was losing patience with the dog. Gary started scolding Luke, 'Get off it already! It's just a damn diesel truck. There's no tennis ball here for you! Don't even think about it. I thought we had gotten past this diesel problem!' Gary continued to give short tugs on the lead, but the dog wouldn't budge. Then Gary had an afterthought and gave Luke the benefit of the doubt. He decided to investigate the truck.

"He circled the truck and didn't see anything unusual, but Luke kept locking up in the alert position. Gary stepped onto the running boards and took a look inside the cab. His worst nightmare was realized. It was loaded with C-4 explosives and

155mm artillery shells. In milliseconds, Gary's brain raced with thoughts of what was about to happen. An insurgent was standing about fifty yards away with the remote triggering device. As Gary jumped off the running board, the insurgent pressed down on the garage-door opener.

"This probably wasn't the time that the insurgent had intended to blow up the bomb. He most likely had planned on waiting until more soldiers were around the trucks, but now, having been discovered, he had no choice. Besides, the explosion would be big enough to engulf everyone around for two hundred yards, and the secondary explosions of other tankers would surely make him an acceptable martyr.

"In another twist of fate, it would be the luck of the draw that the insurgent was either too far away or hadn't used a fresh set of batteries. The signal from the transmitter was too weak to trigger the bomb. Nothing happened. The insurgent had come so close to killing so many, but his trip to heaven was circumvented by an alert dog and a trusting handler."

Explosive ordnance dog teams can't prevent every terrorist bomber from hitting their target. Some U.S. security guards and their dogs have been killed while doing their job. Every morning, David Carlton realizes that this could be the last day for him and Blek. He knows that his life, in large measure, depends on his dog. So, too, do the lives of thousands of other men and women who work in the Al Sadeer complex. The Pink Flamingo is not as pretty as it once was. Nearly all the windows have been shattered by bombers hell-bent on killing people. Thanks to David and his dog, they have killed far fewer than they had hoped.

The stress of this daily existence takes a toll on everyone, and David is no exception. It's time for a week or two back home. David Carlton makes his plans to head back to North Carolina and bids farewell to his friends and his dog. David says good-bye to one of his closest friends, Vince Kimbrell. Vince, a former Spartanburg, South Carolina, police officer is also a security contractor. The two men have a lot in common and share both their law enforcement experience and now the bond of war. The armored SUVs load up, and the U.S. security team, guns at the ready, escorts David to Baghdad International Airport for the trip home.

Back at home, David catches up with family and friends, but more than anything else he misses his friends in Iraq. David remarks, "When you are in Iraq, you know that your buddies there are important to you, but you really realize just how much they mean to you and how much they have become family after you're away from them for a few days.

"I am actually looking forward to going back now. I've had enough peace and tranquility."

The day before his vacation ended, David had to unexpectedly change his return flight. He had heard word that Vince Kimbrell was also coming back home—in a coffin. Vince hit an IED and was killed instantly. David attended the funeral and paid his last respects to his old friend and Vince's family. A day later, David Carlton boarded a plane and returned to Iraq.

David and Blek reunited and got back to doing what they do best, protecting Americans. Shortly after his return, David was in the Pink Flamingo when a massive explosion rocked the building. A suicide bomber had blown up his vehicle a block away at the Sheraton Hotel. David bolted for his designated fighting position on the Pink Flamingo's rooftop. As he raced across the roof, a second bomber detonated his load. The blast knocked him back a few yards. He regained his composure, ran forward, and had only just assumed a shooting position on the roof when a third explosion knocked him into the air and momentarily unconscious. He was still delirious from the concussion, his eardrum shattered and his vision clouded, when he saw a section of a car frame lying next to him on the rooftop eight stories from the ground. He managed to move forward and again take up his position, prepared as best he could to engage the enemy— another day in the life of a bomb dog handler in Iraq.

By December 2005, the time had come for David, now hearing impaired, to arrange for his and Blek's return trip home to North Carolina. Sam Parlin Jr., a retired police officer from Garden City, Georgia, rode along with them to Baghdad International Airport. Sam had lived across the hall from David in Iraq, and the two men had formed a close bond. Sam assisted David and Blek through a steady stream of problems with different airlines unwilling to accommodate Blek. With Sam's help, David persevered in getting Blek loaded up. It was difficult saying good-bye to such a good friend, but David was hopeful about returning to Iraq one day.

Only a few weeks later, while in the U.S. awaiting delivery of his new hearing aid, David heard that Sam had been killed by a roadside bomb on the same airport road they traveled together that last day in Iraq. A few days later, two more colleagues and friends died while on duty. Through all the terrible news from Iraq, David's compulsion to return with Blek only gets stronger.

VI. The Welcome Committee

Chazz (Charles Rudolph) has a guardian angel. As a Crescent security team leader, he has been providing protection for convoys over the last six months and has never been fired upon or hit with an IED. His track record is exceptional. He likes to think of himself as a smart operator, but he also knows that he's been really lucky. Convoys have been repeatedly hit in front of him and behind him. Convoys have been attacked the day before and the day after on the same roads he has been traveling. Chazz's convoys always make it through unscathed.

"We were on Highway 2, about forty miles north of Balad (Camp Anaconda) headed for Irbil," Chazz recalls. "My team— Jason B., Mickey, and Dion—had been running these roads with me in northern Iraq for the last several months. We were a tight group. You might say that we were like brothers. The highway runs right through the center of this little town called Al Ifem. It's a blink of a place that you are in and out of in a minute or so. As we passed through the town, I was getting uncomfortable about the way people were looking at us. We were getting a lot of unfriendly glares. I couldn't put my finger on it, but things just didn't seem right. I could just feel it. The military intelligence we received on this area hadn't indicated anything that we should be concerned about, so we just kept rolling.

"As we exited the north end of the town, I heard a loud explosion. It caught me off guard. An IED detonated somewhere in the convoy behind me. I looked back and could see that Mickey, driving our rear vehicle, had been hit. His SUV was engulfed in a cloud of smoke. I had been operating in Iraq for over six months and in this area for the last two months. I guess, subconsciously, I had started to believe it was never going to happen. The insurgents had targeted our SUVs and not one of the convoy trucks. They were after Americans. Three of my operators were wounded and the vehicle was totaled. We scrambled instinctively through our ambush-reaction drill. We got the wounded out, abandoned the SUV, and headed back down to Anaconda to get some medical attention, get another vehicle, and regroup for another run north. We were shook up but we were intact and still doing our jobs. The injuries weren't terribly serious. Most of the guys would be able to make the run again the next day."

When Scott Schneider learned of the attack, he contacted another Crescent team, Team 2, led by Louie Holguin. Louie's team consisted of Kevin Avery, Jason Holmquist, and several Iraqi operators. They were about a hundred miles south of Camp Anaconda, and Scott directed Louie to head to Anaconda and link up with Chazz's guys. They were told to give Chazz whatever personnel and vehicles he needed and then to remain at Anaconda as a QRF in case Chazz developed more problems on the second attempt to get to Irbil the next morning.

Chazz continues: "So we get back to Anaconda, and aside from some medical patchwork, we were all pretty pumped about our experience. Everyone on the team was pretty happy with themselves about how well we had executed our immediate action drill, recovered the wounded, and got out of the kill zone. I was proud of my guys. They were really professional. I thought to myself, *I've finally busted my cherry in this contractor business and lived to talk about it.* In kind of a perverted way, I was really happy. I mean, imagine spending a year in Iraq as a security contractor and coming home having to say, 'I never got shot at or anything. I just drove a lot of roads.'

"It's not like I ever thought I wanted to be shot at, but stuff like that kind of lingers in the back of your mind. I guess if you gotta be attacked this was probably a good way to get it—no serious injuries and at least one personal war story. What I didn't know at the time is that over the next week I'd have a bunch of personal war stories—more war stories than anyone really needs and certainly more than I wanted." Chazz's guardian angel was about to get overworked.

Chazz continues, "The next morning we load out at Anaconda and we're headed up toward Irbil. As we approach the town of Al Ifem, we go into high alert. I'm running point. Jason B. is now riding with me. We're not about to be caught off guard. I'm expecting another attack, but I'm not expecting it at nearly the exact same place two days in a row. The blast goes off. This time it's my vehicle that's hit. My vehicle is pretty screwed up, and four of my operators are wounded or shell-shocked from the explosion. Jason and I have mild concussions and our Iraqi rear gunner has some shrapnel wounds. Small-arms fire is coming in, and we open up with suppressive fire in all directions until we are out of the kill zone. Our injuries aren't life threatening, but we were pretty screwed up this time. We needed help."

The Crescent QRF, Louie's team, hears of the attack on Chazz's group and learns that he has several wounded guys. They quickly lock and load and launch north out of Anaconda. Scott Schneider is in southern Iraq, near Basra, delivering a package to a power station. They have two SUVs. Scott is driving one and Danny is driving the other. They have a couple of Iraqis with them also. As he learns of this second attack, he knows his guys are going to need every shooter they can get. Scott drops his package at the power station and heads north at speeds more than a hundred miles an hour. What few people realize about security contracting work is that, for the most part, the contractors can't depend on the U.S. military to bail them out of difficult situations. Their first line of reinforcements in battle is usually their own people.

Scott remembers the unfolding events: "As soon as we got word of Chazz's second hit, Danny and I headed north instead of returning to Kuwait. We were on what I call a day trip, that is, we had no plans for an extended stay in Iraq. A sad fact is that I'm the one who always preached to the men to be prepared for anything. I used to say, 'No matter where you are going in Iraq or when you think you might return, always, always, take along extra clothing, ammo, food, and water. Well, needless to say, Danny and I weren't prepared for what turned out to be four days and a whole lot of sweating. Before this was over, we just called it the stink fest. We smelled so badly our eyes watered to even be close to ourselves.

"Louie brought Chazz's guys back to Anaconda. Team number two then took the wounded and the damaged vehicles and headed south for Kuwait. I intercepted Louie on the road while I was headed north. We stopped and talked for a while. Team two brought me up to speed on the enemy activity up north and the status of Chazz's remaining men. Louie had left one of his men, Salty, and a vehicle up at Anaconda. We were going to have to make another attempt to get the convoy to Irbil, and now we would have my two vehicles and Salty's SUV. I radioed Chazz and told him not to move until I got to Anaconda. When I got to Anaconda the next morning, I met with Chazz. He said that he and his men were ready to go north again. I wasn't so sure.

"I spent the day with Chazz's team. They all confirmed that they were willing to make the third attempt. But what I saw in their eyes said otherwise. I decided not to take them. They had been through enough for now. The following morning, I had to tell Chazz that I wasn't taking what was left of his team. Instead, our security shield would consist of Danny, Salty, a couple of our Iraqi shooters, and myself. We would take the three vehicles and leave Chazz's guys to rest up and lick a few wounds. Several days had passed since Chazz's team had hit the second IED. Intelligence reports told us that the area was infested with insurgents and several more convoys had since been attacked in the Al Ifem area. The convoy and their supplies were badly needed in Irbil and this is our mission. No one ever discussed not going at all. We developed a new strategy and tactics that I can't reveal, but we arranged the trucks and loaded up again. The last thing I remember the military intel guys said to us was, 'Expect to get hit.'

"Knowing you are going to get hit, but not having a clue as to where, is pretty unnerving. To further complicate matters, we were told that the insurgents were using radio-activated IEDs, so we would have to observe strict radio silence in the high-danger areas. Our adrenaline was high and we were all doing our own thing to control our fear. As we approach the village of Al Ifem, I can see the stretch that we now call the killing zone. About three kilometers of the road ahead are pockmarked with huge potholes from explosions that have been taking place all week. We initiate our new tactics for getting through this stretch of the village but we are moving very slowly. I am white knuckled and crunched down in my seat. Danny is in the lead vehicle, I'm in the center of our five-truck convoy, and Salty is in the rear. I see people milling around and hope that this is a good sign. We get through about two-thirds of the danger zone, and for some unknown reason, Danny's SUV just stops, right there, still in the killing zone!

"Danny's about one hundred yards in front of me, and still stopped. I'm thinking to myself, *Damn it, Danny, keep moving*. I try to make light of my terror by mumbling to myself, 'I know you're not stopping to shoot pictures. Damn it, just move!' I don't dare use the radio. I just have to sit there and trust that Danny knows what he is doing. I can see Danny pointing at a cluster of vehicles and some homes at about fifty yards, at ten o'clock to his left front. I'm thinking that this has got to be a secondary ambush and we are sitting in the middle of the primary ambush right now. Did Danny just take sniper fire from there? I look back and I can't see Salty's SUV at the rear of the convoy. What happened to Salty? With no communications, fear of the unknown is close to killing me. Pounds of perspiration are pouring off my body. My eyes and lips are soaked with salty fluid dripping off my forehead. I figure that whatever is going on has got to be real bad, because Danny would never just stop like this. He's like sitting right on top of an IED crater.

"Finally, I can't take it anymore. I pull out of the convoy and race up alongside Danny. Just as I get parallel to his vehicle, he begins to move, so I drop back into formation. We pass the cluster of cars and buildings. I prepare myself for small-arms fire and I'm expecting that at any second I will see the flash and hear the boom of an IED. I swallow hard. It's all I can do to keep from just opening fire at everyone standing by the cluster of vehicles. The idea that you have to wait for them to shoot you before you can shoot back is a concept of this war that, at moments like this, is very hard to accept. Nothing happens. About a mile past the town, the convoy pulls over and stops. We all get out to discuss what happened. God, we needed that break. Although no one would ever admit it, I think we all needed to change our underwear. So why did Danny stop right smack in the kill zone? His air filter had plugged and the engine coughed out. We always carried spare air filters, but team number two had needed the one out of the car they left, and in the changeover of drivers and cars we hadn't realized that we were missing the spare filter. That mistake could have cost all of our lives. It didn't this time, but we'll never make that mistake again."

The next morning Scott's team takes another convoy back south to Anaconda. Once again, they confront the challenges of getting back through Al Ifem. It's another dicey trip, but their new tactics work and they make it to Anaconda without incident. Chazz and his team greet them. They are glad to see their buddies back, but you can sense now that this Anaconda-to-Irbil run is their responsibility, not Scott's. They want their mission back. In a way that only men and women in war under-stand, they are anxious to prove themselves and not be bested by some other group. This is their turf.

Chazz has had to replace a couple of Iraqi shooters, but the men who have just been assigned to his team are good men. Crescent is a small company. Chazz knows all of these guys. They have had about a week to rehearse their immediate-action drills, review procedures, and assign responsibilities. They are healed, rested, and anxious. Chazz's team is ready to hit the road. Franco and Scott discuss the missions. Scott gives the green light to the team. Chazz, Mickey, Dion, and Jason B. roll out the gate with another convoy.

Chazz thinks to himself, *Third time's a charm*. Chazz and Mickey are in the point vehicle. Mickey is driving. Chazz rides shotgun. An Iraqi called Bob is in the second row behind Mickey, and Ageel, another Iraqi, is the rear gunner. Tensions are high, but the team is in good spirits and is confident that they will make it this time. Chazz and Mickey, both former marines, are best friends. They pass through Al Ifem without incident. The two men take a deep breath. They have confronted their fears and overcome them. They radio Scott that the convoy has cleared Al Ifem.

Chazz recalls what happened next: "Our convoy was now about fifty miles north of Al Ifem. We were still on high alert and not taking anything for granted when we rounded a curve and noticed a dump truck stopped in the oncoming traffic lane of this narrow two-lane road. As we were just about to pass by the truck, a second dump truck pulled out from behind the stopped one and headed directly at us in our lane. Mickey tried to swerve onto the shoulder, but there just wasn't any time or space to avoid the collision. I knew in an instant that we were going to be hit. I didn't feel any fear; I just watched the event unfold in front of me. The collision was more violent than I had expected. It's hard to say exactly what happened in the following seconds, but when the crashing sounds of steel and glass ended, the dump truck was on its side and on top of our vehicle.

"I was still conscious. I could feel a lot of pressure on my back and I couldn't move my head. The roof of our Chevy Avalanche had collapsed and pinned my head against the dashboard, and my legs were crushed up against my chest. Every part of my body hurt, but all I could think of was that I had to get out. I called out to Mickey. He was alive but he couldn't move either. Then Jason showed up and yanked my side door open. I told him, 'I can't move.' I remember him saying, 'I know, dude, you have a dump truck on your head.'

"I could only see out of one eye. Blood was streaming

over the other eye and obscured my vision. Finally, I was able to move my head a bit, but every time I did, torrents of blood washed down my face. Now I was starting to feel real fear. I was begging everyone to get me out. This wasn't good, and my fear was starting to induce shock. Jason was by my side trying to comfort me. Jason is such a hard ass about everything that his being consoling almost had the reverse effect. I mean, if this guy is being warm and fuzzy, I must really be screwed up. Whenever he walked away, even for a moment, I started hyper-ventilating. It was so strange because I was thinking clearly and I knew I was going into shock but I couldn't stop myself. I started throwing up.

"I had to get out of this damn truck. Trying to free myself from this pinned position, I jerked my head toward the driver's side of the car as hard as I could, and in the process, cut another gash in the side of my skull. But the effort worked and I was able to be pulled from the wreckage. Until that moment of freedom, I thought I was going to die. You wouldn't believe how happy I was to be outside of the vehicle. Jason pulled me up, and in sort of a dry kind of humor said, 'It's good to see you Chazz.' It took about forty-five more minutes to free Mickey from the driver's side. He was OK, with only a cut above his eye. Ageel, our rear gunner, had a few scrapes but he was gonna be alright. Bob, our Iraqi shooter in the back seat, had taken the full impact of the dump truck. He was killed instantly. My jinx on this road was getting to be a bit much.

"Mickey and I spent some time in the hospital and several weeks recovering. Around this time, Dion had been promoted to a team leader and there were several other personnel changes. My team now consisted of Boomhower, Festus, Ricco, and

Mickey. We made the run to Irbil, and this time, finally, we made it without any casualties. So I figured our run of bad luck was over. The next day, on the way back through Al Ifem, you know what happened? We hit another IED. This time it was Boomhower [who] got hit. We were lucky enough to have only minor injuries and just another vehicle totaled. We've now made four attempts at this round-trip and been hit all four times. We never saw the enemy. We never killed any bad guys. We just kept getting blown up. After each explosion, as we were trying to get out our wounded and get the hell out of that town, you could see crowds of people just watching us. They stare, they point, some laugh. As soon as the shooting stops, the scavengers come out of the woodwork ready to pick any vehicle carcass clean. I wonder what they say to each other. I wonder what they think.

"Nothing pisses me off more than an enemy that won't face you," exclaims Chazz.

The team's frustration had built to a boiling point. As with all men and women in combat who continually experience casualties from an invisible enemy, they reach a point where they are overwhelmed with the need to exact revenge. During the Vietnam conflict, Lieutenant William Calley's platoon had been decimated for months by land mines, booby traps, unseen mortar rounds, snipers, and hit-and-run ambushes. When Calley's platoon entered the village of My Lai, they thought they had finally surrounded the enemy. They hadn't, but in the frenzy of the moment, and the burning desire to find and kill the enemy, many unarmed civilians were killed. Soldiers and armed security contractors are supposed to be above such fits of rage.

In conflicts like Vietnam, Somalia, Afghanistan, and Iraq, it is nearly impossible to differentiate between good guys and bad.

If a boy has a garage door opener or a cell phone in his hand, is he a good guy, or a bad guy about to detonate an IED? Never shooting a noncombatant is an easy requirement for academics, politicians, and pundits to pontificate about from the comfort of their lounge chairs. It's entirely another matter for the men and women who watch their friends get blown apart every day. Until now, Chazz's team had somehow managed to contain their anger. Something had to give. They couldn't just keep doing the same thing over and over again and experiencing the same result. As Chazz says, "We were becoming nothing more than ducks in a shooting gallery."

A few days passed, and Chazz, Boomhower, Festus, Rico, and their Iraqi operators were back on the road again. Mickey had to sit this one out. Chazz recalls the mission: "We all knew the dangers around Al Ifem, especially Boomhower, who had been pretty banged up during the last IED. So we planned this trip at a different time. Our hope was to pass through Al Ifem around prayer time. This might catch the insurgents off guard and buy us a narrow window of time to get through the town.

"As we slid through the town, there was an uncomfortable silence. The only thing we could really hear was the call to prayer echoing through Al Ifem. There were almost no vehicles or people on the street. Now and then a vehicle approached us and we threw a water bottle or broke the silence with a warning shot. For a moment, I thought the plan had failed. It just seemed like any second, holy hell would break loose, but nothing happened. I did notice that I had unconsciously slid toward the center of the car. I guess I was just getting myself ready for the door to be blown off. The plan worked, this time.

"We got to Irbil without a problem, but we knew that on

the trip back the same plan wouldn't work twice. Our real concern now was how to get back to Anaconda the next morning. We were sure they'd be waiting for us. We had to pull something new out of the hat. We knew that the only way we were going to live was to be more creative and more aggressive than they were. It was time to get real inventive.

"At the warehouse in Irbil, our team sat down to plan the return. We weren't taking any chances. First, we would leave later than the normal time. Then just outside of Al Ifem we would stop the convoy. Our four SUVs would pull out in front. I would run ahead at point and clear out any traffic on the road. The other three SUVs would move forward ahead of the convoy in a triangular formation. The flank SUVs would be off the road cutting across open terrain. Ricco would run left flank, with Boomhower on the right. Festus would lead the convoy through the first section of the gauntlet.

As the convoy moved through the urban section of Al Ifem, the flank vehicles would look for possible insurgents hiding on either side of the road. Insurgents waiting to detonate IEDs often hide in these areas, fifty to a hundred or so yards off to the side. The convoy trucks had to stay on the road itself. If necessary, the flank vehicles were instructed to fire warning shots at anyone lurking behind a building or berm. About midway into the town, Ricco, Boomhower, and Festus would stop and establish a protective shield around the convoy. When the main body of trucks passed through the security screen, I would lead them a few miles up the road and the rest of the guys would fall in to protect the rear of the convoy. We all agreed—there couldn't be anything timid about this run. Basically, it was, 'When in doubt, light 'em up.'

"So we're about twenty miles from Al Ifem and we stop at an Iraqi police checkpoint. They tell us that an Iraqi police vehicle was just ambushed in Al Ifem. We continue on and stop at another police checkpoint. This time we are just a couple of miles from Al Ifem. They confirm the attack on the Iraqi police. The police vehicle had hit an IED and when the officers tried to get out of their vehicle they were taken under fire by machine guns. All five police officers were killed.

"The convoy rolled south, and now we were about a half mile from the town. According to plan, we stopped the convoy. Our four SUVs pulled up to the front. I called Crescent head-quarters and told them where we were and gave them an idea of what we were about to do. We had a good visual on the town. We could see the smoldering ruins of the Iraqi police vehicle. I wondered if their bodies had been removed. I wondered if the insurgents had dragged them through town in some kind of cele-bratory display. I couldn't help but to pity them, while at the same moment hoping that we wouldn't meet the same fate.

"All of us looked toward the town making mental notes of routes we would take and objects and people that were going to have to be moved. A couple of guys took a perfunctory piss. No one likes going into battle with a full bladder. We shuffled a few grenades, double-checked ammunition, tightened down some straps on our personal gear. We talked briefly about the danger spots that posed the greatest threat. I took a swig of water. I looked at my team. Pucker factors were as high as they have ever been. We were all trying to stay as calm as possible. We all knew what we were about to get into. I said in a very calm voice, 'You guys ready?' 'Yep' was all I recall hearing. I said, 'Alright, let's do this shit.'

"Without another word, everyone loaded up. We rolled into Al Ifem. As we closed on the town, I saw more and more IED craters. Every twenty yards there was another crater. I guess I wasn't the only unlucky bastard to have passed through this place. Shit, the road was like the face of the moon. I was out in front of the security triangle. Vehicles started to slow in front of me. I just plowed them off the road. Then I noticed that vehicles were coming from all directions and swerving and slowing right in front of me.

"I had no doubt about it: they intended on slowing us down enough to detonate their bombs and take us under fire. Vehicles began coming in from the side roads and conveniently stopping on the main drag. I opened fire on them, blasting out their rear and side windows. They were clearly trying to box us in. Finally, they got the message: we weren't fucking around this time. Cars and trucks started clearing the road and heading in reverse to get out of my line of fire. This may have been the first time the insurgents ever took us seriously.

"They were driving off the road and into garages. Garage doors were closing; people were ducking into buildings. Usually, they just stand around and watch us get blown up. We were almost to the center of town, and I radioed the team that this looked like a good spot to establish the security screen. Ricco pulled his vehicle up on the left flank. Boomhower was on the right. Just as Ricco stopped, he reported seeing armed civilians on the rooftops. I guess this was part of the Al Ifem welcome committee. They were probably the same guys [who] killed the Iraqi police officers a few hours earlier. We weren't about to give them a chance to get a good shot at us. We opened fire on the surrounding buildings.

"Ricco, Boomhower, and Festus were all engaged in laying down a shield of suppressive fire. Bullets were coming down at us from all sides of the road. They struck the ground around our feet, and dozens of little pops of dust were kicked up. Ricochets glanced off of rocks and cars and whizzed in every direction. You could hear the sound of safety glass shattering on car windows. Now and then an RPG rocket blew past us and we could only hope that it didn't hit one of our convoy trucks. On the rooftops we could see what looked like sticks waving in the air. They were AK-47s poking up to fire at us.

"Our Iraqi machine gunners in the rear of the Avalanches began a systematic back-and-forth stream of bullets raking across the top edges of the buildings. Their barrels were overheating, they were red hot, but there was no time for a pause or a barrel change-out. If they melted down or we had a cook-off, well, shit happens. As we fired into the buildings, our backs were to the main road. The convoy continued to move through the center of this firestorm. I'm sure our truck drivers were scared to death, but none of them backed out. Not one of them hesitated, stopped, or started to turn around. They did what we had asked of them and kept rolling. We shot our way all the way out of town and cleared the south end of Al Ifem.

"On the way out, Ricco's vehicle got pretty shot up and one of his tires was blown out. He limped his car out of the worst of the kill zone. Boomhower provided security for Ricco while Festus and I provided security for the main convoy. When Boomhower and his operators jumped from their SUV to set up protection for Ricco, they noticed that their vehicle had been seriously perforated with bullets, but it still ran and that's all that mattered. Ricco made a tire-change operation that was damn near as fast as a pit stop at the Indy 500.

"I reported the enemy contact to headquarters. I told them that we had received fire and had to return fire to get through the town. We delivered the convoy safely to Anaconda. I don't know if we killed any insurgents. I don't know we if killed or wounded any innocent civilians. I don't know if there is such a thing. It's hard for me to imagine that Al Ifem really has any 'innocent civilians.' I do know that Al Ifem was ready for us in a big way. I do know that if we hadn't executed the mission the way we had, we probably wouldn't be alive. If there are any armchair quarterbacks out there [who] have a better method, let them make a drive through that hellhole.

"That day, when we drove through the town, it was like it was a completely coordinated event for the townspeople. It seemed like every person and every vehicle was playing some part in the attack. I think, for those people, blowing up Americans is a sports event. How do you explain that back in our country? I hope my guardian angel doesn't have a statute of limitations. I have another convoy to run tomorrow."

So many Americans, both civilians and soldiers, have been risking their lives to give democracy a chance in Iraq. Nearly everyone I met or otherwise interviewed for this book was trying their best to make it work, but many expressed doubts. One U.S. instructor who served at the Jordanian police academy commented, "You must understand that these Iraqis don't have allegiance to their fellow countrymen. It's not like the feelings an American would have toward another American. As long as the person is not affiliated through tribal, family, religious, or personal friendship, they don't seem to have much compassion for other Iraqis. Their world is much smaller. Few of them can relate to national objectives. Even fewer believe anything will change in their lifetime."

In light of this lack of nationalism or sense of connection to fellow countrymen, it should come as no surprise that enemy fighters blow up their own citizens in the marketplace, on the buses, or inside of mosques. While writing this book, I marveled at how some Iraqis working for U.S. security contractors had no compunction about opening fire on other Iraqis. At first, I thought it was because they were determined to defeat the insurgents. In retrospect, I wonder how much of it is about money and power. Sides can change quickly in that country. If you are not family, then you had damn well better be the highest bidder.

There are many credible reports of both Iraqi military recruits and police cadets, after having completed their training, selling their uniforms and equipment and disappearing. Some are just not interested in the job. Some are lazy. Others will serve only in their own community. Still others are known to have defected to the insurgents. Some were insurgents to begin with. The common denominator among these quitters and defectors is that they are not motivated to fight for their country. Their interests are far more personal. The number of "trained" soldiers and police officers is very deceptive. The numbers by themselves tell us nothing. More than anything else, those who remain in the service of their country are poorly led.

The only clear winners in this conflict to date are the Kurds. After many years of oppression by the Iraqi Arab population, they are unquestionably motivated, and they take their military training seriously. Many Kurds believe that one day, the Arab Shiites and Sunnis will again turn against them, and they are quietly preparing for that day. The Kurdish people from northern Iraq have had a taste of their long-awaited freedom, and they have no intention of returning to the previous condition—even if that means having to create their own fortress-like country within Iraq. Because of this, the Kurdish-populated military units are often the most combat-ready of all Iraqi military units.

Further complicating our effectiveness to transition Iraq into a democratic form of government is the nature and conditioning of the people. Democracy may be theoretically attractive, but as a practical matter the Iraqi people simply aren't used to it. People gravitate toward what they know, and what they know in Iraq is that you respect power. This is best summed up in an article written by Elaine Grossman, a writer for *IPW News*. She quotes Middle East expert Hisham Melhem, "Americans have lost *haiba*." Haiba is an Arabic term for a combination of "respect and intimidation." Saddam had haiba. The Iraqis have centuries of conditioning to respond only to those who have haiba. Once you have lost haiba, it is difficult to command respect anywhere in Iraq.

Ted Weekley, of the Jordanian police academy, was right when he said to Donna Kerns, "We're planting seeds." I have no doubt that we are making progress, but perhaps it's like trying to walk up a down escalator. Can we get to the top in any reasonable time frame? Is the job bigger than we are? Is the commitment required longer than anything our government recognizes? It is not that we cannot democratize Iraq, but can we devote the time, money, and lives it may take to implement our vision in that region of the world? Democracy has two very important components: The first, free elections, are taking place with remarkable participation, and that is certainly encouraging. However, the second component, respecting the outcome of those elections, remains to be seen. Many of the soldiers and civilian contractors I met while writing this book truly believe that we will achieve our goals. They have worked so very hard and risked so much. I hope they are right.

Civilian contractors are as necessary on the modern battle-field as soldiers. Whether by design or by default, the United States' wartime strategy now requires large numbers of civilians to go into harm's way. The call to duty echoes beyond the recruiting stations and draft boards. It reaches past the career soldiers, the teens, and the young men and women who wear U.S. uniforms. It reaches into every U.S. industry, every skill, every age group, and every gender and race. The civilian men and women who have answered this call are unrecognized and unappreciated patriots.

Throughout this book we have seen the attenuated problems of an ambiguous policy concerning the deployment, protection, and application of civilians supporting a war effort or covert national objectives. The potential for abuses by overzealous and uncontrolled civilian contractors is abundantly clear. No question, the use of civilians in war has both the potential for good and the potential for bad. It is a matter of policy and organization that can harness the good and limit the bad.

Our ability to anticipate and prepare the military for future conflicts is impaired and challenged by the rapidly changing nature of war, types of potential adversaries, developing technologies, and the sheer number of dissimilar requirements for the use of military force. These exigencies will require vast numbers of civilian contractors on short notice. In many cases, civilian contractors will be less expensive and more efficient than the deployment of regular military units.

Weapons of mass destruction, once thought to be in the exclusive realm of high-intensity conflict, are now a possibility at every level in what the military refers to as the spectrum of conflict. Biological warfare, until recently dismissed as highly unlikely, is now a real probability. Cyber attacks against our banking and economic infrastructure are in the planning and development stages. Religious networks are known to provide direct and indirect support to our enemies. Enemy sympathizers and active combatants live in our neighborhoods, go to our schools, and plan our demise. Our enemies operate in horizontal, and often, independent networks. They employ the latest communication technologies, which are now readily available on the open market. They are able to change methods of operation and adjust to our tactics very quickly.

To respond to these ever-broadening threats, many civilians will be required to participate in the defense of our nation, whether at home or abroad. Nation building in the aftermath of war has become, by our choice, a necessary consequence of our military forays into other countries. Civilian carpenters, electricians, technicians, truck drivers, police officers, cooks, and clerks will be recruited in droves. In the next conflict, we may need computer experts, bioengineers, nuclear physicists, and hazardous-waste-disposal experts. The military cannot conceivably maintain the personnel resources to respond to such a wide variety of threats and reconstruction requirements. These requirements are not all entirely new. Civilians have always been required in post-war reconstruction, but the breadth and scope has changed. And, most importantly, the assumption that these tasks can be accomplished in an environment of relative peace is no longer applicable.

One only needs to Google the term civilian contractors to see how maligned and often despised these men and women and their firms are in the eyes of so many journalists and pundits. Not all of the bad press about defense contractors is unwarranted. Undeniably, some firms have been caught with their hand in the till. Several are under investigation, and some have been found liable for fraud. Improved controls on doling out money to military contractors are desperately needed. However, when disaster strikes, even natural disaster, the rapid flow of money frequently has to take precedent over caution. We will have to deal with the corrupt as best we can later.

The Iron Pony Express civilian truck drivers don't think of their job as glamorous. They don't see themselves as heroes. They just see themselves as a bunch of middle-aged men and women helping soldiers do their job in a war zone. They are the old guys who bring the food, mail, and clothing to our young soldiers in combat. These truckers are confused and frustrated as to why the U.S. government prohibits them from carrying weapons. In October 2005, four U.S. civilian truckers made a wrong turn in the wrong Iraqi town. Two were killed in a hail of bullets, another, after being captured, was executed with a bullet to the back of the head. The fourth truck driver was soaked in gasoline and lit on fire. Mark Taylor (Ugly Puppy) went ballistic. He wrote a scathing article for *Land Line* magazine (a trucking industry publication) asking why this happened. Why weren't those men armed?

Hundreds of U.S. civilian contractors have been killed in Iraq and thousands have been wounded. As a percentage of the total number of Ameicans killed in Iraq, the number of civilian contractors killed and wounded is probably quite shocking. It seems that no one knows exactly what those numbers are. The U.S. government claims to not maintain an accountability of dead and wounded contractors. Contracting firms are generally quiet about the numbers. Strange how the U.S. government can provide figures on how many Iraqi civilians have been killed but have no idea of how many U.S. civilians have died. It's a lot of subterfuge to disguise the true number of U.S. casualties. This practice is dishonest to the public and unfair to the U.S. contractors and their families who have made such a major contribution to the war in Iraq.

In the course of writing this book, I interfaced with hundreds of individual contractors. I met them here in the States, in Kuwait, and in Iraq. I met dozens of their family members. They all wanted their story told. I have never heard one mumble a word of disrespect or resent the attention given to soldiers. To the contrary: they have greater respect and admiration for the U.S. military than most people in the United States.

In most past conflicts, there has been some rear area or some safe haven where both soldiers and civilians could periodically relax and enjoy themselves between major combat encounters. For the civilian contractors in Iraq, who operate outside the wire, there is no such thing. Day after day, month after month, they are risking their lives. As long as they are in country, they run missions every day of the week. There is rarely a day off that they can spend inside the wire. A close call today is history by morning, and each new day will bring another close call, injury, or death.

When death or serious injury does occur, civilian contractors have an unceremonious return home. Even when they come home in one piece, if they share their experiences with friends or neighbors, inevitably they get harangued with questions like, "Why would you go to Iraq? Are you crazy? Do you have a death wish? Are you that desperate for money?" They soon tire of the abusive questions and just avoid discussing the subject. Their closest friends are the civilians and soldiers they served with in Iraq. The difference is that our soldiers will, in most cases, be respected for their participation. Our U.S. civilian contractors deserve nothing less.

Appendix

Security and Training Companies in Iraq

AD CONSULTANCY

www.portaliraq.com/showbusiness.php?id=419

Services: Risk and threat assessment as well as close-protection teams/ bodyguards for personnel in Iraq. Travel and escort security to and from oil and gas facilities as well as surveillance and countersurveillance.

"We support a wide range of clients, such as embassies, law enforcement, military customs, oil and gas companies, financial institutions, cargo organizations, and constructions companies."

Headquarters:

ADC House, PO Box 153, Sutton, Surrey SM39WF, U.K.

Tel: 0870 707 0074, Fax: 0870 707 0075

e-mail: security.services@adporta.com

Contact in Iraq: Ian Grealey, Tel: 0870-707-0074

AEGIS DEFENCE SERVICES

www.aegisdef-webservices.com

Services: Involved in maritime security. Aegis has a contract to provide seventy-five teams of eight men each for security on major Iraqi government projects such as oil and gas fields and water and electricity supplies. Aegis has four divisions focusing on risk analysis, research and intelligence, risk mitigation, strategic protective security, maritime security, and defense assistance.

> *"We have a global reach and work for clients in many sectors including insurance, reinsurance, telecommunications, media, shipping, and logistics. We also provide consultancy services to selected government bodies and international institutions in Europe, the Middle East, Far East, and the Americas."*

Headquarters:

118 Piccadilly, London W1J 7NW, U.K.

Tel: 44 20 7495 7495, Fax: 44 20 7493 3979

e-mail: info@aegisdef.com

Contact in Iraq: Lieutenant Colonel Tim Spencer: 703-343-8136

AIRSCAN

www.airscan.com

Services: AirScan was created in 1989 to provide airborne surveillance security for U.S. Air Force launch facilities. Provides ground, air, and maritime surveillance equipment.

> *"AirScan is a private military company [that] is committed to providing clients with the best air, ground, and maritime surveillance, security, and aviation possible. AirScan strives for professional, timely results in response to clients' worldwide airborne surveillance and aviation requirements."*

Headquarters:

AirScan, Inc., 3505 Murrell Road, Rockledge, FL 32955

Tel: 866-631-0005/321-631-0005, Fax: 321-631-5811

e-mail: airscan@airscan.com

AKE LIMITED

www.akegroup.com

Services: Security risk specialists who provide not only armed security services but also hostile-regions training, political security, intelligence and cultural briefings, and a secure database of security risk and intelligence information. Believed to be employing Australian SAS teams in Iraq.

"In today's uncertain world, the security of businesses and professionals is at a premium. In a high-risk geographical, legal, or technological environment you need to know how to protect your investment, facilities, staff, and yourself. Otherwise, the result could be failed projects, reduced efficiency, additional costs, injury, illness, and even death, along with high insurance premiums."

Headquarters:

AKE Asia-Pacific Pty, Ltd., Level 4, 201 Miller Street, North Sydney, NSW 2060, Australia

Contact in Iraq: Peter Hornett, Tel: 66(0)2 9025 3525

e-mail: operations@akegroup.com

AMA ASSOCIATED LIMITED

www.ama-assoc.co.uk

Services: Security consultancy, aviation security, maritime security, training services.

"AMA Associates Ltd. provides training and consultancy in the following: risk and crisis management; fraud investigation; surveillance; technical counter-surveillance; security management; counter terrorist and hostage release; maritime security; aviation security and air cargo security at all levels; close protection and executive management, and management of aggressive behavior."

Headquarters:

AMA Associates Ltd., PO Box 130,

Chorley, Lancashire, PR7 3GA, U.K.

Tel: 44 (0) 1257 231172, Fax: 44 (0) 1257 231173

e-mail: info@ama-assoc.co.uk

Contact: Sharon Ripley, Business Development Manager

AMERICAN INTERNATIONAL SECURITY

www.aisc-corp.com

Services: Executive protection, crisis management, event security, strike management and security, vulnerability assessments.

"AISC offers a comprehensive set of security services that identify vulnerabilities and implement procedures to reduce and eliminate these risks—all from one trusted source. Drawing from an extensive array of available personnel and services, AISC will develop a highly customized security program for your organization."

Headquarters:

AIS, 60 State Street, Suite 700, Boston, MA 02108

Tel: 617-523-0523, Fax: 617-367-4717

e-mail: info@aisc-corp.com

APPLIED MARINE TECHNOLOGY

www.amti.net

Services: Training and security, corporate security, exercise management, SOF CBRNE, EOD, and IED operations, and integrated information solutions.

"Provides government and private sector customers with professional and technical services in international and homeland security,

266

information systems and communications, and the rapid prototyping of unique technical solutions. This includes the test and evaluation contract for the Predator UAV drone."

Headquarters:

Applied Marine Technology, 2900 Sabre Street, Suite 800,

Virginia Beach, VA 23452

Tel: 757-431-8597, Fax: 757-431-8391

e-mail: desteph@amti.net

Contact: Bill DeSteph, Vice President, Business Development

ARMOR GROUP

www.armorgroup.com

Services: Armor Group operates in Mosul, Baghdad, and Basra, and has ongoing operations throughout Iraq. They provide major corporate and government clients in Iraq with risk assessment and management. Operations include guarding Baghdad headquarters and transport depots of U.S. conglomerates Bechtel and the Halliburton subsidiary KBR.

"Private military company with practices in security planning and management, training, mine action, response center, kidnap and ransom, humanitarian support, information business intelligence and fraud, and intellectual property asset protection."

Headquarters:

25 Buckingham Gate, London SW1E 6LD, U.K.

Tel: 44 20 7808 5800, Fax: 44 20 7233-7434

email: info@armorgroup.com or jmillar@armorgroup.com

Contact in Iraq: John Farr, MBE, Country Manager

Tel: 0088 216 511 20010, e-mail: jfarr@armorgroup.com

ATHENA INNOVATIVE SOLUTIONS

(formerly MZM, Inc.)

www.athenaisinc.com

Services: Veritas Capital acquired MZM through its subsidiary, Athena Innovative Solutions. Athena has a contract to provide linguistics support services. They also provide witness protection services for the Iraqi Provisional Authority witness protection program.

> *"Provides a wide range of consulting services to homeland security clients that complement the company's expertise in intelligence operations, counterintelligence, systems and data management, program management, national security, intellectual and technical development."*

Headquarters:

1523 New Hampshire Avenue, N.W., Washington, DC 20036
Tel: 202-518-5240, Fax: 202-518-5241

BH DEFENSE

www.bhdefense.com

Services: BHD works for the Coalition Provisional Authority Program Management Office. Services in Iraq include providing secure warehousing, logistics support, and convoy escort.

> *"BH Defense has a strong network of partners and allied businesses in Iraq. Through close cooperation with network partners,*
> *BH Defense can offer comprehensive solutions including logistics, airfreight, construction, life support, ground transport, and advanced distribution services."*

Headquarters:

BH Defense, LLC, 2300 9th Street South, Suite 503

Arlington, VA 22204

Tel: 703-553-0561, Fax: 703-553-0562

e-mail: info@bhdefense.com

BLACKHEART INTERNATIONAL, LLC

www.bhigear.com

Services: Provides equipment procurement services, security, and training
to military, law-enforcement agencies, and private clients. It has been
providing these services since 1999. The bulk of its consultants and contracts
are former special operations personnel who were trained on military and
nation-building-related subjects.

Headquarters:

114 East Erie Street, PO Box 10, Linesville, PA 16424

Tel: 814-683-1048, Fax: 814-683-1048, e-mail: support@1stoptacticalgear.com

BLACKWATER USA

www.blackwaterusa.com

Services: Blackwater USA consists of five separate business units:
Blackwater Training Center (the largest private firearms and tactical training
center in the United States), Blackwater Target Systems, Blackwater
Security Consulting, Blackwater Canine, and Raven Development Group.
Blackwater also has relationships with their strategic partners, Aviation
Worldwide Services and Greystone Ltd.

*"We are not simply a 'private security company.' We are a professional
military, law enforcement, security, peacekeeping, and stability*

operations firm who provides turnkey solutions. We assist with the development of national and global security policies and military transformation plans. We can train, equip, and deploy public safety and military professionals, build live-fire indoor/outdoor ranges, MOUT facilities, and shoot houses, create ground and aviation operations and logistics support packages, develop and execute canine solutions for patrol and explosive detection, and can design and build facilities both domestically and in austere environments abroad."

Headquarters:

850 Puddin Ridge Rd., Moyock, NC 27958

Tel: 252-435-2488, Fax: 252-435-6388

e-mail: hr@blackwaterusa.com

BRITAM DEFENCE, LTD

www.britamdefence.com

Services: BritAm was awarded a contract for providing security cover for a humanitarian visit to Basra and Baghdad by executives from Demag Delaval Industrial Turbomachinery Ltd., a wholly owned company of Siemens.

"Our focus is to use our management's considerable expertise in counter-terrorism, insurgency, and public security situations to give clear and objective advice to our clients and provide solutions to their requirements. Whether it is for advice, practical assistance, or training support, the selection of the most appropriate security consultancy is of paramount importance. With our wide spectrum of first-hand experience in a variety of challenging situations, we at BritAm are confident that we have the pedigree to make a real difference."

Headquarters:

BritAm, Marvic House, Third Floor, Bishop's Road

London SW67AD, U.K.

Tel: 44 207 61001111, Fax: 44 207 3859311

e-mail: baghdadoffice@britamdefence.com

CACI

www.caci.com

Services: Homeland security, systems integration, managed network services, information assurance, engineering and logistics, intelligence solutions, knowledge management, vision and solution center.

> *"CACI has rapidly grown into a world leader in providing timely solutions to the intelligence community. Engaged across a wide range of national intelligence disciplines from the most complex space-based operations to human source intelligence, we help America's intelligence community collect, analyze, and share global information in the war on terrorism."*

Headquarters:

CACI House, Kensington Village, Avonmore Road

London, W14 8TS, U.K.

U.S. Headquarters:

1100 North Glebe Road, Arlington, VA 22201

Tel: 703-841-7800, Fax: 703-841-7882, e-mail: rhart@caci.com

CARNELIAN INTERNATIONAL RISKS

www.securitypark.co.uk

Services: Carnelian provides interventions that address conflicts in three distinct responses. 1) Preventive deployment: close protection of key personnel, security drivers, information protection, and/or conflict negotiators. 2) Fact Finding: gathering appropriate evidence to bring the conflict to an end. 3) Advice: Support or advice management on additional conflict factors.

> *"Our services are aimed at domestic and international organizations that may be subjected to all forms of conflict as a result of changing economic, civil, military, or terrorist factors. In such cases where there may be some risk of conflict arising from financial, political, social or environmental factors, Carnelian where possible will operate on behalf of the affected party by negotiating a resolution to the conflict situation. In situations where the conflict is non-negotiable, we will deploy alternative interventions in order to help bring the conflict to an end."*

Headquarters:

Carnelian International Risks, 4 Lubards Lodge

Rayuleigh, Essex SS69QG, U.K.

Tel: 44 1245 380 683, Fax: 44 1245 382 894

e-mail: enquires@carnelian-international.com

CASTLEFORCE CONSULTANCY LTD.

www.portaliraq.com/showbusiness.php?id=464

Services: Provides security services with focus on Iraq.

> *"Route surveys of major and minor supply routes (MSRs) throughout Iraq to include establishment of checkpoints, rally points, alternate routes, communication dead spaces, local checkpoints, coalition checkpoints, and GPS route mapping and tracking data. Fixed-site security surveys. Established Iraqi security contacts*

throughout Iraq to include contacts with the Ministry of Interior, police chiefs. Northern Iraq Peshmerga Militia Forces, Northern Iraq KDP and PUK political contacts, established and proven Iraqi informants, Iraqi Civil Defence Corps (ICDC), Iraqi Facility Protection Services (FPS), Iraqi National Police (INP), and numerous Iraqi private security firms."

Headquarters:

CFC, Town Lane, Bebington, Wirral CH63 5JF, U.K.

Tel: 32 48445 8672

CENTURION RISK ASSESSMENT SERVICES

www.centurion-riskservices.co.uk

Services: Hostile-environment training, emergency first-aid training, specialist first-aid training.

"Centurion prepares people both mentally and practically for dangerous work in extreme conditions. These people are usually in the news media, international organizations, humanitarian aid agencies, charities, and other non-governmental organizations (NGOs), and commercial businesses."

Headquarters:

Centurion, PO Box 1740, Andover, Hants, SP11 7-E, U.K.

Tel: 44 0 1254 355255, Fax: 44 0 1264 355322

COCHISE CONSULTANCY, INC.

www.cochiseconsult.com

Services: Cochise is pursuing contracts in security and VIP protection for major U.S. companies doing business in Iraq. They have a contract to help provide security for an ammunition-clearing operation.

> *"Cochise Consultancy Inc. specializes in planning, implementing, and managing security and training programs for government and commercial clients worldwide."*

Headquarters:

5202 Silverado Way, Valrico, FL 33594

Tel: 813-643-0022, Fax: 813-643-1007

e-mail: cochiseconsult@aol.com

COMBAT SUPPORT ASSOCIATES

www.csakuwait.com

Services: Divided into three companies, CSA provides logistics, maintenance, technical support, security, and environmental support services. They also support military testing and training activities.

> *"The CSA partners currently have projects at a dozen OCONUS locations where they provide technical training, base operating support, supply services, logistics and infrastructure support, transportation, and environmental support. The three companies have a combined global workforce of seven thousand employees and revenues exceeding one billion dollars."*

Headquarters:

CSA Human Resources, Unit 69905, APO AE 09889-9905

Tel: 965-486-5338, Fax: 800-783-3220

e-mail: csajobs@kuwait.com

CONTROL RISKS GROUP

www.crg.com

Services: Hires armed guards to protect officials from Whitehall, aid workers, and businesses. CRG has an office in Baghdad providing clients with a range of services including security management, discreet armed protection, and information support.

> *"Control Risks has thirty years of experience in successfully advising clients about the risks they face and the solutions they can implement. This expertise is called upon by companies, governments, and nonprofit organizations all over the world. We group our skills into ten service areas that together can address the issues that your organization is confronting."*

Headquarters:

83 Victoria Street, London, SW1H OHW, U.K.

Tel: 44 20 722 1552, Fax: 44 20 7222 2296

Contact in Iraq: James Blount, Country Manager,

Tel: 914-822-9502, e-mail: james.blount@control-risks.com

CRESCENT SECURITY

www.crescentsecurity.com

Services: Convoy escort, personal protection services, site security, medical training.

> *"Crescent Security operates a 'Hybrid' Security Company, offering clients a choice of 100 percent Western Security Operators or a mix of Iraqi and Western operators dependent upon client requirements. Crescent utilizes modified and up-armored civilian vehicles utilizing the latest technology to provide tracking and communications, ensuring total peace of mind to clients with sensitive cargo*

movements or VIP escorts. Crescent Security employs professional
former military and specialist law enforcement personnel. Many of
whom have specialist courses and qualifications specific to the
security business and transportation."

Headquarters:
Crescent Security Group, PO Box 4584
Kuwait City, Kuwait 13046
Tel: 965-390-3184, Fax: 965-390-3164
e-mail: group@crescentsecurity.com
Contact in Kuwait: Scott Schneider

CRITICAL INTERVENTION SERVICES

www.cisworldservices.org

Services: CIS is a protection firm operated by experienced security professionals, whose backgrounds include law enforcement, corporate security, intelligence, and force protection/antiterrorism. They also have a staff of consultants with expertise ranging from crime prevention through environmental design (CPTED) to chemical and biological terrorism. CIS professionals also act as regular consultants for the news media.

"CIS has provided protective services for high-profile individuals,
including Senator Bob Dole, actor Steven Seagal, news anchorwoman
Paula Zahn, talk show host Sally Jesse Raphael, and civil rights leader
Archbishop Desmond Tutu, and to governmental agencies, such as
the Florida Department of Insurance during fraud investigations and
court-ordered receiverships."

Headquarters:

Critical Intervention Services, 1261 South Missouri Avenue

Clearwater, FL 33756

Tel: 727-461-9417, 800-247-6055

Hillsborough: 813-910-4247

Fax: 727-449-1269

24-hour operations center: 813-221-1911

Contact: Debra Osmun, e-mail: cisdoc@cisworldservices.org

Employment: 727-461-9417

Contact: Lesley Palmer, e-mail: employment@cisworldservices.org

CUSTER BATTLES

www.custerbattles.com

Services: Global risk consulting, security services, business intelligence, litigation support, emergency support services, explosive detection. Security services include life supports, construction, logistics, transportation, and personal security details.

> *"Custer Battles offers personal security detail (PSD) to provide close protective escort support to client personnel in hostile environments. The service includes a 'meet and greet' upon arrival, transportation to the clients' facilities, and protective armed PSD accompaniment when required."*

Headquarters:

Custer Battles, 8201 Greensboro Drive, Suite 214

McLean, VA 22102

Tel: 703-356-2424, Fax: 703-356-3001

e-mail: cbaumann@custerbattles.com

DECISION STRATEGIES (part of Vance Global)

www.decision-strategies.com

Services: Specializes in all aspects of corporate, criminal, and financial investigations, background and due-diligence inquiries, security audits, protecting proprietary information, and gathering litigation intelligence.

> *"Our highly trained consultants and operational personnel have strong backgrounds as former law enforcement officers within federal agencies, the military, and private sector firms, and have undertaken assignments in more than eighty countries. Our executive protection agents receive rigorous training in logistics and protective operations, weapons proficiency, emergency medical response, evasive driving, tactical communications, surveillance recognition, and special intelligence."*

Headquarters:

Decision Strategies, 31 Old Burlington Street, 2nd Floor
London W1S 3AS, U.K.

U.S. Headquarters:

33 East 33rd Street, New York, NY 10016
Tel: 800-759-7402 Fax: 212-935-4046
e-mail: nick.copeland@vance.spx.com

DILIGENCE MIDDLE EAST

www.diligencellc.com

Services: Risk advisory consulting, competitive due diligence, close protection, site security, and security escort services for multiple international clients and contractors

> *"Whether in Iraq or Yemen, and from Saudi Arabia to the United Arab Emirates, DME provides our clients with a wealth of experience and a*

*far-reaching network of sources and contacts. DME's mission is to
ensure our clients in the Middle East have the information, analysis,
connections, and security that they need to minimize risk and make
the most profitable and efficient business decisions."*

Headquarters:

Diligence Middle East, 1275 Eye Street, NW

Washington, DC 20005

Tel: 202-659-6210, Fax: 202-659-6210

Contact in Iraq: Ken Josey, Country Manager

Tel: 914-822-9746, e-mail: kjosey@diligenceiraq.com

DS VANCE IRAQ:

www.iraqitradecenter.com/companies/?inc=comvw&coid=162

Services: General security, convoy protection, close protection, and asset
protection. It is recognized by the Coalition Provisional Authority as a "force
protection" security company.

*"We can deploy a variety of specialist teams to serve and protect
personnel and assets. Our international specialists and/or local
security staff provide the following range of security services:
Executive close protection (CP) and crisis response. Executive escort—
cross border from Jordan or Turkey into and out of Iraq. Convoy
protection—specialists for cross border and in-country convoys.
Protective advance reconnaissance—routes, buildings, access points.
Facilities security and asset protection—site security guards for all
sizes of facilities."*

Headquarters:

DS Vance Iraq, 31 Old Burlington Street, London W1S 3AS, U.K.

DYNCORP INTERNATIONAL, LLC

www.dyncorprecruiting.com

Services: DynCorp, purchased by CSC, is involved in a wide variety of Iraqi military and police training as well as security operations.

> *"We provide major support to protect American diplomats and diplomatic facilities as well as key allied leaders in high-threat countries. We provide services to eradicate illicit narcotics crops and support drug-interdiction efforts in South America and Afghanistan. We are engaged in the removal and destruction of land mines and light weapons in Afghanistan. We have vast international experience and operate on all continents except Antarctica. Our business office in Dubai serves the Middle East region, where we've operated for some thirty years."*

Headquarters:

CSC, 132 National Business Parkway

Annapolis Junction, MD 20701

Tel: 866-472-1837

EOD TECHNOLOGY

www.eodt.com

Services: EOD is on contract to the U.S. government to dispose of tons of unexploded ordnance in Iraq. They also provide security for oil fields in southern Iraq.

> *"Our range of expertise includes risk assessment, demining, range residue and scrap processing and disposal, target replacement, construction support, security, environmental sampling, geophysical survey and investigation, geographic information system development, and public relations and community involvement."*

Headquarters:

EOD Technology, PO Box 24173, Knoxville, TN 37933

Tel: 865-988-6063, Fax: 865-988-6067

e-mail: eodt@eodt.com

ERINYS INTERNATIONAL

www.erinysinternational.com

Services: An expatriate Iraqi-based security service employing thousands of Iraqi security guards under the direction of former British and South African soldiers. In addition to protecting oil infrastructure, they provide personal protection for U.S. Army Corps of Engineers personnel service, indigenous or expatriate, encompassing overt high-threat environments.

> *"Erinys can provide a global personal protection through to more covert scenarios requiring tact and discretion. Operatives, male and female, are fully trained and, where applicable, their weapon-handling skills and counter-surveillance techniques are current. In all cases individuals act within the law of the country in which they are deployed and abide by appropriate regulatory requirements."*

Headquarters:

Erinys Middle East, Old Bank Building, Deira, Dubai, U.A.E.

Tel: 971 4 22 33 646, Fax: 971 4 22 70 099, e-mail: uae@erinysinternational.com

GENRIC

www.genric.co.uk

Services: Genric has constructed a secure facility in the Basra region of Iraq. They provide armed site security and armored and nonarmored vehicles for hire or purchase.

"Genric UK Ltd. assists with security and risk assessment by providing an assessment of security threats that may affect the client's operating aims allowing them to be effective in the proactive and reactive risk management of their business."

Headquarters:

Genric, Hereford House, East Street, Hereford, HR1 2LU, U.K.

Tel: 44 1432 379083, Fax: 44 1432 370786, e-mail: nick.duggan@genric.co.uk

GLOBAL RISK STRATEGIES, LTD.

www.globalrsl.com

Services: Security, logistics, and facilitation services in post-conflict Iraq. Company employs many former British army Gurkhas and is working under several U.S. defense contracts for personal and facility security.

"We offer strategic level consultancy, assessment, and project management services in challenging environments. Our proven record of performance includes: management of the Voter Registration Election Programme in Afghanistan; providing security services in Iraq; delivering logistical support to commercial oil and gas extraction projects in Africa; designing specialist insurance and finance products."

Headquarters:

GRS, 6 Stratton Street, London W1J 8LD, U.K.

Tel: 44 20 7491 7492, e-mail: info.uk@globalgroup.com

Contact in Iraq:

Tel: 964 790 2517315, e-mail: info.iraq@globalgroup.com

GLOBAL SECURITY SOURCE

www.esi-lifeforce.com

Services: At last report, Global Security is affiliated with Executive Security International and is engaged in providing guards and personal protection for the American embassy in Iraq.

> *"ESI is the oldest intelligence-based executive protection, bodyguard training academy in the world. ESI offers two thousand hours of peer-reviewed certification programs for protection and security specialist in special operations, executive protection, protective intelligence, and investigation. ESI's premier program, security specialist combines our core training curriculum in intelligence and protection into on integrated program."*

Headquarters:

ESI, Gun Barrel Square, 2128 Railroad Ave.

Rifle, CO 81650

Tel: 888-718-3105, e-mail: ESI@esi-lifeforce.com

GROUP 4 FALCK A/S

www.group4falck.com

Services: Static and mobile guards, close protection, and air marshals.

> *"Group 4 Securicor forms one of the largest global networks of security operations worldwide, with 360,000 full- and part-time employees. Group 4 Securicor operates in more than one hundred countries on six continents."*

Headquarters:

Group 4, Falck A/S, Panchwati, 82-A, Sector 18

Gurgaon 122016 (Haryana), India

Tel: 91 124 2398888, Fax: 91 124 2397131

e-mail: reg.office@group4falckmesea.com

Contact in Iraq: Abrahem Ghazarian

Tel: 971508131680, e-mail: brahem@group4falckmesea.com

HALO GROUP

www.halointernational.com (website offline)

Headquarters:

Halo Group, PO Box 1095, Clayton, CA 94517

Tel: 888-997-3275

e-mail: info@halointernational.com

HART SECURITY

www.hartsecurity.com

Services: Marine counter-terrorism, maritime interdiction, intervention forces, internal security, customs, and border control.

> *"We bring extensive international experience in counter-terrorism and internal security to the task of training national security forces. Hart has a recognized track record in recruiting and training local forces and populations to meet identified security needs and provide solutions. Forces established and developed by Hart continue to serve governments and companies around the world."*

U.K. Headquarters:

Tel: 44 (0) 207 751 0771, Fax: 44 (0) 207 384 0501

U.S. Headquarters:

Hart Security Inc., 1750 Tysons Blvd., 4th Floor

McLean, VA 22102

Tel: 703-744-1345, Fax: 703-744-1344

HENDERSON RISK, LTD.

www.hrlgroup.org

Services: Security, political risks analysis and control, crisis and contingency planning.

> *"HRL provides rapid response to increasing security threats: this could mean the hardening of existing security programs or it could mean managing the evacuation of company personnel from a volatile environment."*

Headquarters:

Henderson Risk Ltd., 7 Barton Buildings, Old King Street

Bath, BA1 2JR, U.K.

Tel: 44 (0)1225 470099, Fax: 44 (0)1225 448566

e-mail: info@hendersonrisk.com

HILL & ASSOCIATES, LTD.

www.hill-assoc.com

Services: This firm has been in Iraq since June 2003. They have offices in Baghdad and are focused on providing clients in Iraq with services to include executive protection, information services, and security audits.

> *"Members of Hill & Associates' executive protection team have a strong police and counter-terrorism background and are specially selected for their expertise, experience, and proven integrity. Detailed planning and appropriate deployments surround the client with a reassuring safety zone."*

Headquarters:

Hill & Associates Ltd., 2201-05 Shell Tower, Times Square, 1 Matheson Road

Causeway Bay, Hong Kong

Tel: 852-2802-2123, Fax: 852-2802-2133

e-mail: info@hill-assoc.com

ICP GROUP, LTD.

www.icpgroup.ltd.uk

Services: Personal security, corporate security, corporate training, investigations and intelligence collection, and high-tech security.

> *"Executive close protection, individual escort and teams. Harassment and stalking threat management. Personal protection and safety training for individuals, staff, and family. Spouse and family safe escort, domestic and overseas. Event security management. Risk profiling surveys and assessments for VIPs and key personnel."*

Headquarters:

2 Old Brompton Road, London SW7 3DQ, U.K.

Tel: 44 0 207 591 4411, Fax: 44 0 207 584 1460

e-mail: iraq@icpgroup.ltd.uk

ISI

www.isiiraq.com

Services: Secure services, communications, secure housing, and logistical support across Iraq.

> *"ISI has been a specialist in the field of Iraqi security since spring 2003, after winning the Baghdad Convention Centre contract. The first post-invasion contract was to supply and vet an all-Iraqi team to provide round the clock security alongside coalition forces within the Green Zone."*

Headquarters:

ISI Baghdad Compound, Al Mansour, Baghdad

Tel: 964 1 541 7668, e-mail: admin@isiiraq.com

JANUSIAN SECURITY RISK MANAGEMENT, LTD.

www.janusian.com

Services: Founded by a former British SAS soldier, Janusian has been providing security details in Iraq since April 2003.

"As companies find themselves increasingly confronted by inventive and aggressive new security threats, Janusian offers a genuine alternative in security risk management. Our reputation is for challenging the conventional, and for delivering solutions that are innovative, flexible, and effective."

Headquarters:

Russell Square House, 10–12 Russell Square

London WC1B 5EH, U.K.

Tel: 44 0 20 7578 0009, Fax: 44 0 20 7578 7855,

e-mail: general@janusian.net

KROLL SECURITY INTERNATIONAL, LTD.

www.krollworldwide.com

Services: Kroll Security has a contract to protect USAID employees in Iraq.

"Kroll's experts in security, protection, engineering, business continuity, and emergency management help clients prevent, prepare for, and respond to the many threats they face at home and abroad."

Headquarters:

Kroll Security, 900 Third Ave., 7th Floor, New York, NY 10022

Tel: 212-593-1000, Fax: 212-593-2631

MANTECH INTERNATIONAL CORP

www.mantech.com

Services: Maintains a telecommunications base in Iraq.

> *"ManTech is one of the U.S. government's leading providers of innovative technologies and solutions for mission-critical national security programs supporting the Department of Defense, the intelligence community, the Department of State, the Department of Justice, the Department of Homeland Security, and other federal government agencies. Our expertise covers software development, enterprise security architecture, information assurance, intelligence operations support, network and critical infrastructure protection, information technology, communications integration, and engineering support."*

Headquarters:

ManTech, 12015 Lee Jackson Hwy., Fairfax, VA 22033, Tel: 703-218-6000

METEORIC TACTICAL SOLUTIONS

Services: Reportedly this South African firm has had several contracts with Britain and Switzerland to provide security services for installations inside of Iraq. At one time, they had a contract with the United States to assist in the training of Iraqi police. Two owners of the company, Hermanus Carlse and Lourens Horn, were arrested in Zimbabwe for their part in a coup attempt in Equatorial Guinea. Information concerning their current status is not readily available.

Contact in Iraq: Lourens Horn (Louwtjie) Tel: 914-360-3113
e-mail: louwtjieh@hotmail.com

MEYER GLOBAL SECURITY, INC.

www.meyerglobalforce.com

Services: Provides personal security, intelligence, kidnap and ransom operations, convoy escort and executive protection, helicopter transportation, and airborne operations. Meyer reportedly boasts the ability to interface directly with insurgent groups.

"Operating as a private military company we provide complete security and protection services for government organizations and private sector companies including executive protection, bodyguards, security guards, convoy escorts, and all risk-management components. We have transportation available including 4x4 SUVs, sedans, armored and rapid response vehicles as well as aircraft support."

Headquarters:

Meyer Global Security, 105 N. Main, PO Box 1800
Joshua, TX 76058
Tel: 817-426-1199, Fax: 817-558-4868

MPRI

www.mpri.com

Services: MPRI is a division of L3 Communications. Their primary focus in Iraq, Jordan, and Kuwait is the training of coalition force military units, Iraqi army soldiers, and Iraqi police cadets. They also provide Arabic interpreters.

"We serve the national security needs of the U.S. government, selected foreign governments, international organizations, and the private

sector with programs of the highest standards and methodologies of proven effectiveness. Our core competencies center on security sector reform, institution-building, the development of leaders at all levels, training, education, and emergency management."

Headquarters:

MPRI, 1201 E. Abingdon Drive, Suite 425

Alexandria, VA 22315

Tel: 703-684-7114, Fax: 703-684-3528

e-mail: info@L-3com.com

OLIVE SECURITY, LTD.

www.olivesecurity.com

Services: Provides extensive security services throughout Iraq. Services include convoy escort, personal bodyguards, key point security, site survey, threat and risk assessment. Major client is Bechtel.

> *"We protect affluent and high-profile individuals and sports teams through security measures tailored to the client's unique requirements based on an extensive assessment of their lifestyle, daily regime, place of residence, office, and other activities. We also manage every aspect of security for international travel."*

Headquarters:

Olive Security, 2 Charles Street

Mayfair, London W1J 5DB, U.K.

Tel: 44 0 207307 0540, Fax: 44 0 207307 0542

e-mail: info@olivegroup.com

OPTIMAL SOLUTION SERVICES

www.portaliraq.com/showbusiness.php?id=360

Services: Security guards, personal protection, convoy escort.

> *"Our emphasis is on maintaining the highest industry standards with our security personnel adhering to safety and health regulation and best work practices."*

Headquarters:

Optimal Solution Services, 4/35 Spencer Street

Fairfield NSW 2165, Australia

Tel: 61297555840, Fax: 61297559835

OVERSEAS SECURITY & STRATEGIC INFORMATION, INC./ SAFENET-IRAQ

Services: Personal security, convoy escorts, training for local security personnel, threat and intelligence reporting, and provision of combat medics and equipment.

> *"We provide in-country 'hands on' management of highly trained and experienced South African security personnel by former U.S. intelligence officers with paramilitary backgrounds. Services include close protection of VIPs, general personal security of employees, convoy escorts of personnel and equipment, training of local security personnel, provision of armored and unarmored vehicles, threat and intelligence reporting, and provision of combat medics with proper equipment. Our approach is responsive, personalized, and cost-effective."*

Headquarters:

OSSI, PO Box 52067, Atlanta, GA 30355

Tel: 404-307-4072, Fax: 413-208-6069, e-mail: ossiinc@hotmail.com

PILGRIMS GROUP

www.pilgrimsgroup.co.uk

Services: Security officers, dog services. Specialties include training the media to cope with challenges in dangerous countries.

> *"Our management and our training teams have been carefully selected from a wide range of backgrounds including special forces, military, police, customs, security services and other complementary backgrounds. This gives us a comprehensive experience and knowledge base from which our procedures, advice, and systems are developed."*

Headquarters:

Pilgrims House, PO Box, 769, Wokin, Surrey GU21 5EU, U.K.

Tel: 44 0 1932 349 943, e-mail: security@pilgrimsgroup.com

RAMOPS RISK MANAGEMENT GROUP

www.ramops.com

Services: Security services, close protection, site security, communications security, information technology security, uniformed security, risk assessment.

> *"All RamOPS security consultants have military special operations or federal security service backgrounds; they are also required to maintain their training in order to recognize emerging threats and advances in the industry. All RamOPS security personnel have military or law enforcement backgrounds augmented with training from today's top security academies."*

Headquarters:

RamOPS, 7312 Hihenge Court, Suite 8, Raleigh, NC 27615

Tel: 919-740-4597, e-mail: careers@ramops.com

RONCO CONSULTING CORPORATION

www.roncoconsulting.com

Services: Mine clearing, security services, environmental remediation. Ronco is also involved in training Iraqi mine-clearing teams.

"Ronco Consulting Corporation, involved in the design and implementation of mine clearance operations since 1989, has developed an integrated humanitarian demining system that is highly accurate, safe, and cost-effective in mine-infested countries."

Headquarters:

Ronco, 2301 M Street, Suite 400, Washington, D.C. 20037

Tel: 202-785-2791, Fax: 202-785-2078, e-mail: jobs@ronco.com

RUBICON INTERNATIONAL SERVICES

www.rubicon-international.com

Services: Asset protection, personal protection, investigation and intelligence, security training.

"Whatever the security challenge, we can provide a combination of intelligence and threat assessments, security surveys, staff training, technical security equipment, and contingency planning to equip you with the inner resources needed to be confident that you are ready to react."

Headquarters:

Rubicon, 70 Upper Richmond Road, London SW 15 2RP, U.K.

Tel: 44 0 20 8874 0055, Fax: 44 0 20 8874 5522

e-mail: info@rubicon-international.com

SALADIN SECURITY

www.saladin-security.com

Services: Bodyguards, security officers, security consultants, crisis management.

> *"Using its specialist knowledge, Saladin has the capability of looking at the situation from a terrorist's point of view to identify the weaknesses which would be exploitable. In addition, the company utilizes past experience to recommend the most appropriate technology and equipment to counter such weaknesses."*

Headquarters:

Saladin Security, 7 Abingdon Road, London, W8 6AH, U.K.

Tel: 020 7376 2655, Fax: 020 7 937 5805

e-mail: saladin@saladin-security.com

SCG INTERNATIONAL RISK

www.scgonline.net

Services: Provides security, intelligence, technical, and training solutions.

> *"SCG International Risk provides the highest caliber security personnel available. Our people are recruited from the world's elite military organizations and further trained to provide your organization with services unmatched by any other risk mitigation firm."*

Headquarters:

SCG, PO Box 6671, Virginia Beach, VA 23456

Tel: 757-689-2148,

Fax: 703-995-4550,

e-mail: info@scgonline.net

SOC-SMG

www.soc-smg.com

Services: International force protection, personal security details, convoy security operations, security consulting, and threat assessment training.

"Our core services include international force protection, consulting, security services, armed protection, threat management, investigation, and large-scale security operations. We provide clients with comprehensive solutions to special problems. These include counter-terrorism expertise, surveillance, electronic countermeasures, explosive device detection, and weapons of mass destruction (WMD) specialties, covert video, overseas special operation protective teams, and intelligence gathering, among others."

Headquarters:

SOC-SMG, 2393 Heybourne Road, Minden, NV 89423

Tel: 866-369-9100, 775-783-9366,

e-mail: employment@soc-smg.com

STEELE FOUNDATION

www.steelefoundation.com

Services: Business investigations, executive security, behavioral sciences, crisis management, information security, environmental services.

"The Steele Foundation specializes in the areas of physical threat assessments, social contingency planning, crisis management, architectural and personal safety and security, information and intelligence management, and corporate program development."

Headquarters:

Steele Foundation, 388 Market Street, 5th Floor

San Francisco, CA 94111

Tel: 415-781-4300, e-mail: info@wwwsteele.com

SUMER INTERNATIONAL SECURITY

www.thesandigroup.com

Services: Infrastructure development, logistical support, security teams, contracting services. Sumer International Security has been prominent in providing security for media teams.

> *"In Iraq, Sumer International Security has held a prominent role in real estate development and trading for over a century. This responsibility has been handed down through the generations and today's leadership is ably continuing Iraq's infrastructure improvements and modernization efforts."*

Headquarters:

SIS, 1733 Connecticut Avenue NW,

Washington, DC 20009

Tel: 202-483-5900, Fax: 202-438-9710

e-mail: contact@thesandigroup.com

TITAN CORPORATION

www.titan.com

Services: L-3 Communications has acquired the Titan Corporation, which provides translators for U.S. agencies operating in Iraq.

> *"L-3 Communications Titan is a leading provider of comprehensive information and communications products, solutions, and services for national security. Serving the Department of Defense, intelligence agencies, and other government customers, L-3 Communications*

Titan's business focus includes homeland security, transformational programs, enterprise information technology, and C4ISR technology."

Headquarters:

Titan Corporation, 3033 Science Park Road, San Diego, CA 92121

Tel: 858-552-9500, Fax: 858-552-9645

TOR INTERNATIONAL

www.torinternational.com

Services: Security and crisis management, convoy protection, executive escort, first-aid training, facilities security, emergency evacuation.

"We assist people on the ground by facilitating, supporting, protecting, and by simply getting things done behind the scenes when others cannot. We help their organizations by increasing efficiency and productivity and by improving personnel retention."

Headquarters:

TOR, PO Box, 3455, London WC1N 3XX

Tel: 44 0 20 419 8753, Fax: 44 0 207 831 9489

e-mail: enquiries@torinternational.com

TRIPLE CANOPY, INC.

www.triplecanopy.com

Services: Security services, assessment, training.

"Triple Canopy excels in executive protection, site security, and convoy security. Our operators have an average of more than twenty years in the most elite military special operations units and are the highest quality personnel in the industry. Our services range from discreet

travel companions to heavily armored, high-profile convoy escort. From security assessments to tactical training to direct security work, Triple Canopy has the solution."

Headquarters:

Triple Canopy, 2250 Corporate Park Drive, Suite 300, Herndon, VA 20171

Tel: 703-673-5000, Fax: 703- 673 5001

UNITY RESOURCES

www.unityresourcesgroup.com

Services: Security consulting, training, and support services.

Recently purchased Security Solutions–Asia.

"Emergency Medical services, emergency supply chain management, insurance options for complex/hostile environments, medical evacuation key personnel extraction, operational communications and IT infrastructure, project verification, monitoring, and evaluation, remote technical survey, satellite tracking, secure logistics, specialist protective security services, specialist procurement and equipment supply, water purification."

Headquarters:

Unity Resources, Level 6, 140 George St.

Museum of Contemporary Art Building

Sydney, NSW 2000, Australia

Tel: 61 2 9252 5259, Fax: 61 2 9252 5258

U.S. Contact:

Mike Fiacco, Tel: 314-244-1501, e-mail: mfiacco@unityresourcesgroup.com

USA ENVIRONMENTAL

www.usa-environmental.com

Services: Location, identification, removal, disposal, and avoidance of unexploded munitions. This firm has teams of weapons and explosive experts in Iraq.

> *"USA Environmental, Inc. (USA) is a small business that is solely focused on providing munitions response services, including characterization and remediation of federal and nongovernment sites that are contaminated with munitions and explosives of concern (MEC)."*

Headquarters:

5802 Benjamin Center Dr., Suite 101, Tampa, FL 33634

Tel: 813-884-5722, Fax: 813-884-1876

e-mail: cbirner@usatampa.com

VANCE INTERNATIONAL

www.vancesecurity.com

Services: Provides security for multinational companies doing business in Iraq. Additionally, they provide security for their client companys' visiting executives and their employees.

> *"Vance Iraq has managed the security of client projects throughout Iraq since 2003. Current tasks include protecting a multitask telecommunications project for a major European engineering company, providing executive protection for a U.S. consulting company, and securing multiple worksites for an international power company. We are specialists in the north of Iraq and have offices throughout, such as Erbil and Sulaymaniyah, along with a representative Baghdad presence."*

Headquarters:

10467 White Granite Drive, Oakton, VA 22124

Tel: 703-385-6754, 800-533-6754, Fax: 703-359-8456

e-mail: info@vancesecurity.spx.com

VINNELL CORPORATION

www.vinnell.com

Services: Vinnell, a division of Northrop Grumman, has a major contract to train the Iraqi army. Vinnell advertises that they can conduct combat service support training, command and control training, live-fire exercises, after-action reports, field medical training, and training support.

> *"Vinnell Corporation is a recognized leader in facilities operation and maintenance, military training, educational and vocational training, and logistics support in the United States and overseas. Since its modest beginnings during the Great Depression, Vinnell has successfully completed projects on five continents and in over fifty countries for a variety of government and commercial customers."*

Headquarters:

Vinnell, 12150 Monument Drive, Suite 800

Fairfax, VA 22033

Tel: 877-270-8339, Fax: 703-218-5230

WADE-BOYD & ASSOCIATES

www.wade-boyd.com

Services: Provides armed close-protection teams and K-9 dogs for explosive detection and armored vehicles.

> *"Wade-Boyd & Associates LLC has provided convoy protection services,*

residential security protection, and close protection teams for United States and foreign corporation representatives, and United States government contractors all throughout the war-torn country of Iraq and for contractors from Kuwait. Our undercover operatives/investigators work details for world class clients and law firms."

Headquarters:

Wade-Boyd, Main Street, Suite 116, Lawler, IA 52154

Tel: 641-330-4581, Fax: 270-518-5780

e-mail: wbaprotection@yahoo.com

WORLDWIDE LANGUAGE RESOURCES, INC.

www.wwlr.com

Services: Interpretation, language training, translations, in-country language and cultural immersion programs. WWLR offers extensive foreign language and international language services.

"Among WWLR's many services are: interpreters/linguists/cultural advisors, simultaneous, consecutive, escort and conference level interpreters. WWLR also provides interpreters for field or combat operations in support of the Global War on Terrorism. WWLR conducts training in the U.S. and abroad to include customized language training programs to meet the customers' individualized needs. Translation services are offered in over more than languages, most dialects, and all levels of expertise."

Headquarters:

WWLR, PO Box 125, Andover, ME 04216

Tel: 207-364-5866, Fax: 207-364-5867

e-mail: info@wwlr.com